BEYOND THE IDEAL

Recent Titles in
Contributions in Latin American Studies .

Authoritarianism in Latin America since Independence
Will Fowler, editor

Colombia's Military and Brazil's Monarchy: Undermining the Republican Foundations
of South American Independence
Thomas Millington

Brutality and Benevolence: Human Ethology, Culture, and the Birth of Mexico
Abel A. Alves

Ideologues and Ideologies in Latin America
Will Fowler, editor

Family and Favela: The Reproduction of Poverty in Rio de Janeiro
Julio César Pino

Mexico in the Age of Proposals, 1821–1853
Will Fowler

Reinventing Legitimacy: Democracy and Political Change in Venezuela
Damarys Canache and Michael R. Kulisheck, editors

Sugar and Power in the Dominican Republic: Eisenhower, Kennedy, and the Trujillos
Michael R. Hall

Tornel and Santa Anna: The Writer and the Caudillo, Mexico 1795–1853
Will Fowler

Exiles, Allies, Rebels: Brazil's Indianist Movement, Indigenist Politics, and the
Imperial Nation-State
David Treece

One of the Forgotten Things: Getulio Vargas and Brazilian Social Control, 1930–1954
R. S. Rose

The Abolition of Slavery in Brazil: The "Liberation" of Africans Through the
Emancipation of Capital
David Baronov

BEYOND THE IDEAL

Pan Americanism in Inter-American Affairs

Edited by
DAVID SHEININ

Contributions in Latin American Studies,
Number 18

GREENWOOD PRESS
Westport, Connecticut • London

Library of Congress Cataloging-in-Publication Data

Beyond the ideal : Pan Americanism in Inter-American affairs / edited by David Sheinin.
    p.   cm.—(Contributions in Latin American studies, ISSN 1054–6790 ; no. 18)
     ISBN 0–313–31470–5 (alk. paper)—ISBN 0–275–96980–0 (pbk. : Praeger Publishers :
alk. paper)
    1. Pan-Americanism.   2. Latin America—Relations—United States.   3. United
States—Relations—Latin America.   I. Sheinin, David.   II. Series
F1410.B585   2000
303.48'28073—dc21   99–462055

British Library Cataloguing in Publication Data is available.

A paperback edition of *Beyond the Ideal* is available from
Praeger Publishers, an imprint of Greenwood Publishing Group, Inc.
(ISBN 0–275–96980–0).

Library of Congress Catalog Card Number: 99–462055
ISBN: 0–313–31470–5
ISSN: 1054–6790

First published in 2000

Greenwood Press, 88 Post Road West, Westport, CT 06881
An imprint of Greenwood Publishing Group, Inc.
www.greenwood.com

Printed in the United States of America

The paper used in this book complies with the
Permanent Paper Standard issued by the National
Information Standards Organization (Z39.48–1984).

10 9 8 7 6 5 4 3 2 1

For Micaela

Contents

Acknowledgments   ix

1   Rethinking Pan Americanism: An Introduction   1
     David Sheinin

2   Pan Americanism and Slavery in the Era of Latin American
     Independence   9
     Peter Blanchard

3   The First Conference of American States (1889–1890) and the
     Early Pan American Policy of the United States   19
     Joseph Smith

4   Leo Stanton Rowe and the Meaning of Pan Americanism   33
     David Barton Castle

5   A Greater America? Pan Americanism and the Professional
     Study of Latin America, 1890–1990   45
     Mark T. Berger

6   Rubén Darío and Literary Anti-Americanism/Anti-Imperialism   57
     Alberto Prieto-Calixto

7   Hispanismo versus Pan Americanism: Spanish Efforts to Counter
    U.S. Influence in Latin America before 1930   67
    Richard V. Salisbury

8   In Four Languages But with One Voice: Division and Solidarity
    within Pan American Feminism, 1923–1933   79
    K. Lynn Stoner

9   The New Pan Americanism in U.S.–Central American Relations,
    1933–1954   95
    Thomas M. Leonard

10 "Its Most Destructive Agents": Pan American Environmentalism
    in the Early Twentieth Century   115
    David Sheinin

11 Pan American Shift: Oswaldo Aranha and the Demise of the
    Brazilian-American Alliance   133
    W. Michael Weis

12 The Theory and Practice of Inter-American Literature:
    An Historical Overview   153
    Earl E. Fitz

13 The Myth of Pan Americanism: U.S. Policy toward Latin
    America during the Cold War, 1954–1963   167
    Stephen M. Streeter

14 Ecuador and the Organization of American States: A Less Than
    Perfect Union   183
    Jeanne A. K. Hey

15 The Inter-American Human Rights System: A Force for Positive
    Change in the Americas   195
    Jo M. Pasqualucci

16 Eclectic Ideal: Bringing a Positivist Order to the Literature of
    Pan Americanism   213
    David Sheinin

Index   219

About the Editor and Contributors   223

Acknowledgments

None of this would have made much sense without the rich discussions along the way—with Bill Berman at Bayview Village, Dani Fridman at Plaza Once, Isaac Traiber in Paternal, Dale Graden in the Moscow arboretum, Carlos Mayo on the bus to La Plata, and the many others. I thank colleagues, family, and friends who have backed this project in all sorts of ways. They include Daniela Sheinin, Gabriela Sheinin, Micaela Sheinin, David Glassco, George Mac-Dougall, Carlos A. Mayo, Bill Hoglund, Tom Paterson, Erin Goodman, Minister Carlos A. Dellepiane, Carmen Rebagliati, José Luis Rebagliati, Marilou Rebagliati, Mariano Lafont, Javier Lafont, Claudio Lafont, Juan Carlos Areso, Claudio Blanchart, Ivana Elbl, Teresa Traiber, Guille Traiber, Patricia Pavlovsky, Ricardo Pavlosky, Sara Fridman, Analia Fridman, Javier Rusansky, Raquel Weinstein, Rolfi Weinstein, Roberto Spangenthal, Graciela Szyber, Emilio Levin, Rosita Levin, Antonio Peralta, Rose Sheinin, and Joe Sheinin. Librarians and archivists at the Robarts Library (University of Toronto), the Bata Library (Trent University), the Library of Congress (Washington), the Biblioteca Nacional (Buenos Aires), the Smithsonian Institution Archives (Washington), and the Columbus Memorial Library (Washington) were enthusiastic in their helpful advice and guidance.

I am grateful for the high professionalism and thoughtful assistance of Heather Ruland Staines, and for the financial support of the Social Sciences and Humanities Research Council of Canada.

1

Rethinking Pan Americanism: An Introduction

David Sheinin

Pan Americanism is elusive. At its simplest, it defines a movement started in the 1880s by diplomats, business leaders, and politicians from many countries. Spearheaded principally by the United States, Pan Americanism was meant to organize the Western Hemisphere republics into an international cooperative body. However, this definition is limiting and has been recognized as such by scholars, political leaders, and others. At the opening of the 1923 Pan American conference in Chile, President Arturo Alessandri urged delegates to think of Pan Americanism "beyond the ideal," as a movement that combined important geographical, historical, and political imperatives. Critics Victor Raúl Haya de la Torre and Manuel Ugarte were more dismissive, linking Pan Americanism with Theodore Roosevelt's "Big Stick" and a U.S. "Ministry of Colonies," respectively. Indeed, despite the active participation of Latin American political and business leaders in the Pan American Union, Latin Americans quickly came to associate Pan Americanism with a U.S. agenda for political, strategic, cultural, ideological, and economic influence in the hemisphere; Pan Americanism has always been U.S. led, the friendly face of U.S. dominance in the hemisphere.

As a vision for friendly inter-American exchange, Pan Americanism had its origins in the Monroe Doctrine, other early-nineteenth-century expressions of anti-European sentiment, and the Congress of Panama (1826), the first international meeting of delegates from the newly independent Latin American republics. In a series of successive gatherings, Spanish American countries forged what some called a Pan American movement for peaceful exchange in the hemisphere. At times, Latin American exponents of inter-American solidarity were critical of the United States and of what seemed to be a U.S. unwillingness to subscribe to this early Pan American ideal. At the Continental Congress of Santiago (1856), for example, Chile, Ecuador, and Peru signed a mutual defense pact directed against the United States, in response to the U.S. William Walker's Nicaragua filibuster (1855–1856). At the Juridical Congress of Lima (1877–1879), the United States would not participate in an inter-American codification of legislation on the grounds that U.S. law was incompatible with that of Latin American states.[1]

Between 1881 and 1938, policy makers in the United States and in many Latin American countries placed new emphasis on the Pan American cooperative ideal. Although U.S. and Latin American leaders advanced themes in cultural, educational, and scientific cooperation, the new Pan Americanism was U.S. led, and directed primarily at improved and stabilized economic ties in the Americas. In 1881, Secretary of State James G. Blaine was the first high-ranking U.S. official to speak of Pan Americanism as a means of achieving inter-American commercial and cultural cooperation. Blaine proposed a Pan American conference (the First Conference of American States), eventually held in 1889–1890. The U.S. invitation to participants combined the notion of peace and cooperation with the first of many U.S. proposals for the standardization and simplification of inter-American terms of trade. In keeping with earlier suspicions of U.S. motives, the Cuban writer José Martí was one of many Latin Americans who viewed Blaine's Pan Americanism with concern because it seemed to be less focused on hemispheric cooperation than on the expansion of U.S. trade and financial interests.[2]

In some respects, the most important result of the First Conference of American States was the formation of the Commercial Bureau of American Republics (later, the Pan American Union) and the creation of a new inter-American system of regular international meetings. At the Second (1901–1902) and Third (1906) Conferences of American States, Latin American delegates voiced their dismay over the increasing military interventionism in U.S. policy, seemingly at odds with the Pan American objective of peaceful exchange. Keen on distancing itself from the dollar diplomacy of President William Howard Taft, the administration of President Woodrow Wilson revived Blaine's effort to link cultural and commercial cooperation in a Pan American ideal. Like that of Blaine, however, Wilson's Pan Americanism was directed primarily at improving economic ties in the Americas. As such, it differed little from the dollar diplomacy of the Republicans. At the First Pan American Financial Conference in 1915, Secretary of the Treasury William Gibbs McAdoo brought together tens of bankers and diplomats from throughout the hemisphere. Under the banner of Pan Americanism, those present revived Blaine's project for uniform rules of trade and finance in the region. Once again, many Latin Americans, including the Argentine author Manuel Ugarte, accused U.S. authorities of invoking Pan Americanism as a cover for their support of U.S. businesses with interests in Latin America.[3]

At the Fifth (1923) and Sixth (1928) Conferences of American States, Latin

American delegates spoke more boldly and directly than they had in the past about U.S. military intervention in the Caribbean basin as a betrayal of the Pan American ideal. Even so, the Clark Memorandum (1928) and the Good Neighbor policy of the 1930s highlighted Pan American values of cooperation and peace; this shift in U.S. policy provided an important impetus for the accomplishments of several Pan American meetings in the next decade. At the Seventh Conference of American States (1933), the Argentine delegation introduced a successful resolution that denounced the interference by one state in the internal affairs of another. At the Eighth Conference of American States (1938), delegates affirmed the principle of continental solidarity in the event of war. Ironically, between 1938 and 1945, the growing emphasis on mutual defense agreements within the Pan American movement led to the marginalization of Pan Americanism in the foreign policies of the United States and other hemispheric states, which were now explicitly concerned with inter-American relations in a context of global strategy and warfare.[4]

During World War II, the inter-American system was decreasingly characterized by a multifaceted Pan American ideal and increasingly dominated by new military and security alliances. With the creation of the Organization of American States (OAS) in 1947–1948 in the context of Cold War anticommunism, Pan Americanism came to signify inter-American strategic concerns—a shift that was emphasized in the replacement of the Pan American Union by the OAS. The 1948 OAS charter highlighted the threat of international communism, and from the toppling of Jacobo Arbenz in Guatemala in 1954 through the Cuban and Nicaraguan Revolutions, the work of the OAS became bound up in Cold War imperatives. At the same time, obscured by the high-level negotiation of inter-American security, Pan Americanism functioned behind the scenes in a variety of important areas. The Inter-American Indian Institute, for example, emerged as an early defender of the rights of Native peoples in many countries. Environmentalists established Pan American bureaucracies to help create national parks and preserve wildlife. In the 1980s, the Inter-American Human Rights Commission established new standards for the prosecution of human rights violations in the region and on a global level. Ironically, while Pan Americanism proved unsuccessful at times in its twentieth-century diplomatic initiatives—including, for example, the mediation of the longstanding Peru-Ecuador boundary dispute, and during the Central American civil wars of the 1980s—it registered important successes in its less public functions around the environment, in human rights, and in promoting scientific and technical cooperation.

In the scholarly literature since World War II, Pan Americanism has frequently been associated with power politics and inter-American security. Despite Alessandri's early warning about probing beyond the ideal, what has counted for most authors in defining Pan Americanism has been the highest levels of diplomatic activity in a Cold War, anticommunist context. Indeed, our understanding of Pan Americanism has been shaped by scholars writing in a Cold War context that has placed tremendous emphasis on the post-1945 era, security, defense, and high-level diplomacy while sidelining problems other than those of inter-American security. This collection of new scholarship on Pan Americanism challenges the limiting assumptions of three prominent genres of Cold War-era scholarship: works on defense and security; those supportive of the Cuban revolution and hostile to U.S. foreign policies during the Cold War; and the boosterism of studies by OAS insiders.[5] This volume builds on recent works that have begun to examine Pan Americanism in a variety of contexts, including, for example, the empathy for Mexican culture manifest in the United States as an explanation for 1930s Pan Americanism in Washington, Pan Americanism as an information industry, and Pan Americanism as a moderating force against strongman dictatorial rule.[6] At the same time, this book includes important current literature that addresses strategy, inter-American defense, and high-level diplomacy.

Peter Blanchard's "Pan Americanism and Slavery in the Era of Latin American Independence" establishes important links between the origins of a Pan American ideal and a crucial moral and economic question of the nineteenth century, the abolition of slavery. As Latin American nations secured independence in the early nineteenth century and some independence leaders contemplated the creation of a wider, inter-American political entity, one of the problems they faced was citizenship. Who would be citizens in the new countries? Status, birth, and property would determine citizenship for the wealthy, but what about the poor? What rights would slaves enjoy in the new states? Would there be a common response to black slavery from nation to nation? In the long run, political and economic concerns outweighed humanitarian ones. In the 1820s, Latin American blacks contended with an entrenched slave system and associated prejudices. Pan Americanism drifted away from its links to slavery and abolition.

In "The First Conference of American States (1889–1890) and the Early Pan American Policy of the United States," Joseph Smith offers a detailed overview of the U.S. political approach to the founding of modern Pan Americanism. Hosted and organized in large measure by the United States, the first Inter-American conference was held in Washington in 1889–1890. U.S. organizers had high hopes for the meeting. In part, they wished to supplant British commercial and financial preeminence in Latin America. While the conference served to affirm the preeminent political role of the United States in the Americas, its achievements were also seen as disappointing and insubstantial. Smith considers the workings and accomplishments of the first Pan American meeting—including the creation of the Commercial Bureau of American Republics, which eventually became the Pan American Union and a physical embodiment of Pan Americanism—in the context of domestic U.S. political imperatives.

David Barton Castle's "Leo Stanton Rowe and the Meaning of Pan Americanism" is a subtle exploration of the ideas and practice of Pan Americanism. A long-standing director of the Pan American Union (1920–1946), Rowe participated in many aspects of U.S.–Latin American relations. Along with other

U.S. scholars of Latin America, Rowe thought of Latin America as backward. He believed that the United States should devote its energies to bringing progress to the region. His resulting Pan American philosophy combined elements of cultural sensitivity, ethnocentrism, and progressive ideals. No ideologue, Rowe backed a program of U.S. investment and commerce in Latin America toward modernization and development. He called for political stability in the hemisphere, which he thought would be achieved through centralization of federal powers and authoritarian rule. At the same time, he opposed U.S. military intervention in Latin America. Rowe's missionary faith in Pan Americanism stressed a common commitment in the hemisphere to U.S. ideals of democracy and freedom—and, by default, the triumph of U.S. values.

"A Greater America? Pan Americanism and the Professional Study of Latin America, 1890–1990" by Mark T. Berger takes a harsher view of the ideological foundations of twentieth-century Pan Americanism. Berger reasons that after World War I, new versions of Pan Americanism cast the Americas as having a shared history, heritage, and commitment to democratic values. This view was linked to a tendency among U.S. scholars and policy makers to project U.S. ideas about a common past and future on the Americas. The emergence of Pan Americanism in the early part of the century coincided with the rise of the professional study of Latin America in the United States; Pan American assumptions became central to the institutionalization of that study. Against a backdrop of rising twentieth-century U.S. hegemony in the hemisphere, Pan Americanism, along with liberal developmentalism and modernization theories, increasingly provided key assumptions for the dominant professional discourses on Latin America and for U.S. policy in the region.

If Leo Rowe can be thought of as an intellectual progenitor of the movement, Rubén Darío was at the forefront of a literary current that directly and indirectly challenged the underpinnings of U.S.-led Pan Americanism. In "Rubén Darío and Literary Anti-Americanism/Anti-Imperialism," Alberto Prieto-Calixto explores one component of the critical literary response to Pan Americanism. At the turn of the twentieth century, the Modernist literary stream emerged to comment on the political and social upheaval that had captured the region. Prieto-Calixto counters a long-standing criticism leveled at the Modernists and at Darío more specifically: that their work reflected an escape from political concerns. Darío's writing points to a hunt for aesthetic regeneration, which in turn takes issue with the political and ideological status quo. The chapter assigns particular importance to the poems "Salutación del optimista" and "A Roosevelt," in which Darío proclaims against U.S. imperialism and its Pan American ideology.

In "Hispanismo versus Pan Americanism: Spanish Efforts to Counter U.S. Influence in Latin America before 1930," Richard V. Salisbury explores a different sort of challenge to Pan Americanism and U.S. preeminence in the hemisphere. Defeat at the hands of the United States in 1898 removed Spain as an imperial presence in the Caribbean basin, but Spain was reluctant to accept U.S. hegemony in the hemisphere. Accordingly, Madrid embarked on a policy of

Hispanismo, or cultural, economic, and political approximation with Spanish America. Spanish policy makers were careful to avoid any direct challenge to the United States, but Spanish diplomats did try to convince Latin Americans that common ties of race, religion, language, and historical tradition should continue to reaffirm a spiritual and commercial unity within Spain's former empire. Such efforts at approximation were apparent in Spain's efforts to secure influence at the Pan American meetings in 1923 (Santiago) and 1928 (Havana) and to create a trade opening in the Americas at the expense of Pan American business initiatives.

In her chapter "In Four Languages But with One Voice: Division and Solidarity within Pan American Feminism, 1923–1933," K. Lynn Stoner examines the formation of the Inter-American Commission of Women within the Pan American Union. With reference to the cooperation between the U.S. and Latin American feminists, she argues that the Commission clashed with male-dominated Pan American diplomacy and offered a forum that allowed women to transcend national and regional avenues for feminist praxis.

In "The New Pan Americanism in United States Central American Relations, 1933–1954," Thomas M. Leonard focuses on problems of Pan Americanism and dictatorship. After thirty years of intervention in Central America, the United States withdrew its troops in 1933. Almost immediately dictators surfaced in El Salvador, Guatemala, Honduras, and Nicaragua. For Central American elites, this was true Pan Americanism—both the republics and the United States were committed to nonintervention in the political affairs of other nations, even in the face of dictatorial rule. Over the next generation, global change brought close cooperation between the Central American nations and the United States: the worldwide depression of the 1930s; events leading to World War II and the war itself; and postwar cooperation and the onset of the Cold War. Traditionally, historians have argued that between 1933 and 1954 the United States imposed its will on Central Americans. By contrast, this chapter suggests that Central American governments advanced their own foreign policies; only when U.S. objectives were beneficial did they cooperate wholeheartedly with them. When U.S. policy did not benefit them, the Central American nations effectively resisted U.S. projects, both Pan American and others.

U.S. dominance within the Pan American movement was clearer on the problem of wildlife preservation. Between 1900 and 1940, American scientists and environmentalists applied Pan American assumptions on governance, ethnicity, and competence to conservation. In " 'Its Most Destructive Agents': Pan American Environmentalism in the Early Twentieth Century," David Sheinin explores the perceptions and the realities of environmental decay in Latin America, the movement to conserve wildlife in the hemisphere, its insertion into the Pan American movement by U.S. politicians, and its ties to domestic U.S. political and environmental issues.

If Leo Rowe can be seen as an archetype of the U.S. Pan Americanist, the Brazilian diplomat and politician Oswaldo Aranha embodied wartime pro–Pan

American sentiment in Latin America. W. Michael Weis shows in "Pan American Shift: Oswaldo Aranha and the Demise of the Brazilian-American Alliance" that as ambassador to the United States (1934–1937) and as foreign minister (1938–1944), Aranha had a decisive role in marshalling a unanimous recommendation at the Pan American foreign ministers meeting in Rio de Janeiro (1942) that diplomatic relations with the Axis powers be broken. Aranha's influence and advocacy persisted in the early postwar years, but because of the Cold War and his growing discontent with U.S. development strategies for Brazil, Aranha drifted from Pan Americanism. He began to advocate a more neutralist foreign policy for Brazil and an end to the "special relationship," or "unwritten alliance," between the United States and Brazil. Because the alliance was a cornerstone of diplomatic Pan Americanism in the first half of the twentieth century, its end meant that the United States could no longer achieve its hemispheric goals through inter-American diplomacy and so began to rely increasingly on ties to military regimes in Latin America.

"The Theory and Practice of Inter-American Literature: An Historical Overview" is chronologically more sweeping than the other chapters in this collection. Earl E. Fitz reasons that Pan Americanism is both an intellectual and a cultural progenitor of inter-American literature. A synthesis of inter-American literary study, this work addresses several ongoing methodological problems and controversies. These include how scholars and writers have defined the geographical and cultural boundaries of inter-American literature—often setting aside regions and nations from assessments of the whole—and a program of meaningful literary analysis for the future. Fitz suggests that a broad range of themes and methodologies might inform an expansion of Pan American literature, including Native literatures, the novel of the land, the immigrant novel, the concept of the West and westward movement in the Americas, and the "New Novel" of the 1960s.

Stephen M. Streeter's "The Myth of Pan Americanism: U.S. Policy toward Latin America during the Cold War" analyzes Washington's liberal development models as a panacea for Latin America's ills. U.S. officials frequently explained their policies toward Latin America during the Cold War by using the discourse of Pan Americanism: What's good for the United States, Assistant Secretary of State for Inter-American Affairs John Moors Cabot told many audiences, is good for Latin America. Streeter challenges the notion that Pan Americanism operated in the 1950s and 1960s as anything other than a propaganda device for convincing the public of Washington's benign intentions. The United States pursued policies in the name of Pan American ideals that protected long-standing U.S. economic and strategic interests, and this helped to deepen Latin America's economic woes.

The next two chapters incorporate excellent samples of the current literature on two areas of Pan Americanism: recent diplomatic initiatives and international human rights. In "Ecuador and the Organization of American States: A Less Than Perfect Union," Jeanne A. K. Hey suggests that Ecuador and the OAS share an inconsequential status in regional and global contexts dominated by powerful states and other actors. Because Ecuador carries little weight in the inter-American system and the OAS holds little authority at a global level, they have a mutual interest in backing one another in regional and global affairs. A history of Ecuador's participation in the OAS bears this out. This chapter traces Ecuador's participation in and use of the OAS as an important part of Quito's foreign policy. It also considers whether the relationship between Ecuador and the OAS is guided by mutual self-interest or is a genuine reflection of international legal principles that promote and recognize the activities of small states like Ecuador and multilateral institutions like the OAS.

"The Inter-American Human Rights System: A Force for Positive Change in the Western Hemisphere" by Jo Pasqualucci offers a review of the inter-American human rights system, recent progress on promoting human rights, the American Convention on Human Rights, specific human rights problems in the hemisphere, and the unique responses to those problems that have been developed by the Inter-American Commission on Human Rights and the Inter-American Court of Human Rights.

The final chapter, "Eclectic Ideal: Bringing a Positivist Order to the Literature of Pan Americanism," revisits major themes in the book, considers the difficulties in defining Pan Americanism, and provides a short bibliographical essay.

NOTES

1. Samuel Guy Inman, *Inter-American Conferences, 1826–1954: History and Problems* (Washington, 1965).

2. Bill J. Karras, "José Martí and the Pan American Conference, 1889–1891," *Revista de Historia Americana* 77 (1974): 77–100.

3. Mark T. Gilderhus, *Pan American Visions: Woodrow Wilson in the Western Hemisphere 1913–1921* (Tucson, 1986).

4. Leslie B. Rout, *Politics of the Chaco Peace Conference, 1935–1939* (Austin, 1970).

5. See Alonso Aguilar, *El panamericanismo de la Doctrina Monroe a la Doctrina Johnson* (Mexico City, 1965); Ezequiel Ramos Novoa, *La farsa del panamericanismo* (Lima, 1955); Germán Arciniegas, *OEA: La Suerte de una institución regional* (Bogotá, 1985); Alejandro Orfila, *The Americas in the 1980s: An Agenda for the Decade Ahead* (Lanham, MD, 1980); Heraldo Muñoz, "A New OAS for the New Times," in *The Future of the OAS*, edited by Viron Vaky and Heraldo Muñoz (New York, 1993); Gordon Connell-Smith, *The Inter-American System* (New York, 1966).

6. Helen Delpar, *The Enormous Vogue of Things Mexican: Cultural Relations between the United States and Mexico, 1920–1935* (Tuscaloosa, 1992); Ricardo D. Salvatore, "The Enterprise of Knowledge: Representational Machines of Informal Empire," in *Close Encounters of Empire: Writing the Cultural History of U.S.–Latin American Relations*, edited by Gilbert M. Joseph, Catherine C. LeGrand, and Ricardo D. Salvatore (Durham, 1998), 69–104; Roland H. Ebel, Raymond Taras, and James D. Cochrane, *Political Culture and Foreign Policy in Latin America: Case Studies from the Circum-Caribbean* (Albany, 1991).

2

Pan Americanism and Slavery in the Era of Latin American Independence

Peter Blanchard

In July 1826, delegates at the Congress of Panama approved a treaty of unity and perpetual alliance that included an article calling for the abolition of the African slave trade.[1] The treaty linked two issues that had emerged from the Latin American wars for independence: Pan Americanism and the abolition of slavery. The two were also tied by having been aggressively promoted by the dominant figure of the independence period, Simon Bolívar. Bolívar's primary concern was the creation of a political entity uniting the newly freed states; at the same time, he passionately believed in the abolition of slavery and urged its consideration by conference delegates. Despite his support, neither objective was achieved. The controversies and inconsistencies surrounding the issues, many of them linked to Bolívar himself as well as to regional differences and hostilities that had arisen from the wars, undermined both initiatives, leaving Pan Americanism and abolition goals for later generations. The pressure for abolition may not have affected the support for Pan American unity, nor is there evidence that the reverse was true. Yet the two issues were interrelated: the abolition of slavery and related problems of citizenship were conceived around a larger Pan American vision of a modern union of states. Both issues also revealed the social, racial, and political divisions that weakened the new republics during much of the nineteenth century.

Pan Americanism had significant support in the early nineteenth century. A postindependence union incorporating former Spanish American colonies had its roots in the colonial framework. For some, it was an attempt to re-create colonial ties without the domination of Spain—a reflection of the commitment to continuities that underlay the struggles for independence. Although independence figures such as Francisco de Miranda, Bernardo de Monteagudo, José de San Martin, and Bernardo O'Higgins envisioned some sort of Spanish American unity after the freeing of the continent, it was Simon Bolívar who took on the issue as his own and carried it forward. Bolívar was committed to the idea from an early date. In September 1810 he publicly advocated a Latin American confederation. He saw it as a means to ensure internal stability, obtain outside recognition, profit from the common interests and background of the Spanish American peoples, and warn off opponents and outside aggressors.[2] His major concern was to create a strong entity that could defend its component parts from outside powers. "Union under one supreme government will give us strength and make us formidable to everyone," he argued in 1813.[3] The following year he repeated the point: "We require our nation to have the strength to resist successfully any aggression prompted by European ambition."[4] By 1826 concerns about U.S. ambitions also colored his thinking. His hope was that the delegates to the Panama Conference would enunciate an international policy and foment closer relations among the American nations in what he called "a nation of republics"—what the historian John Lynch has referred to as a "supranational" structure.[5]

The desire to create a confederation was also sparked by Bolívar's conflicts with local political strongmen. The *caudillos* had challenged the unification component of Bolívar's independence drive, challenged his military efforts, prolonged the independence wars, and prevented the rapid establishment of strong nation-states. Bolívar and other independence-era leaders believed that strong centralized rule and a dominant executive would disarm what they viewed as the disorder of the *caudillos*.[6] The idea for a Pan American confederation can be seen as an extension of this idea, an attempt to create order out of what seemed to be extensive and crippling divisiveness in South America. It would incorporate each of the nations that Bolívar had freed, with Gran Colombia at the union's center. Formal political unity was out of the question, as Bolívar recognized. In his 1815 Jamaica Letter he noted the following:

It is a grandiose idea to think of consolidating the New World into a single nation, united by pacts into a single bond. It is reasoned that, as these parts have common origins, language, customs, and religion, they ought to have a single government to permit the newly formed states to unite in a confederation. But this is not possible. Actually, America is separated by climatic differences, geographic diversity, conflicting interests and dissimilar characteristics.[7]

Even so, he pressed for a Pan American tie that would be looser than formal nationhood, perhaps hoping that it would lead one day to a more formal structure. His long and bitter struggle to maintain the unity of Gran Colombia attested to this belief in the desirability of and need for larger political units.[8]

Just as the political entity Bolívar envisioned was to be inclusive, so too was the human element of that entity. Like Pan Americanism, the abolition of slavery was conceived by Bolívar as a sociopolitical development that would break down regional divisions, invest Latin Americans with a political and juridical stake in the new republics, and enhance the stability and strength of an independent Latin America. He wrote of "a common Latin American citizenship"[9] that would include the white elite minority but would also extend to other classes and races—and, as such, strengthen the polity. Before independence, white elites had developed a closer attachment to the colony than to Spain, creating a national identity that became an important factor in the emergence of secessionist movements; Alexander von Humboldt was among a number of visitors who identified Creoles as "citizens of Spanish America."[10] Bolívar's vision of citizenship, however, crossed class lines to include a body of inhabitants who would understand and appreciate their identities vis à vis the new states. Because he regarded loyalty to the new order as essential, military service became an accepted route to citizenship. In 1813, he declared that any foreigner who "fought in the ranks of the liberation army was automatically a citizen." Foreigners with needed skills and who would occupy vacant lands were also to be offered citizenship along with the rights and the protections of the law. Bolívar was even prepared to accept his enemies as citizens. He called a halt to his declared "war to the death" on the Spaniards, partly to attract royalists into his new republic of Colombia.[11]

Bolívar also indicated a willingness to include the poorer sectors of society as citizens. At the Congress of Angostura in February 1819, he proposed that citizens should be those "who have the necessary qualities and abilities, even if they have no wealth."[12] Did this apply to those at the very bottom of the social ladder, to the large slave population? Would they be permitted to play a role in the new nations and in the Pan American superstate? The answer was a qualified yes. Where slavery is concerned, Bolívar was inconsistent and even contradictory. His writings reflect his own slaveholding background, his philosophical commitment to abolition, and a pragmatic recognition of countervailing political pressures. During the independence struggles he insisted that it was "madness that a revolution for liberty should try to maintain slavery."[13] He promised the president of Haiti that he would free the slaves in the lands that he liberated. In addition, he came to realize that military victory in parts of Spanish America was impossible without slave support.[14] In May 1816 he decreed freedom for Venezuela's slaves. A month later he announced that "natural justice and political coherence demand the emancipation of the slaves. From now on, there will be only one class of men in Venezuela: citizens."[15] Bolívar's 1826 constitution for Bolivia gives further evidence of his commitment to the area's slaves, the stability of nation-states, and a common set of principles around citizenship and governance: "All those who until now were slaves are Bolivian citizens: as such, they are set free by the publication of this Constitution: a special law will determine the amount of compensation to be paid to their former owners."[16] Blacks were to be part of what Bolívar conceived of as a new Pan American race, "a blend of all the races . . . which will produce homogeneity."[17]

However, Bolívar's writings also reveal a man who was suspicious of blacks, a man who had reservations about granting ex-slaves equal rights and citizenship. The constitutions he wrote may have offered freedom to slaves, but they also defended property rights over slaves. Bolívar's creation of manumission *juntas* and banks to purchase the freedom of slaves only partly resolved the problem of abolition, leaving many slaves expecting but, in the end, not receiving their freedom.[18] That inconsistency was evident in Bolívar's Angostura speech of 1819: "The man who cannot write, who does not pay taxes, who has no known occupation, is not a citizen."[19]

Bolívar's legacy is clouded further by his seeming interest in reducing the black population to ensure white rule: "Is it not proper," he asked, "that these slaves should acquire their rights on the battlefield and that their dangerous numbers should be lessened by a process both just and effective? In Venezuela we have seen the free population die and the slave survive."[20] The British consul in Peru described Bolívar as being a firm believer in albocracy, since "experience has taught him that though South America is at length freed from her oppressors, if the principles of liberty are too rapidly introduced, anarchy and the destruction of the white inhabitants will be the inevitable consequence."[21] The slave revolution in Haiti and his personal experiences with slaves led Bolívar to believe that it was not possible to "create united nations from slave societies" and that the "incorporation of blacks and coloreds into society" would be fatal.[22] His failure to attract slaves into his army with the promise of freedom and their continuing support for the Crown prompted his 1816 admonishment that blacks were "ignorant and stupid."[23] He repeated the characterization in 1825 when he told an English sea captain that South America was unsuited to "a republican form of government because the population consists of Indians and Negroes who are even more ignorant than the Spanish. . . . A country ruled by such a class is headed for certain disaster."[24] Bolívar seemed to fear slaves. He described them in 1815 as descended "from a savage race" and expressed his concern that "colored people [might] rebel and destroy everything."[25] His views may have been influenced by the continuing slave unrest and resistance in postindependence Venezuela. Bolívar had turned to slaves to help secure independence, and he imagined their freedom and citizenship in a Pan American context, but he never entirely trusted them or viewed them as equals.

The inconsistencies of Bolívar and other leaders on race and citizenship undermined the possibility for creating strong, citizen-based nation states at an early stage and an effective supranational confederation in the 1820s. Even so, black slaves helped to push independence forward across Latin America. The wars were transnational, pitting Spanish against American forces, and Americans against other Americans. Social fears ensured that although independence was a goal of many Creoles, the majority at first adamantly opposed an end to colonialism. In a situation where the vast majority of the population comprised exploited groups of Indians, mestizos, black slaves, free blacks, free and enslaved mulattos, and various other racial groupings, wealthy Creoles feared that rebellion or civil war might unleash social revolution. However, the wars quickly eroded racial exclusiveness and forced multiclass alliances.

A shortage of soldiers caused generals on both sides to set aside fears of a race war in Latin America and recruit slaves. A precedent had been set in 1806 and 1807 when Argentine Creoles had enlisted slaves in local militias.[26] With the outbreak of the independence wars, royalists in Montevideo, Venezuela, and Peru turned to slaves. Republicans quickly followed suit. Both offered freedom in return for military service. The potential importance of slaves as soldiers was particularly evident in Venezuela, where they took advantage of the divisions among elites and the unrest that followed the Creole takeover of the government in 1810 to rebel. Their actions assisted in the destruction of the first republic in 1811, and their continuing loyalty to the Crown translated into support for the royalist guerrilla army of José Tomas Boves. That backing was instrumental in the destruction of the second republic in 1814. Attempting to win them over, or at least to neutralize them, Bolívar offered freedom to those between fourteen and sixty years old who joined his army. He later complained about the small number that accepted, but after 1816 slaves no longer opposed the independence forces as they had in the past, removing what had been a significant obstacle to independence and to a Pan American confederation of new states.[27]

Accompanying recruitment initiatives were laws that attacked slavery. Of these the most important were laws abolishing the African slave trade and declaring free the children of slaves born after a certain date. Authorities in Buenos Aires ended the African slave trade in 1812 and issued a "free womb" law the following year, along with other antislavery legislation.[28] In July 1821, the New Granada Congress of Cúcuta issued a constitution with equivalent antislavery provisions, and in the same year José de San Martín issued decrees ending the slave trade and freeing newborns in Peru.[29] Each of these acts severely weakened slavery by all but preventing the internal and external renewal of the slave population. They reflect the liberal thrust of the age as well as the desire to win over slaves and to attract British support for the cause of independence. They were a response to slave activism during the wars, a gesture to repay slaves for their contributions to the patriot forces, and an indication of the early Pan American character of abolitionism in its constitutional, military, and moral significance.

The result was significant slave participation in the various armies of liberation. Many slaves volunteered. Some fled their owners to secure the promised personal freedom.[30] In Venezuela, despite his complaints, Bolívar managed to attract numerous volunteers, men like Joaquin Vivas, who joined the patriots in 1814 and served in the zapaderos and in the cavalry, and José Ambrosio Surárregui, who took up arms in Caracas in 1817 and served in the navy for several years.[31] San Martín's forces attracted slaves after his invasions of Chile and Peru; Peruvian slaves continued to volunteer in what became a multinational army until the final battles.[32] However, far more slaves had to be recruited, often forcefully, indicating their unwillingness to risk their lives for what they saw as a "creoles' war"[33] and their lack of confidence in the patriots' likelihood of success. Their reservations also reflected the mixed message on slavery that they heard from Creoles. Recruitment was most effective in the Rio de la Plata, where slaves were enrolled to meet immediate military needs and to prevent them from joining the royalists or engaging in activity that could hurt the patriot cause. Some 2,000 slaves were recruited between 1813 and 1818. They served in campaigns throughout the former viceroyalty, as well as in the Army of the Andes, which under San Martín helped to free Chile in 1818 and invaded Peru in 1820. Bolívar also actively recruited slaves. In 1819, after the Battle of Boyacá that freed New Granada, he planned to build new army units with freed slaves who would, in return, serve two years in the military. Those who were recruited served in both the militia and the regiments of the line. Many slaves may have served unwillingly and deserted when the opportunity arose, but they continued to arrive, helping Bolívar to defeat the remaining Spanish armies in Venezuela, Ecuador, and Peru.[34]

Because slaves played such a significant role in the military, moral, and political thrust of the independence struggles—across what would become the national boundaries of the new republics—it is not surprising that when the first Pan American conference (the Congress of Panama) met in 1826, the issue of slavery was on the agenda. Bolívar had called for a meeting in a letter from Lima in December 1824. He invited delegates from Mexico, Peru, Chile, and Buenos Aires to meet with representatives from New Granada. The program focused primarily on an issue that would be at the core of Pan Americanism for two centuries—mutual defense—with treaties signed for union and perpetual alliance, defense, and the establishment of a transnational army.[35] There was a proposal for entrenching equality among the member states. In addition, the slave presence during the wars pressed the question of abolition onto the agenda. Delegates proposed abolishing racial discrimination and ending the slave trade. Bolívar's instructions to the Colombian delegates recommended that their goals include the abolition of slavery and the end of the African slave trade. Slavery as a Pan American concern was also shaped by the abolitionist thrust coming from Europe. Bolívar wrote that "the interest which the civilized world had shown for the abolition and suppression of the African slave trade also demands that the Assembly of American states consider it. This subject presents our republics with a fine opportunity to offer a splendid example of liberalism and philanthropy."[36] Prospects thus seemed favorable for Spanish America's black populations; delegates approved Article 26 of the Treaty of Union, League, and Perpetual Confederation that called for cooperation in ending the African slave trade and declaring as pirates those involved in the trade.[37]

However, as most Latin American countries had already abolished the slave trade and passed "free womb" laws, and some had even ended slavery, Article 26 amounted to very little. Pan Americanism failed to secure abolition, citizenship rights for blacks, and racial equality because of various factors. For one thing, Bolívar's absence from the congress weakened its potential to establish transnational legislative direction. Conference attendance was poor. Only Gran Colombia, Peru, Mexico, and Guatemala sent delegates; in the latter two countries, slavery had already been abolished, lessening the importance of abolition as a conference imperative. In Gran Colombia and Peru, on the other hand, slavery remained very much alive. There were still some 40,000 slaves in Peru and Venezuela, and slightly fewer in Colombia.[38] They not only represented a vital labor force but were also a notable source of income and a status symbol for their owners. As a result, slaveholders, who constituted a large part of the governing elite in many regions, were not prepared to willingly give up their slaves. Slaveholder strength was evident in Venezuela, where owners managed to block abolition legislation. The president of the new republic, José Anonio Páez, had a personal stake in the slavery debate: his vast landholdings were worked by large numbers of slaves. In Peru the situation was similar. From the late 1820s, slaveholders successfully flexed their muscles, ignoring or reversing liberal legislation that favored slaves and undermining abolitionist pressures.[39]

Slavery survived, therefore, despite the abolitionist pressures, the antislavery politics of the independence movement, and Pan American conference dictates and proposals. Blacks were still not accepted as equals in the new states. Indeed, white attitudes toward them had hardly changed. Discrimination and abuse continued. Many slaves who had volunteered and risked their lives for the freedom of the *patría* quickly learned that there would be no reward for their efforts. On reentering civilian life they found themselves reduced to destitution.[40] Even their personal freedom was not assured. Years after their service, ex-slaves were compelled to go to the courts to challenge former owners who had reenslaved them or were claiming them back as property. Venezuela's José Ambrosio Surárregui was one of these ex-slaves, protesting before the courts, "A man who defends this sacred right [freedom of his country] with his blood and with his life could not be a slave."[41] In Venezuela, appeals such as these tended to be decided in the soldier's favor, but only if they could prove they had served in the military.[42]

The failure of abolition as a Pan American mandate reflected the self-interest of the independent nations' new rulers, which also helped to undermine Pan Americanism more generally in the decades after independence. The Pan American conference could not produce unity around any issue. Indeed, Pan Americanism ran headlong into national and regional political leaders whose primary concern was consolidating internal unity, often at the expense of national or international arrangements. Hostilities aroused by the wars soon split apart the larger political entities, including Bolívar's Gran Colombia, and set the nations that he had helped to free in conflict. Separation from Spain not only produced a break from the mother country but also unleashed national and regional animosities that—unlike in the United States—set the former colonies against one another. Civil wars that marked the independence struggles continued. Instability, warfare, and inward-looking regimes conspired as well against abolitionism. As regional *caudillos* and national leaders determined to minimize opposition in a time of unrest, they avoided antagonizing slaveholding elites. Moreover, they rejected what Bolívar had proposed, what later generations of Latin American leaders would revive, and what early republican leaders in the northeastern United States took as a given: the idea of an informed, equal citizenry.

Pan Americanism was revived later in the century in a new context and with a more complex agenda than it had in 1826, even though Bolívar's name was invoked frequently as a founding father of the Pan American ideal. While advocates of Pan Americanism faced new problems after 1880, including the potential dominance of a new foreign power in Latin America, most states had gone a long way to resolving the regionalism and civil unrest that had undermined Pan American initiatives at independence. Although slavery was finally abolished by 1888, Pan Americanism would provide a forum in the decades that followed for renewed debate around race, ethnicity, and civic equality.

NOTES

1. For details of the Congress of Panama, see Rafael Caldera, *Pedro Gual: el Congreso de Panamá, y la integración latinoamericana*, 3d ed. (Caracas, 1983); Mariano J. Drago, *El Congreso de Panamá* (Buenos Aires, 1970); Samuel Guy Inman, *Inter-American Conferences 1828–1954: History and Problems*, edited by Harold Eugene Davis (Washington, 1965), chap. 1; Vicente Mendoza Lopez, *El Congreso de Bolivar y el panamericanismo* (Buenos Aires, 1926); Antonio de la Peña y Victor Reyes, ed., *El Congreso de Panamá y algunos otros proyectos de unión hispano-americana* (Mexico City, 1971).

2. J. L. Salcedo-Bastardo, *Bolivar: A Continent and Its Destiny*, edited and translated by Annella McDermott (Atlantic Highlands, NJ, 1977), 81–103; de la Peña y Reyes, iii–x; Caldera, 11.

3. Quoted in John Lynch, *The Spanish American Revolutions 1808–1826*, 2nd ed. (New York, 1986), 253.

4. Quoted in Salcedo-Bastardo, 88.

5. Lynch, 253–54.

6. Lynch, 246, 285–86; John Lynch, *Caudillos in Spanish America 1800–1850* (Oxford, 1992), 62–68; John Lynch, "Bolivar and the Caudillos," *Hispanic American Historical Review* 63, no. 1 (1983): 3–35.

7. Vicente Lecuna, comp., and Harold A. Bierck, Jr., ed., *Selected Writings of Bolivar*, vol. 1 (New York, 1951), 118.

8. Gerhard Masur, *Simon Bolivar*, rev. ed. (Albuquerque, 1969), 315–316; Lynch, *Spanish American Revolutions*, 254.

9. Salcedo-Bastardo, 94.

10. Lynch, *Spanish American Revolutions*, 1; Salcedo-Bastardo, 60.

11. Salcedo-Bastardo, 99, 100; Masur, 285.

12. Quoted in Salcedo-Bastardo, 62.

13. Lynch, *Spanish American Revolutions*, 213.

14. John V. Lombardi, *The Decline and Abolition of Negro Slavery in Venezuela. 1820–1854* (Westport, 1971), 41.

15. Quoted in Salcedo-Bastardo, 104.

16. Quoted in Salcedo-Bastardo, 105, 109.

17. Quoted in J. B. Trend, *Bolivar and the Independence of Spanish America* (London, 1946), 181; Masur, 275. See also Salcedo-Bastardo, 101.

18. Robin Blackburn, *The Overthrow of Colonial Slavery 1776–1848* (London, 1988), 362.

19. Quoted in Salcedo-Bastardo, 61.

20. Lynch, *Spanish American Revolutions*, 213; José Marcial Ramos Guédez, "Simón Bolivar y la abolición de la esclavitud en Venezuela," *Ultimas Noticias, Suplemento Cultural* (Caracas), 31 July 1994, 6–7; Lecuna and Bierck, 223; Bolivar to Santander, no. 230, 4 April 1820, *Cartas Bolivar-Santander 1820*, vol. 2 (Bogotá, 1988), 87–88.

21. Ricketts to Canning, no. 2, 25 April 1826, File 61/7, Foreign Office Files, Public Record Office, London.

22. Lester D. Langley, *The Americas in the Age of Revolution, 1750–1850* (New Haven, 1996), 243–44.

23. John V. Lombardi, "Los esclavos en la legislación republicana de Venezuela," *Boletín Histórico, Federación John Bolton*, no. 13 (January 1967): 51.

24. Quoted in Masur, 403.

25. Lombardi, *Decline and Abolition*, 40; quoted in Masur, 424.

26. George Reid Andrews, *The Afro-Argentines of Buenos Aires, 1800–1900* (Madison, 1980), 115.

27. See Lynch, *Spanish American Revolutions*, chap. 6.

28. Lynch, *Spanish American Revolutions*, 85.

29. Peter Blanchard, *Slavery and Abolition in Early Republican Peru* (Wilmington, 1992), 7.

30. For details of Argentine slaves who fought, see Guerra, Rescate de esclavos, 1813–1817, vol. X-43-6-7; Solicitudes Militares, 1812, vols. X-6-5-7; X-8-7-4, X-8-7-5, 1815; vol. X-12-167, 1822, Archivo General de la Nación, Buenos Aires, Argentina (AGN-A); Andrews, *Afro-Argentines*, 48, 115–16; Núria Sales de Bohigas, *Sobre esclavos reclutas y mercaderes de quintos* (Barcelona, 1974), 64.

31. For examples of slaves who fought in the patriot forces, see "El Sindico Procurador municipal de este canton demandando al Señor Domingo Vargas la libertad de Andrés Vargas, su siervo, por haber servido en los Ejercitos de la Republica, 1828," Civiles, IRV, 1828, File 3; "Expediente seguido por José Ambrosio Surárregui, reclamando su libertad por haber servido a las tropas de la República, 1829," Civiles, LRST, 1829, File 6; Archivo de la Academia Nacional de la Historia, Caracas, Venezuela (AANH-V); "Copiador de oficios de la Comandancia General de la Columna de Retaguardia del Ejercito Libertado, a cargo del Coronel Manuel Manrique, 22 de noviembre de 1820," Gran Colombia, Papeles de Guerra y Marina, vol. 1, 1820–1821, Folio 48; "Oficio de Soublette al General Paéz—Caracas, 1 de marzo de 1823," Gran Colombia, Intendencia, Papeles de Guerra y Marina, vol. 53, 1823, Folio 16, AGN-V.

32. John Miller, *Memoirs of General Miller in the Service of the Republic of Peru*, 2nd ed. (London 1829), vol. 1, 287–88, 305, 352–53, vol. 2, 105–6; Timothy E. Anna, *The Fall of the Royal Government in Peru* (Lincoln, NE, 1979), 172, 196, 202; Blanchard, 11–12; *El Peruano* (Lima), no. 10 (5 May 1855), no. 11 (19 May 1855), no. 13 (29 May 1855).

33. Lynch, *Spanish American Revolutions*, 213.

34. Bolivar to Santander, no. 169, 8 February 1820, and Santander to Bolivar, no. 298, 7 July 1820, in *Cartas Santander-Bolivar 1820*, vol. 2, 1–2, 219–21; Bolivar to Santander, no. 451, 5 January 1822 in *Cartas Santander-Bolivar 1820–1822*, vol. 3, 181–

83; Lecuna and Bierck, 222; Masur, 197–198, 275; Fernando Jurado Noboa, *Esclavitud en la costa pacífica: Iscuandé, Barbacoas, Tumacoy Esmeraldas, siglos xvi al xix* (Quito, 1990), 393–94.

35. de la Peña y Reyes, vi, xiii–xiv, 3–5, 54–56, 90, 94.

36. Masur, 413; Salcedo-Bastardo, 96–97, 107; Drago, 253.

37. de la Peña y Reyes, 63–64.

38. Santiago Tavara, *Abolición de la esclavitud en el Peru* (Lima, 1855), 29; Blackburn, 364, 365; Sales de Bohigas, 105.

39. Lynch, *Caudillos*, 104, 281–83; Blackburn, 360–68; Blanchard, 13–14, chap. 3; Tavara, 10–21.

40. Sales de Bohigas, 64.

41. "Expediente seguido por José Ambrosio Surrárregui reclamando su libertad por haver servido a las tropas de la Republicá, 1829," Civiles, LRST, 1829, Expediente 6, AANH-V.

42. For cases of ex-slaves who fought to claim their freedom, see "Lino Rodrigues, sargento, pide se le declare libre de servidumbre por sus servicios puestados a la República, 1825," Civiles, BCGJMPRT, 1825, Expediente 7; "El Señor Candelario Espinosa cobrando al Estado el valor de su esclavo, Silvestre, que tomó las armas en defensa de la República, 1829," Civiles, ACEF, 1829, Expediente 3, AANH-V; "Expediente promovido por D. Vicente del Castillo solicitando le se devuelto un esclavo negro de su propiedad llamado Manuel del Castillo, enrolado en la artillería," O.L. 145–561, 1826; "D. Mariano Reyna sobre la devolución de un esclavo suyo que está sirviendo a la Patria, y en la actualidad en el Resguardo Militar del Callao," P.L. 6–189, 1826, Archivo General de la Nación, Lima, Peru.

3

The First Conference of American States (1889–1890) and the Early Pan American Policy of the United States

Joseph Smith

The terms *Pan American* and *Pan Americanism* came into popular use in the United States as a result of the International American Conference, or First Conference of American States, held in Washington from October 2, 1889, to April 19, 1890.[1] For most of the nineteenth century the United States showed little interest in inter-American gatherings, preferring friendly but detached diplomatic ties with Latin America. The most frequent contact came by way of trade, although commercial relations remained modest, representing less than one quarter of the annual U.S. trade abroad. Preoccupied with internal territorial and economic development, the United States saw Latin America as geographically remote, economically backward, politically unstable, and unworthy of much attention. However, U.S. attitudes began to change during the 1880s. There was a growing perception by business interests and politicians of the value of Latin America as an accessible market to help absorb the worrying surplus caused by U.S. agricultural and industrial overproduction.

Contemporary foreign observers believed that economic motives were responsible for the Washington conference. According to Cuban nationalist José Martí, who reported on the conference for the Buenos Aires daily *La Nación*, the United States was "glutted with unsaleable merchandise and determined to extend its dominions in America."[2] Mindful of the exclusion from the conference of the American colonies of European powers, the *South American Journal* warned British commercial interests that the central object of the gathering for the United States was to capture the European–South American trade.[3] U.S. historians William Appleman Williams, Walter LaFeber, and others have also stressed the American economic agenda for Washington;[4] Latin American writers have generally concurred, describing the late nineteenth century as a period in which prodigious American economic growth resulted in a new expansionism south.[5] Modern Pan Americanism, then, began not in a context of inter-American cooperation but as a function of U.S. political and economic expansionism in the Americas. Although the conference affirmed U.S. leadership in the Western Hemisphere, the gathering's commercial accomplishments were limited, and regarded at the time as disappointing—a "complete failure," according to the editor of the *South American Journal*.[6] Recommendations of the conference lapsed. The one tangible achievement of the gathering was the creation of the Commercial Bureau of American Republics. The Bureau would become the Pan American Union and operate as the permanent secretariat for the organization of inter-American conferences during the first half of the twentieth century.

Few multinational conferences had been staged in the Western Hemisphere during the nineteenth century. The most important remained the 1826 Congress of Panama, convened by Simon Bolívar to provide the opportunity for an historic first meeting of the newly independent nations of Latin America. The Congress of Panama was often described subsequently as a symbol of the Bolivarian ideal of hemispheric partnership.[7] Three unrelated conferences followed, involving only a handful of Spanish-American states: Lima in 1847–1848, Santiago de Chile in 1856, and Lima in 1864–1865. Attendance at each was slight, the purpose not to promote hemispheric union but to discuss collective defense. The United States stayed away from all three meetings. Indeed, because the United States had traditionally stressed unilateral diplomacy, the idea for the Washington conference seemed to contradict the history of U.S.–Latin American relations before 1889, and it came as a surprise to many.[8]

To be sure, the United States had taken an interest in hemispheric multilateralism before 1889. Promulgated in the 1820s, and like the Bolivarian ideal, the Monroe Doctrine proposed a separate hemispheric system of nations. But unlike Bolívar, Monroe conceived of that system as protected and promoted by the United States. In practice, during the nineteenth century, the United States reacted to conflict between Latin American states as a mediator. During the War of the Triple Alliance, for example, the U.S. Congress suggested that the belligerents send representatives to Washington to discuss a peace settlement. The more ambitious idea for a full inter-American conference emerged unexpectedly in 1881 on the initiative of Secretary of State James G. Blaine. Blaine called for a peace congress to meet in Washington in 1882, hoping to resolve territorial disputes between Mexico and Guatemala and between Chile and Peru. Delegates would also be charged with creating a system of arbitration to prevent future wars. Though vague on the mechanics of the peace congress, Blaine's proposal restated the tenets of the Monroe Doctrine, asserting the need for peace in the hemisphere and the preeminent role of the United States in achieving this end.

However, Blaine's suggestion came without the backing of the Latin American governments involved in the conflicts. It also came within a short time of his departure from office and was attributed by his critics to self-serving personal ambition. The result was considerable political controversy in the United States over the meeting, which led to the formal rejection of the scheme by the new secretary of state, Frederick Frelinghuysen, in August 1882.[9] Blaine kept the issue alive in the press with a rhetorical style reminiscent of Bolívar; he insisted that the conference might have fostered a closer relationship between the United States and Latin America and allowed a chance for the United States to exert a "moral influence" that would be "beneficent and far-reaching" in promoting peace and civilization throughout the hemisphere.[10] Blaine became identified in the American public mind as the leading advocate of Pan Americanism.[11] But his Pan American idealism aroused a mixed response and was dismissed by critics such as Carl Schurz, who pointed to the practical and moral dangers of overseas entanglements for the United States. He argued the following:

This republic would have to become practically the arbiter and protector of the whole sisterhood, enforcing its decision with a strong hand [and] then we would see a fine selection of adventurers from the little republics hanging around our State Department and the lobbies of Congress, trying to involve our Government in their intrigues and our public men in their schemes.[12]

A more politically influential and timely argument for an inter-American conference was the prospect of substantial commercial benefits. Although the 1881 proposal had been primarily concerned with peace and diplomacy, Blaine argued retrospectively that he had also intended the meeting to help American merchants reconquer markets in Latin America that had been lost to European competitors, especially the English. "If the commercial empire that legitimately belongs to us is to be ours," Blaine asserted in 1882, "we must not lie idle and witness its transfer to others."[13] Blaine's advocacy of commercial expansion provoked little dissent. But his failure to win the presidential election in 1884 meant that the U.S. politics of Pan Americanism shifted to Congress. Through the 1870s, Congress had regularly debated financing improved steamship, mail, and other commerce-related ties to Latin America. But these measures met with mixed results because they invariably aroused a partisan political response, especially in the House, where Democrats regularly denounced Republicans as wasteful spenders for advancing mail subsidies.[14]

Even so, bipartisan backing in Congress for a Pan American commercialism began to take shape after 1880. Democrats and Republicans increasingly saw exports as a means of alleviating the economic recession of 1882–1885 and the associated problem of chronic agricultural overproduction. A widely circulated 1884 report revealed that the United States held only 18.9 percent of Latin America's foreign trade and suggested that the United States had fallen behind its European competitors in the region.[15] Congress responded by funding a trade commission to visit Latin America and by showing new interest in a customs union modeled on the Prussian Zollverein to include all the nations of the hemisphere. Speaking in April 1888, Democratic Congressman Richard Townshend echoed Blaine on Pan Americanism:

The largest and most inviting field for enterprise on earth exists in the countries south of us on the American continent. Their natural resources are incalculably valuable, and their trade and commerce are capable of immense extension. . . . We should not only have a larger share of that trade than any country but we should be able to control most of it. It is the only great market left for our surplus products. We can and ought to have it. But in order to meet with the fullest measure of success statesmanship must precede and open the way for the producers, tradesmen, and capitalists of the United States. The most effectual and surest means that can be devised to this end is the establishment of an American Zollverein or commercial union as contemplated in the measure before us.[16]

The measure referred to by Townshend was a U.S.-organized conference of American nations stressing trade and business. It would be similar to the commercial expositions regularly held in the United States. Bills sponsored by Democratic Congressman James McCreary of Kentucky and Republican Senator William Frye of Maine were approved in May 1888 by a joint House-Senate conference. The resulting act of Congress instructed the president to invite Latin American governments to an International American Conference to be held in Washington during 1889. Agenda items would include a customs union, steamship and railroad communications, a uniform system of customs regulations and weights and measures, laws to protect copyrights and trademarks, and a common silver coin for the Americas. Congressmen linked peace and stability to trade; they kept a component of Blaine's 1881 proposal by calling on conference delegates to discuss the implementation of a system of arbitration to preserve hemispheric peace. An appropriation of $100,000 was approved to cover costs.

The McCreary-Frye Act attracted slight public attention and was over-shadowed by congressional debate over a controversial, and not unrelated, Democratic bill to stimulate the economy and boost internal and external trade by reducing the tariff.[17] Nevertheless, at a time of fierce division between Republicans and Democrats, passage of the McCreary-Frye bill was remarkable. José Martí believed that Democratic misgivings had been subordinated to electoral considerations.[18] The British minister to Washington believed that the Act reflected a political maneuver by which the Democratic majority in the House had backed it in the name of freer trade, while the Republican majority in the Senate supported McCreary-Frye to help alleviate pressure against the protective system.[19] Once the Act was passed, the executive branch took the initiative in bringing the conference to fruition, naming American delegates and inviting Latin American governments to send representatives. In order to counter possible animosities in Latin America over U.S. leadership in conference organization, U.S. Secretary of State Thomas Bayard appointed the diplomat John G. Walker as a special commissioner charged with touring South America and persuading all governments, especially those in Argentina and Chile, to accept the U.S. invitation. On his travels, Walker reassured government leaders that each country would have an equal vote at the conference, that the United States had no desire "to extend unduly its influence upon the continent," and that conference deliberations would lead to "practical advantage."[20]

However, Latin Americans remained suspicious of U.S. intentions. From Mexico, British minister Francis Denys reported that the government was showing little interest in the conference and did not expect to derive much benefit from attendance. Mexicans were traditionally wary of their powerful neighbor and believed that commercial discussions would not make much progress because a reduction in U.S. customs duties was highly unlikely. Indeed, the opposite occurred in the summer of 1889, when the U.S. Congress imposed a new duty on silver-lead ores. The increase was seen as a direct blow to the Mexican mining industry and, according to Denys, "has rendered the Mexican Government very averse to promoting or helping in any way the commerce of the United States."[21] At the same time, Brazil would not confirm its conference attendance. Peruvian officials indicated that they anticipated nothing of value to emerge from the meeting, and Chileans were openly suspicious of the United States. Chile was still disappointed that the United States had expressed a pro-Peruvian position at the time of the War of the Pacific. The *Buenos Ayres Herald* argued that few Argentines thought of or cared much about the United States.[22]

Despite these and other queries, delegates from seventeen Latin American nations assembled in Washington in October 1889. Their motives for attendance varied, but foremost in the minds of many were business opportunities that might come with a renewed Pan Americanism. Brazil was rumored to be eager for a commercial treaty with the United States to boost its declining sugar industry. Chileans hoped for regular steamship traffic to the United States and supported a common silver currency for the hemisphere. At the same time, most countries saw the conference as an opportunity to air a variety of grievances and initiatives. Venezuela publicized its boundary dispute with Britain over Guyana. Ecuador, Colombia, and Paraguay highlighted access to the sea and the free navigation of rivers. Chileans saw their presence as a hedge against Peru, which, they suspected, might advance its claims in the Tacna-Arica boundary dispute.[23]

Appointed Secretary of State by incoming U.S. president Benjamin Harrison, Blaine returned to the helm of Pan Americanism, elected as president of the conference assembly. But much of the conference administrative work fell to William E. Curtis, a journalist from Chicago and secretary of the 1884–1885 Latin American Trade Commission. Curtis tried to counter public ignorance of the meeting. "A good many people," observed the *Indianapolis Journal*, "seem to have got the conference which meets in October mixed up with the exposition that is to be held in 1892."[24] Curtis publicly praised the "phenomenal foresight" of Bolívar in convening the 1826 Congress of Panama and, although it distorted the historical record, traced a direct link between that meeting, Blaine's revival of the idea in 1881, and the subsequent congressional act of 1888. Excepting the arbitration issue, Curtis stressed that the conference would avoid political matters. There would be no entangling leagues or confederations. "The primary purpose of this congress," he explained, "is international fellowship, as desired by Bolivar."[25] The concept of all the delegates working together to create a hemisphere of prosperous and democratic sister nations reflected the popular view of Pan Americanism in the United States. The meaning of the term remained vague, but its appeal is reflected in the preference of the U.S. press to adopt the term "Pan American Conference" instead of the official title of "International American Conference."

The Harrison administration enhanced the profile of the conference with a lavish opening ceremony in Washington, followed by a deluxe railroad tour of the United States for the visitors. Delegates visited New England, then journeyed west to Chicago and St. Louis before returning to Washington to begin conference business. A second tour was scheduled for after the conference to cover the southern states. The preconference excursion was tailored to impress Latin American delegates with the industrial prowess of the host country. "They will be shown," enthused Curtis, "the mills of New England, the forges and furnaces of Pennsylvania, the farms of the prairies, and the plantations of the South."[26] Yet despite the proclaimed desire to promote international fellowship, the itinerary of the excursion underlined the commercial significance attached to the conference by the Harrison administration. Moreover, the Latin Americans were joined on the trip by American delegates Charles Flint and Andrew Carnegie, whose business backgrounds and fame reinforced the commercial nature of the exercise. In sharp contrast to the composition of the Latin American delegations, made up primarily of diplomats, jurists, and statesmen, only two of the ten American delegates were nonbusinessmen.

The journey of some six thousand miles was completed in a hectic six weeks. As *The Nation* remarked, Curtis's apparent insensitivity seemed to pervade the excursion:

It may be said that its planning showed other motives than delicate consideration for the nation's guests. Most of them are men of mature years, for whom six weeks of life in railroad cars, in a changeable climate, is not exactly a luxury. Besides, there is in the thing almost an implication against their intelligence—as if it would be a good thing to treat them as the Government used to treat the Sioux chiefs Red Cloud and Crazy Horse—take them to Washington, show them the sights, and so impress them with Uncle Sam's power that they would see no hope in opposing him. These delegates are traveled gentlemen, who are not easily awe-stricken.[27]

The press reported that delegates were suffering from exhaustion. Such was the dissatisfaction among delegates with the trip that only two signed on for the postconference excursion. Blaine also had difficulty exerting influence over the business of the conference, which the British Foreign Office had judged a "rather fantastic" scheme. There were no English-to-Spanish translations made of opening conference speeches. Only two members of the U.S. delegation had a speaking knowledge of Spanish, while a minority of the Latin Americans could speak English. The inexperience and ethnocentrism of Blaine and Curtis were evident in a conference agenda that proved far too ambitious. The vague wording of the agenda, which had been an advantage in persuading governments to attend, became a liability when the conference came into session. Apart from the question of arbitration, commented *The Nation*, "Mr. Blaine had absolutely no program, and left his delegates wholly uninstructed, his idea appearing to be that instead of a gathering of representatives of several governments, under careful instructions, the Congress was a sort of town meeting where personal views were to be freely ventilated."[28]

Discussion of substantive items was further hindered by the intrusion of domestic political pressures, especially from a newly elected U.S. Congress, which came into session in December 1889. Congress made known its opposition to a common silver coinage. Under the chairmanship of Republican Congressman William McKinley, the House Ways and Means Committee prepared a new tariff bill that would raise duties on a number of key Latin American exports; Blaine wrote McKinley that these were "a slap in the face of the South Americans with whom we are trying to enlarge our trade."[29] The effect on conference discussion was to nullify the promotion of inter-American trade. According to Curtis, developments in Congress over the McKinley Tariff provided the delegates with "a topic of daily conversation more interesting and important than the questions under consideration in their own councils."[30] Lack of progress at the conference was most evident in the failure of the customs union proposal; the conference committee assigned to report on the item soon decided that it was simply too ambitious and impractical. The committee recommended instead the negotiation of bilateral commercial agreements toward an eventual free trade area. Curtis singled out Latin American financial policies as the roadblock in the way of the customs union—impossible "because all of the nations of Central and South America depend entirely upon their customs revenue for support."[31]

Latin American delegates had other explanations. Argentine Roque Saenz Peña noted that most Latin American trade was with Europe, not the United States: "to secure free trade from markets which exchange nothing between themselves would be a luxurious display of utopy and an illustration of sterility."[32] Others complained that as long as the United States maintained a high protective tariff on imports, it could hardly be regarded as a sincere champion of free trade. The Uruguayan Alberto Nin, who left the conference before its close, declared that before the United States could establish closer relations with Latin America, its delegates would have to "make some concessions in order to obtain the advantages they profess to be so anxious to secure."[33] Thus, despite the references to international fellowship and Pan American cooperation that had preceded the conference, delegates remained suspicious of U.S. motives and willing to press national agendas over an abstract hemispheric ideal. Dissensions surfaced between Latin Americans; Nicaragua and Costa Rica clashed over the location of a future Central American canal. Reflecting the suspicions of Mexico on the part of small Central American states, Guatemala advanced a land claim against Mexico. Determined to block Peru and Bolivia from pressing territorial claims arising from the War of the Pacific, Chile stood against creating the machinery for the arbitration of international disputes, which Chilean delegate Emilio Varas observed "belongs . . . to the realm of illusions."[34] A more tense conflict emerged between Argentina and the United States over a resolution to condemn the right of conquest. The United States believed that the measure was an attempt to reopen the question of territory ceded by Mexico to the United States. During a plenary session a heated personal exchange erupted between Blaine and Argentine delegate Manuel Quintana.[35] In the end, the right of conquest was deleted from resolution language. Delegates recommended that nations should have an automatic recourse to arbitration in a conflict—a vote on which Chileans abstained, mindful of having acquired Bolivian and Peruvian territories a generation before.

Despite disagreement over the customs union and arbitration, on April 19, 1890, the conference closed on a cooperative note, having laid the groundwork for future agreement on copyrights and trademarks, improved transportation in the Americas, and the creation of a Pan American Union. However, there was little to show in concrete actions taken by delegates for more than six months of meetings. The American minister at Bogotá underlined a mood of disappointment in Latin America when he reported that the Colombian government "is of the opinion that the results of the International Conference cannot be considered as already realized" and that "the greater part of the measures are reduced to propositions, in which is recommended the adoption of certain methods, laws and regulations."[36] The two most ambitious measures, arbitration and the customs union, had not attracted sufficient support. Lavished with praise by Blaine as a "new Magna Charta,"[37] the arbitration convention lapsed when no government was willing to proceed with the necessary ratification. There were suspicions of U.S. predominance. Martí disliked the associated plan for a permanent court in Washington and warned of a U.S. design to dominate the nations of Latin America. Mexicans worried about "a limitation of their independence by placing in the hands of the United States a certain control over their actions."[38]

After the meeting, the United States pressed forward with the proposed alternative to the customs union: bilateral reciprocal trade agreements. Treaties were signed with Brazil, Spain (for Cuba), the Dominican Republic, Guatemala, Honduras, El Salvador, Costa Rica, Nicaragua, and Britain (for the British West Indies). U.S. negotiators, however, were unable to conclude treaties with Mexico, Argentina, Venezuela, and Colombia. This aspect of the Harrison administration Pan American policy did not quite cover the whole hemisphere. Even so, it expanded U.S. trade and economic influence.[39] Other recommendations approved by the conference held out the prospect of increasing American involvement in Latin American economic affairs. These included the creation of an inter-American bank and the establishment of specialist commissions to study railroad and steamship communications. Their implementation, however, depended on financial subsidies from the U.S. Congress. Democratic congressmen bridled at being asked to approve schemes in whose making they had not participated or been consulted. Funding that materialized proved insufficient and hedged with unworkable conditions. The Pan American initiatives collapsed.[40] Given little public attention at the time, one tangible symbol of Pan Americanism that emerged from the conference was the formation of the International American Union, whose administrative office, the Commercial Bureau of the American Republics, would become the Pan American Union.

The idea of a Pan American commercial bureau originated as one of several recommendations in the Report of the Committee on Customs Regulations. The stated aim was for the systematic collection and distribution of useful information relating to the exterior navigation and commerce of the conferring powers and to the changes in their customs laws and regulations. The Report stressed also that "the expense of maintaining such a Bureau would be inconsiderable and its benefits inestimable."[41] Conference delegates unanimously accepted the committee's recommendation. They established the Commercial Bureau in Washington under the supervision of the U.S. secretary of state for a period of ten years. Its first director was William E. Curtis. The Bureau's staff in 1890 numbered ten.[42] In practice, Curtis was merely continuing the work he had been doing during the summer of 1889 in preparation for the conference. He answered inquiries from businessmen and published a series of bulletins and handbooks on Latin American commercial conditions. Despite the routine nature of its work, the Bureau attracted some unfavorable comment and criticism. In effect, its early history was analogous to that of the Washington conference. Just as Latin American governments had found it awkward to turn down their invitations to the conference, they felt similarly unable to resist the offer of the United States to organize and locate the Bureau in the U.S. capital. Although created ostensibly "at the common expense, for the common benefit,"[43] the Bureau was seen by many as a purely U.S. creation, with Curtis as director and no provision for Latin American oversight or participation in Bureau activities. Moreover, much of the Bureau's day-to-day work and many of its contacts were inevitably with business leaders and companies in the United States rather than from distant Latin America.[44]

The Latin American nations, therefore, took little interest in the Bureau. The most open opposition came from the Chilean government, which declared that it had no reason to maintain a formal association with the Bureau. Other Latin American governments expressed no overt criticism of the Bureau, and with the exception of Paraguay all paid their dues in the first year of its operation. In subsequent years, Bolivia, Peru, Colombia, Argentina, Mexico, and El Salvador defaulted on their obligations. In part, Latin American nonpayment was a response to uncertainty over whether the U.S. government could meet its financial obligations to the Bureau. The principal threat to the work of the Bureau came from domestic political factors in the United States. Congressional support for the 1888 act to set up the Washington conference had reflected bipartisan political action. The meeting had been managed by the Republicans; Harrison and Blaine had sought maximum political benefit for their party and packed the U.S. delegation with Republican loyalists and business leaders. In the process the bipartisan consensus was dissolved. Democrats reacted by reviving traditional political party battle lines and accused their opponents of manipulating the conference to satisfy ulterior financial motives. "The fact is," alleged *The New York Times*, "that Mr. Blaine's Pan American Conference and the fanciful scheme of which it was a part never had any attraction for the Republican leaders except as a device for promoting subsidies."[45]

Democratic wrath focused on requests for appropriations to fund inter-American railroad and shipping schemes, but the Bureau also became a direct target for criticism. The appointment of Blaine's protégé, Curtis, as director was seized upon as an opportunity to condemn the organization as a Republican securement. More significant, by accusing the Bureau of wasting public money, the Democrats questioned the financial competence of the Harrison administration. This charge acquired added force when it became known that some of the Latin American nations were unwilling to contribute their share of the Bureau's expenses.

In 1892 the Democrats exploited their control of the House Committee on Foreign Affairs to include in the annual Diplomatic and Consular Appropriation Bill a proposal to reduce the Bureau's grant from $36,000 to $25,000 and to make payment of the U.S. contribution contingent upon the receipt of dues owed by the other members. At one point opponents of the Bureau sought to pass an amendment that would withdraw U.S. financial support entirely. "I want to abolish this Bureau," Congressman James Blount openly admitted. Just as he had similarly denounced Republican designs to misappropriate steamship subsidies, Blount alleged that the Bureau was a place for somebody to occupy and represented "one of the numerous sores to be found in every Department of the Government."[46] To counter the Democratic onslaught, Curtis organized a campaign to save the Bureau. Letters and petitions from business interests reached Congress praising the Bureau and protesting its abolition. The bipartisanship of the 1880s also came to the rescue. The cosponsor of the 1888 Act, James McCreary, spoke out against his fellow Democrat James Blount. In an effort to deemphasize party politics while promoting hemispheric cooperation, McCreary declared, "I regard the International American Conference as one of the grandest conferences ever held in the world."[47] Curtis feared defeat, but a vote of 143 to 75 in May 1892 reinstated the $25,000 appropriation. This was hardly a stunning success, however. *The New York Tribune* attributed the victory to the modest appropriation amount and the desire of Democratic congressmen to avoid "the odium of attempting to cripple the work of the Bureau of American Republics."[48]

Political pressure continued. Indeed, the future of the Bureau was again brought into question by Grover Cleveland's victory over Benjamin Harrison in the 1892 presidential election. The Democratic triumph compelled Curtis to resign as director in May 1893. His successor, Clinton Furbish, possessed no particular knowledge of Latin American affairs and secured the appointment purely as a reward for political services performed on behalf of the Democratic party during the 1892 election.[49] The Bureau's future remained uncertain. In July 1894 the Democratic majority in Congress reduced the U.S. appropriation to $10,000, although an additional $5,000 was voted specifically to cover the cost of Bureau publications. One congressman predicted that the vote pointed to "a slow death" for the Bureau.[50]

The attack on the Bureau in 1894 was part of a larger Democratic strategy to reverse the protectionist policies of the Republicans, symbolized most of all by the 1890 McKinley Tariff, which had raised customs duties to a record level. The main business of Congress in 1894, therefore, was to debate and pass the Wilson bill, named after Democratic Congressman William Wilson of West Virginia, which proposed a thorough reduction of existing tariff schedules. The bill also deliberately sought to nullify the Pan American policy of the Harrison administration by including the unilateral abrogation of all the reciprocal trade agreements that had been signed since 1890. The person widely regarded as the architect of that policy, James G. Blaine, had died in January 1893, but Republican Senator John Sherman of Ohio claimed that the Democrats were intent on seeking posthumous political revenge. He confessed to being puzzled by the desire to destroy the treaties and observed: "The only reason which can be given in a political sense is that they were brought about by a Republican administration, mainly through the influence of a gentleman who is now dead and gone."[51] Republicans also stressed that abrogation of the treaties would seriously damage relations with Latin America. Senator Redfield Proctor of Vermont argued the following:

Reciprocity under the existing laws has met every reasonable expectation of its friends. Its prospects for the future were even brighter. And yet, in utter disregard of the positive advantages thus secured to our producers, it is proposed to throw these advantages entirely away. It is proposed, too, to effect these changes at once, and arbitrarily, in a manner well calculated to wound the sensibilities of those neighbors with whom we ought to cultivate the most frank, consistent, and friendly relations.[52]

Pan American goodwill, however, was not a political priority in Washington. The Democratic majority was sufficient to pass the Wilson bill in August 1894, including the section abrogating the reciprocity treaties with Latin American countries. In the meantime Congress had also examined whether the United States could enact legislation to permit a similar termination of the Bureau of American Republics. Secretary of State Walter Q. Gresham reported that the agreement made at the Washington conference had established the Bureau for a period of ten years and had also stipulated that no country should cease its membership during that period. As long as a majority of the members continued to support the Bureau, Gresham concluded that "this Government cannot in good faith withdraw from the organization."[53] In effect, a legal technicality prevented Democratic politicians from dismantling the Bureau in 1894.

The troubles affecting the early years of the Bureau highlighted the constraining influence exerted by U.S. politics upon the formulation and execution of Pan American policy at the close of the nineteenth century. To aim for peace and friendship was appealing and unobjectionable, but U.S. politicians showed their most active interest in Pan Americanism when it promised commercial growth. This was exemplified in congressional approval for the Washington conference. Economic factors had limited influence on politicians, however. The fragile bipartisan consensus collapsed when the conference became too closely identified with the Republican party. When the Democrats secured victory in the 1892 elections, they used their majority in Congress to nullify the Pan American policy of Blaine and Harrison. In the process, they abrogated the reciprocity treaties and almost terminated the Bureau of American Republics. A similar conflict was evident in Latin America, where traditional suspicion of U.S. motives clashed with the desire for more contact with the growing economic power of the "colossus of the north." The Washington conference was useful in promoting inter-American fellowship, but Latin American governments generally adopted a negative attitude toward implementing its recommendations.

The one tangible achievement of the Washington conference was the establishment of the Bureau of American Republics. Although the Bureau was "of small consequence to anybody,"[54] its continued existence, however precarious, provided a living embodiment and symbol of hemispheric cooperation throughout the 1890s. Indeed, the fact that the initial ten-year term of the Bureau was set to expire in 1900 directed attention to the future of Pan Americanism and was one of the reasons for President McKinley's recommendation in 1899 that a second inter-American conference should be scheduled. That the Second Conference of American States was held successfully in Mexico City in 1901–1902 enhanced the significance of the Washington conference. Instead of appearing solitary and unsuccessful, the 1889–1890 meeting became the first of a series of Pan American conferences representing a system that the United States manipulated to extend its hegemony over Latin America. In retrospect, it appeared to some that Blaine's 1881 initiative and the Washington conference were part of a calculated and systematic Pan American policy. In reality, the political consensus that had formed during the 1880s, and which had brought the Washington conference into being, fell apart during the 1890s, nullifying much of the work of the conference. Nevertheless, despite the limitations and inconsistency of Pan American policy, that the Washington conference was held after decades of neglect was notable in demonstrating the political preeminence and economic influence of the United States in the hemisphere, and that country's impressive capacity to alter the historical pattern of inter-American relations.

NOTES

1. The first use of "Pan American" in connection with the 1889 conference was in *New York Evening Post*, 7 September 1889, cited in Jesús María Yepes. *Philoso-*

phie de Panaméricanisme et organisation de la paix—le droit Panaméricain (Paris, 1945), 25.

2. Cited in Philip S. Foner, ed., *Inside the Monster: Writings on the United States and American Imperialism by José Martí* (New York, 1975), 340. See also Peter Turton, *José Martí: Architect of Cuba's Freedom* (London, 1986), 86–93.

3. "The United States and the South American Nations," *South American Journal*, 14 September 1889.

4. See William Appleman Williams, *The Roots of the Modern American Empire* (New York, 1969) and Walter LaFeber, *The New Empire: An Interpretation of American Expansion, 1860–1898* (Ithaca, 1963).

5. Josefina Z. Vazquez and Lorenzo Meyer, *México frente a Estados Unidos* (Mexico City, 1981), 97.

6. "The American Congress," *South American Journal*, 19 April 1890.

7. A. Curtis Wilgus, "James G. Blaine and the Pan American Movement," *Hispanic American Historical Review*, 5 (1922), 662–63.

8. A Chilean described the event as the first step by the United States "away from its traditional route of isolation." See Alejandro Magnet, *Orígenes y antecedentes del Panamericanismo* (Santiago, 1945), 331; Stephen C. Topik, *Trade and Gunboats: The United States and Brazil in the Age of Empire* (Stanford, 1997), 38–39.

9. David M. Pletcher, *The Awkward Years: American Foreign Relations under Garfield and Arthur* (Columbia, 1962), 59–86.

10. James G. Blaine, "Foreign Policy of the Garfield Administration," *Chicago Weekly Magazine*, 16 September 1882.

11. Joseph B. Lockey, *Pan-Americanism: Its Beginnings* (New York, 1920), 4.

12. Carl Schurz, "Mr. Blaine's Manifesto," p. 99. *The Nation*, 9 February 1882; Robert L. Beisner, *Twelve against Empire: The Anti-Imperialists, 1898–1900* (New York, 1968), 18–34.

13. James G. Blaine, *Political Discussions* (Norwich, CT: 1887), 419.

14. *Congressional Record*, 45th Cong. 3rd sess., 2131.

15. House, 48th Cong. 1st sess. 1884, H. Doc. 1445.

16. *Congressional Record*, 50th Cong., 1st sess., Appendix, p. 308.

17. Joanne Reitano, *The Tariff Question in the Gilded Age* (University Park, PA, 1994), 18.

18. Foner, 348.

19. Julian Pauncefote, Memorandum, 15 February 1890, FO 5/2085, Public Record Office, London (PRO).

20. Bayard to Walker, 18 January 1889, Instructions, Record Group (RG) 59, National Archives (NA) of the United States, Washington.

21. Denys to Salisbury, no. 27, 11 July 1889; Denys to Salisbury, no. 21, 6 September 1889, FO 50/469, PRO.

22. Untitled editorial, *Buenos Ayres Herald*, 7 September 1889.

23. Robert N. Burr, *By Reason or Force* (Berkeley, 1965), 188.

24. "Mistaken Notions," *Indianapolis Journal*, 20 September 1889.

25. "The Congress of American Nations," *Frank Leslie's Illustrated Newspaper*, 8 June 1889, p. 1. This article was published anonymously by Curtis.

26. Ibid.

27. "A Preliminary Blunder," *The Nation*, 17 October 1889, p. 304.

28. "Romero on the Pan American Congress," *The Nation*, 4 September 1890, p. 183.

29. Blaine to McKinley, 10 April 1890, cited in Ida M. Tarbell, *The Tariff in Our Times* (New York, 1911), 204.

30. William E. Curtis, *The United States and Foreign Powers* (New York, 1899), 73.

31. William E. Curtis, *Trade and Transportation between the United States and Spanish America* (Washington, 1889), 285.

32. International American Conference, 1889–1890, *Minutes of the Conference* (Washington, 1890), 304. See also Miguel Angel Scenna, *Como fueron las relaciones argentino-norteamericanos* (Buenos Aires, 1970), 83.

33. Untitled editorial, *South American Journal*, 8 March 1890.

34. International American Conference, 711.

35. Carlos Márquez Sterling, "1890: The First International Conference of American States," *Américas* 4 (1970): 12.

36. Abbott to Blaine, no. 107, 6 August 1890, Colombia Dispatches, 45, RG 59, NA.

37. International American Conference, 857.

38. Spenser St. John to Salisbury, no. 6, 19 February 1890, FO 50/474, PRO.

39. Lincoln Hutchinson, "The Results of Reciprocity with Brazil," *Political Science Quarterly* 18 (1903): 282–303; Topik, 210–11.

40. John A. Caruso, "The Pan American Railway," *Hispanic American Historical Review* 31 (1951): 608–39.

41. International American Conference, 535.

42. James F. Vivian, "Four Missing Men: Directors of the Bureau of American Republics, 1893–1899," *Inter-American Review of Bibliography* 24 (1974): 48.

43. International American Conference, 535.

44. Curtis to Blaine, 31 October 1891, in Bureau of American Republics, *First Annual Report 1891* (Washington, 1892), 7.

45. "Mr Blaine's Ambition," *New York Times*, 25 June 1890.

46. *Congressional Record*, 52nd Cong. 1st sess. 3672.

47. Ibid., 3673.

48. "Report from Washington," *New York Tribune*, 4 May 1892.

49. Vivian, 33–35.

50. *Congressional Record*, 53rd Cong., 2nd sess., 4148; LaFeber, 202.

51. Ibid., 6987.

52. Ibid., 5437.

53. House, 53rd Cong., 3rd sess., H. Doc. 116, 4–5.

54. Untitled editorial, *New York Mail and Express*, 31 July 1897.

4

Leo Stanton Rowe and the Meaning of Pan Americanism

David Barton Castle

In a 1935 radio address, Leo Stanton Rowe spoke with great enthusiasm about the success of the Pan American movement. "In these moments of world-wide uncertainty and misgiving," he began, "it is with a feeling of genuine relief that one turns to the international situation on the American Continent." In contrast to Europe, where distrust, antagonisms, and enmities were the dominant themes, the relationships between the American republics "reflected a spirit of cooperation, of mutual confidence and helpfulness which is growing stronger with each year." Rowe was convinced that Pan Americanism was one of the most significant movements of his time and that it was "destined to have far-reaching consequences both for the civilization of the Americas and for their influence in world affairs."[1] Throughout his career Rowe gave hundreds of such inspirational talks, each reflecting his faith in the ideals of Pan Americanism and his belief that a commitment to those ideals would benefit the entire hemisphere. Rowe's vision of Pan Americanism combined elements of progressive thought, a faith in the benefits of international cooperation, and his own theories of political and economic development. The realization of this vision, he believed, would result in mutual understanding between the United States and South America, political stability throughout the hemisphere, and Latin America's economic development.

Leo Rowe was one of the most significant figures in the Pan American movement during the first half of the twentieth century. Between 1900, when he was appointed to the U.S. Commission to Revise and Compile the Laws of Porto Rico, and his death in 1946, Rowe was involved in almost every aspect of U.S.–Latin American relations. He was a respected scholar of Latin American history and politics and wrote several books about the region. He taught for many years at the University of Pennsylvania, where he trained a number of other historians of Latin America, including Dana Gardner Munro. Between 1901 and 1917, he served as a member or delegate to nine inter-American commissions and conferences. During a brief career with the U.S. government, he worked first as assistant secretary of treasury (handling Latin American trade and other international financial issues) and later as chief of the Latin American division of the State Department. Rowe left the State Department in 1920 to become director general of the Pan American Union, a post he held until his death twenty-six years later.

At the time of his death, Rowe was eulogized by many as one of the principal architects of inter-American cooperation and as the personification of Pan Americanism. But despite this contemporary acclaim, historical treatments of Rowe are few; there have been no biographies of Rowe, nor is he prominent in the histories of U.S.–Latin American relations for this period.[2] The chief reason for Rowe's virtual absence from the history books is that his raison d'etre, Pan Americanism, is widely considered to have been a mere tactic employed by the United States either to impose and maintain U.S. economic hegemony over Latin America or to gain hemispheric security.[3] The discrepancy between Pan American ideals and the reality of U.S.–Latin American relations has prompted scholars to assess Pan Americanism harshly. Rowe's idealism has been dismissed as rhetoric, cynically designed to boost domestic and hemispheric support for the Pan American movement and for U.S.–Latin American policy in general. Even historians who have viewed the movement more sympathetically have underplayed its ideas and usually concluded that Pan Americanism was ineffectual.[4] Many studies simply ignore Pan Americanism.

There is some truth in the negative assessments. Inter-American security was certainly a fundamental component of Pan Americanism, particularly in the late 1930s and during World War II, when the threat of Nazi Germany convinced U.S. policy makers to seek new hemispheric alliances. Security remained an overriding priority during the Cold War; hemispheric defense against communism seemed essential to Washington policy makers.[5] Furthermore, a primary function of the Pan American movement was to promote U.S. trade and increase U.S. investment in Latin America. Still, it would be a mistake to dismiss the rhetoric behind the movement as unimportant or to attribute U.S. enthusiasm for the movement to cynical self-interest alone. For Rowe and other intellectuals, Pan Americanism involved more than realpolitik concerns about hemispheric security and the continued growth of U.S. trade. It also embodied notions that reflected a sense of noble purpose and, to a certain extent, altruism; these included the philosophy of internationalism, the Western Hemisphere idea, and "progressive" economic theories. In that regard, Pan Americanism provided intellectuals with an outlet for the "missionary impulse" that has long been a component (albeit a sometimes subordinate one) of U.S. foreign policy.[6]

The purpose of this chapter is not to prove that the idealism behind the Pan

American movement was more important than pragmatic motives. That cannot be demonstrated and, at any rate, is probably not true. The intent is to examine some of the ideas behind the Pan American movement, particularly the conceptual framework with which Rowe approached Pan Americanism and thought about U.S.–Latin American policy. Such an examination should shed some light on the climate of opinion within which U.S. policies were formulated and reveal some of the intellectual assumptions behind Pan Americanism.[7]

Along with most other "experts" on the region, Rowe saw Latin America's main problem as being one of "backwardness," and he shared with them a conviction that it was the United States' responsibility to alleviate that condition. In that sense, Rowe fits Mark Berger's model of intellectuals dominated by a "powerful mixture of assumptions" that included Anglo-Saxon racism, reform Darwinism, and a sense of U.S. mission.[8] However, Rowe's approach to Latin America was more subtle. He developed a philosophy of Pan Americanism that would accomplish modernization without overt U.S. interference in the affairs of its neighbors. The core ideas in his philosophy were nonintervention by a nation in another nation's internal affairs; hemispheric trade and U.S. investment in Latin America; and cultural and intellectual exchange between Latin America and the United States.[9] Together they constituted a comprehensive conceptual approach to the related issues of Latin American's development and U.S.–Latin American relations. Rowe was convinced that commitment to these principles would result in peace, prosperity, and mutual understanding between North and South America, accelerate Latin America's development, and advance what he believed to be the "mission" of the Americas: to provide the rest of the world with an example of the benefits of international cooperation.

Rowe developed two key concepts that influenced his approach to Latin America. One was the importance of the environment in shaping human character and as a means of promoting social progress. The other was the idea that political systems were relative, in the sense that the nature of political discourse and the applicability of political institutions changed for different eras and for different places within the same period.[10] The main subject here was the role of cities in promoting progress and social and cultural advancement. Rowe's enthusiasm for the city extended to an association of urbanization with progress. He often returned to the idea of a positive manipulation of the environment when confronting the problems of Latin America. He also emphasized the interplay between political ideas, political forms, and political problems. For cities to have a healthy political system, political institutions had to be adapted to political and social conditions rather than to political ideals. He argued that the emphasis should be on political forms that would work, as opposed to idealized democratic forms that proved inefficient, even if the result would be a movement away from pure "democracy" and toward increased government centralization and authority.[11]

Rowe believed in political relativism. He thought it was a mistake to elevate features unique to one society as general principles applicable to all. Rowe's ideas on political relativism and the influence of local conditions on political forms were influenced by the writings of the English economic and political theorist Walter Bagehot (1826–1877). Bagehot wrote about the social psychology of economic and political development. He emphasized the importance of customs to the organization of society and maintained that fundamental differences existed between societies. As a result, there were no universally applicable economic or political principles. The principles of representative democracy, for example, were not necessarily valid for all societies and nations. According to Bagehot, economic and political behavior was rooted in cultural, social, and psychological factors.[12] Like Rowe, he believed that societies could gradually progress toward ideal political forms.

The idea of nonintervention was supported by many Pan Americanists as either an abstract principle of international cooperation or, more concretely, as a means of limiting U.S. unilateralism in Latin America. Although Rowe agreed that a commitment to nonintervention would advance the cause of internationalism and improve hemispheric relations, he also believed that it was a prerequisite to Latin American progress. His belief followed from his concept of political relativism and his theory that stable government was necessary for social and economic advancement. Rowe believed that the keys to Latin America's advancement were political stability and economic growth. The latter could be dependent on the former in that the international capital necessary for economic development would not be available to a nation suffering from chronic political upheaval. Because stability was crucial, it was essential that the nations of Latin America establish political institutions and systems that were in harmony with their historical traditions and social structures. U.S. interventions designed to impose constitutionalism were counterproductive, interfering with stability.

It was clear to Rowe that political forms for Latin America would involve government centralization, national leadership by an educated elite, and a tendency toward strong executive authority, not representative democracy as it was known in the United States. In his recommendations about the structure of Puerto Rico's government, Rowe advocated a retention of the Spanish practice of centralized authority rather than the establishment of local autonomy. In the aftermath of the island's cession to the United States from Spain, many Puerto Ricans demanded full political rights (as they existed in the United States) and an end to local subservience to the central government.[13] Rowe argued against such rights. He reasoned that the island needed to retain the system of central control over the towns and rural areas until Puerto Ricans had developed the ability to handle the freedom of local autonomy. Otherwise, efficiency and stability would break down and further delay the island's progress. Rowe championed Pan Americanism because he hoped that the success of the movement would mean a triumph for the principle of nonintervention, putting an end to the misguided efforts of the United States to force constitutional democracy on unstable Latin American republics.

Only after a nation had established stable government would it be able to attract the foreign investment and trade that was critical to its development. This investment and trade would, Rowe argued, bring about social and economic progress. He wanted more hemispheric trade and increased U.S. investment in Latin America, not because it would accrue economic advantages to the United States but because he thought it would help to advance the region's "backward" nations. Industrialization, for example, would encourage habits of efficiency, promote urbanization, and lead to the rise of a middle class.[14] In 1927, when describing the role of North American companies in Latin America, he partially explained how this occurred: U.S. corporations not only created better living conditions for their laborers but also taught workers and their wives

how to live better, to increase the variety of their food, [and] to create a home environment which will make the laborer feel that this is the place where he wants to stay and which will make it necessary for the laborer, in order to enjoy the higher standard of living, to work and not roam about from place to place.[15]

Social changes triggered by industrialization were a natural phenomenon rather than the result of intentional policies, although change could also be accomplished through intentional action, such as progressive legislation. Like Bagehot, Rowe believed that values (Bagehot's "cake of custom") would change through the introduction of variations in economic and social relations and habits, and industrialization represented one such variation. The association between values and the process of development (including industrialization and urbanization) was common in Rowe's day although, like the term *progress*, the links were imprecisely defined. The idea owes much to Spencerian theories of social evolution but is also evident in the writings of progressive urban reformists.[16] The connection between economic growth and progress was also made by Rowe's contemporary, economist Edwin R. A. Seligman. In his influential analysis of the economic interpretation of history, Seligman agreed that the "chief considerations in human progress are the social considerations, and that the important factor in social change is the economic factor." Industrialization, he concluded, was essential to the development of a modern society.[17]

Rowe was not unaware of the dangers inherent in his formula for Latin America's progress. Rowe recognized that economic growth in Latin America could be misdirected, resulting in serious inequities of wealth. Another problem was that centralized and authoritarian governments could become too rigid and thus be unable to adapt to changing political conditions. According to Rowe, this is what had happened in Mexico under Porfirio Díaz. Díaz was so successful in "establishing order . . . favoring economic development and discouraging political agitation" that a middle class had indeed developed. This new class, instilled with modern values and having strong political interests, chafed under his repression. Díaz failed to understand that this dissent was an indication of progress, and so he did not liberalize his regime accordingly. The result, Rowe argued, was the Mexican Revolution.[18]

Rowe considered cultural and intellectual exchange between Latin America and the United States to be as important as nonintervention and expanded economic ties. He was especially concerned about the widespread ignorance among his own countrymen regarding the rest of the hemisphere and their tendency to view Latin American society with prejudice and disdain. The United States, he claimed, treated its southern neighbors with an "attitude of ill-feigned contempt" and showed little understanding of Latin American culture. Meanwhile, Latin Americans reacted to the United States with distrust and suspicion. Intellectual cooperation would smooth commercial relations between North and South America, not only by removing mutual antagonism but also by familiarizing North Americans with the needs, culture, and tastes of their Latin American trading partners. Rowe hoped that cross-cultural exchange would also assist in the abandonment of intervention, once the United States understood the nature of political development in Latin America and realized that its republics were "slowly, but with firmness and wisdom, working out their [own] political salvation."[19]

Rowe's enthusiasm over Pan Americanism also stemmed from his belief that the diffusion of ideas was critical to the progress of civilization. Thus, intellectual interchange was one of the most effective ways that the United States could assist Latin America's development. Rowe accepted the underlying premise of the Western Hemisphere idea: the notion that the nations of the Western Hemisphere were united in a special relationship based upon both geography and a shared historical and political heritage. The Western Hemisphere idea had its origins in the seventeenth century and Europe's conception of the New World, but it was not really developed by North and South Americans (among them, Jefferson and Bolívar) until the early nineteenth century. The idea was revitalized in the early twentieth century by Herbert E. Bolton, one of the leading Latin Americanists in the United States.[20]

To most North Americans, the Western Hemisphere idea meant that the republics of Latin America would become more like the United States and that U.S. economic and political values would eventually triumph throughout the hemisphere. Some took this idea a step further and advocated that the United States actively impose its values on the rest of the hemisphere. This view was articulated by Herbert Croly in his widely read book, *The Promise of American Life*. Croly fused the Western Hemisphere idea with the concept of Manifest Destiny when he called for hemispheric solidarity to be developed within a "stable American international system." He acknowledged that the "forcible pacification of one or more centers of disorder" might be necessary in order to establish this system, but he argued that the "great work" of civilizing Latin America justified the use of force.[21]

Rowe differed from Croly and others who wanted to see those ideas forced on recalcitrant Latin American republics. In fact, he warned against such impatience and criticized the North American "missionary spirit."[22] Rowe argued that such forced changes would be out of harmony with political and social conditions and would probably result in greater instability. A society's exposure to new ideas, however, could help in the development of more "progressive" values, thus accelerating (albeit slightly) the process of development. Rowe worked to promote increased trade and commerce between the United States and Latin America by giving lectures to business groups and by writing articles. He often emphasized the importance of U.S. capital in the form of loans and credit to Latin America. Without this investment, the construction of infrastructure and the process of industrialization could not occur. Latin Americans, he wrote, had not yet developed "habits of thrift" and did not have sufficient native capital to carry out these programs on their own. He also touched on the ancillary benefits of international trade, which included closer intellectual and cultural ties, and provided some practical advice on doing business in Latin America.[23]

Rowe thought that the State Department should adopt a more active role in monitoring the activities of U.S. business interests in Latin America. In doing so, the government would improve the coordination between U.S. foreign policy and private U.S. economic and industrial policy. It would also serve to check the power of U.S. financial interests in the region. Rowe recognized that U.S. corporations had tended to become involved in the internal affairs of Latin American countries, even to the point of funding revolutions. In a bit of an understatement, he acknowledged that this was a great source of mistrust between Latin America and the United States. For that reason, he felt that the State Department should discourage American corporations from "attempting to secure monopolistic privileges,"[24] but it should also be emphasized that Rowe was not opposed to the extension of U.S. economic influence in Latin America. As we have seen, he was convinced that economic development was the engine of social change, and he was just as certain that U.S. business enterprises were a critical factor in the social improvement and industrial progress of the nations in which they invested.

In contrast to his recommendations regarding the dangers of political intervention, Rowe's economic policies seem both paternalistic and intrusive. However, given his theories of progress, a "hands off" policy in terms of political intervention was not at all inconsistent with a manipulative one in terms of economic development. Whereas political solutions had to reflect indigenous traditions, economic conditions could be influenced by outside forces in a positive way. Hence, Rowe could reject political interference but remain committed to economic penetration as a means of implementing social development.

When he became director general of the Pan American Union, Rowe continued to try to implement his ideas. He agreed on economic policy with the State Department, but he was no tool of Wall Street. Rowe saw no conflict between his role as the spokesman for the inter-American movement and efforts on behalf of U.S. business interests; he was confident that he was working for the betterment of both Latin America and Pan Americanism. Rowe endorsed the State

Department's policy of loan supervision for private loans between U.S. bankers and Latin American governments. He believed that an active role on the part of the government would give U.S. bankers "an added sense of security" and strengthen financial cooperation with the countries of Latin America.[25] He also backed State Department attempts to impose financial reorganization on the debt-ridden republics of Central America. At times Rowe disagreed with U.S. policy. He resisted attempts by the United States to impose control over the agencies of inter-American cooperation. In the early 1920s, he fought Herbert Hoover's efforts to make the Inter-American High Commission a subsidiary of the Commerce Department. Rowe had been the executive secretary for the Commission since its inception and remained in that post after 1920. He had always insisted that it maintain strict neutrality and a complete independence from U.S. politics. Despite Rowe's strenuous objections, Hoover succeeded in absorbing the High Commission into the Commerce Department and soon began exercising close control over it. Rowe resigned as executive secretary, Latin Americans lost interest in the Commission, and by 1935 it had effectively ceased to function.[26]

Rowe also pursued an independent course on political and military intervention in Latin America. He criticized Woodrow Wilson's actions in Mexico and the Caribbean in the 1910s, and in the 1920s he continued to warn against interfering in the political development of Latin America's republics. He rejected not only efforts to impose U.S. versions of democracy and self-government on Latin American nations but also attempts to cajole them toward constitutional rule. Here his views brought him into conflict with official policy and particularly the State Department's policy of nonrecognition. In the 1920s, the general practice of the United States was to refuse diplomatic recognition to governments in Latin America that had come to power through revolution or any other nonconstitutional means. By the mid-1920s Rowe argued that the United States should simply recognize de facto governments. To do otherwise was interference in the region's natural political development. U.S. citizens had to divest themselves of the notion that they were the "teachers of self-government on the American continent" and the "champions of constitutional government."[27]

Rowe continually spoke out against intervention and advised the State Department to address the unpopularity of the Monroe Doctrine in Latin America, but as director general of the Pan American Union he had little influence on U.S. policy. He might have had more had he been willing to see the Pan American Union strengthened so as to address political issues, including Latin America's concerns regarding intervention. The nations of Latin America hoped to use the inter-American movement to circumscribe the power of the United States, but to do so the Pan American Union had to have real authority. Rowe discouraged any such expansion of the organization's responsibilities. He was not, in this case, simply following the lead of the State Department (which also opposed such an expansion). Rowe was afraid, with justification, that the introduction of sensitive political issues into Pan American debates would fatally fracture the inter-American movement. As early as 1906, he warned that political questions that might "arouse sensibilities and antagonisms" should be avoided at inter-American conferences.[28]

Despite its limitations, Rowe vigorously defended the movement against its opponents. Rowe and the State Department were in better agreement on the importance of cultural and intellectual contact. In the 1920s such efforts were still considered the province of private groups and international organizations; the State Department did not actively promote or implement cultural and intellectual exchange programs of its own. Nevertheless, individuals in the State Department believed in the efficacy of such an approach and encouraged the Pan American Union to promote closer ties between the republics of Latin America and the United States through inter-American conferences, faculty and student exchanges, and a host of other programs. Rowe wanted the movement to succeed so badly, however, that he refused to acknowledge its real weaknesses and instead constantly emphasized its symbolic triumphs. He could take a relatively minor accomplishment, such as the establishment of overseas telephone communications between Cuba and the United States or the building of the Columbus Memorial Lighthouse in the Dominican Republic, and proclaim it as an event of "far deeper significance" than it might appear, since it invariably represented the "spirit of continental unity and solidarity" or marked "a step forward in the growth of mutual understanding and goodwill."[29] Underlying Rowe's optimism was his conviction that the republics of Latin America and the United States would grow closer as they became culturally and economically entwined. Although his conviction was based on reasoned theories of progress, development, and the nature of international relationships, it appeared to most observers to be simply a naive faith in the idealistic possibilities of Pan Americanism. As a result, Rowe became an increasingly marginalized participant in debates in the United States on Latin America.[30]

Rowe's faith in the Pan American movement as a panacea for the hemisphere's problems proved unfounded. The reality of Pan Americanism never matched Rowe's praise for the movement, nor did it accomplish the goals he had set for it. Even during the period of President Franklin D. Roosevelt's Good Neighbor policy—when Rowe's ideas on nonintervention, cultural exchange, and U.S. capital investment in the region were adopted as the basic framework of U.S.–Latin American relations—mistrust and antagonism between the United States and Latin America continued. Neither the Good Neighbor policy nor Pan Americanism could bring the political development and economic progress that Rowe had claimed they would. While authoritarian regimes became the norm throughout the hemisphere in the 1930s, there was little evidence of any political development that would lead to the replacement of these dictatorships by democratic governments. Meanwhile, most of Latin America's republics remained poor, underdeveloped, and economically dependent on the United States. In the end, Rowe's ideas provided additional intellectual justification for U.S. hegemony over both Latin America and the Pan American movement. In fact, Rowe helped to reinforce this hegemonic trend by aggressively promoting U.S. economic and cultural expansion in Latin America, with the Pan American movement as the agency of that expansion, and by opposing the grant of any real power to the inter-American organization. The Latin American policies of the United States remained interventionist, albeit more through cultural and economic influences than gunboats and marines. The result was that Pan Americanism, though championed by Rowe and others as an idealistic effort at hemispheric cooperation, became another manifestation of U.S. imperialism.

NOTES

1. Leo S. Rowe, "The Present Day Significance of Pan Americanism," (Radio address delivered before the George Washington University Forum, Washington, D.C., 13 December 1935), *Bulletin of the Pan American Union* 81 (April 1947): 253–55.

2. Two dissertations provide the only exceptions: Gustav Sallas, "Leo S. Rowe, Citizen of the Americas" (Ph.D. diss., George Washington University, 1956), and Donald Joseph Murphy, "Professors, Publicists, and Pan Americanism, 1905–1917: A Study in the Origins of the Use of 'Experts' in Shaping American Foreign Policy" (Ph.D. diss., University of Wisconsin, 1970).

3. See, for example, Mark T. Berger, *Under Northern Eyes: Latin American Studies and US Hegemony in the Americas, 1898–1990* (Bloomington, 1995); Alonso Aguilar, *Pan Americanism from Monroe to the Present: A View from the Other Side* (New York, 1968).

4. See John Edwin Fagg, *Pan-Americanism* (Malabar, FL, 1982); and Samuel F. Bemis, *The Latin American Policy of the United States* (New York, 1943).

5. Roger R. Trask, "The Impact of the Cold War on United States–Latin American Relations, 1945–1949," *Diplomatic History* 1 (1977): 271–84; "Conference for the Maintenance of Peace and Continental Security" (Rio de Janeiro, 1947) and "Ninth Inter-American Conference" (Bogotá, 1948) in Samuel Guy Inman, *Inter-American Conferences 1826–1954: History and Problems*, (Washington, 1965), 224–52.

6. Frederick Merk and Lois Bannister Merk, *Manifest Destiny and Mission in American History: A Reinterpretation* (New York, 1963), 261–66.

7. See Michael H. Hunt, *Ideology and U.S. Foreign Policy* (New Haven, 1987), xi; Michael H. Hunt, "Ideology," in "A Round Table: Explaining the History of American Foreign Relations," *Journal of American History* 77 (June 1990): 99–107, 108–15; Frank Ninkovich, "Interests and Discourse in Diplomatic History," *Diplomatic History* 13 (Spring 1989): 135–61; and Berger, 1–19, 25–55.

8. Berger, 35–37.

9. See "Possibilities of Intellectual Cooperation," 1908, and "Memorandum on the Latin American Situation," 16 October 1933, Box 9, *Papers of Leo S. Rowe*, Organization of American States (OAS), Washington.

10. Leo S. Rowe, "American Political Ideas and Institutions in Their Relation to the Problem of City Government," *Municipal Affairs* 1 (June 1897): 317–28.

11. Leo S. Rowe, "Problems in Political Science," *Annals of the American Academy* 10 (September 1897): 165–86.

12. Walter Bagehot, *Physics and Politics: or, Thoughts on the Application of the*

Principles of "Natural Selection" and "Inheritance" to Political Society (New York, 1893).

13. Leo S. Rowe, *The United States and Porto Rico: With Special Reference to the Problems Arising out of Our Contact with the Spanish-American Civilization* (New York, 1904), 172–73, 238–40; Leo S. Rowe, "The Reorganization of Local Government in Cuba," *Annals of the American Academy* 25 (March 1905): 320–21; House, *Report of the Commission to Revise and Compile the Laws of Porto Rico*, vol. 1, 57th Cong., 1st sess., 1901, H. Doc. 52, 54–58.

14. Leo S. Rowe, "The Mexican Revolution and Its Causes and Consequences," *Political Science Quarterly* 27 (June 1912): 281–97; "The Progress and Prosperity of Central America," n.d. Box 13, *Rowe Papers*, OAS.

15. "Discussion of the Action of the Latin American Nations toward the United States by a Brief Summarized Statement of the Present Influences Both Favorable and Unfavorable Affecting the Attitude of the Latin American Countries toward the United States," 24 October 1927, Box 22, *Rowe Papers*, OAS.

16. See David Wiltshire, *The Social and Political Thought of Herbert Spencer* (Oxford, England, 1978), 192–256; Michael H. Frisch, "Urban Theorists, Urban Reform, and American Political Culture in the Progressive Period," *Political Science Quarterly* 97 (Summer 1982): 295–315.

17. Edwin R. A. Seligman, *The Economic Interpretation of History* (New York, 1903), 67.

18. "Mexico: Problem in Political Science," Box 9, *Rowe Papers*, OAS.

19. Leo S. Rowe, "Our Interest in a United America," *North American Review* 189 (April 1909): 588–91.

20. Arthur P. Whitaker, *The Western Hemisphere Idea: Its Rise and Decline* (Ithaca, 1954), 1–2; Herbert E. Bolton, *Wider Horizons of American History* (New York, 1939).

21. Herbert Croly, *The Promise of American Life* (New York, 1963), 289–307; William E. Leuchtenburg, "Progressivism and Imperialism: The Progressive Movement and American Foreign Policy, 1898–1916," *Mississippi Valley Historical Review* 39 (1952): 483–504.

22. "Attitude of the Latin-American Peoples toward the United States," [n.d. 1906–1912], Box 12, *Rowe Papers*, OAS.

23. Leo S. Rowe, "Latin America as a Factor in International Relations," in *The History and Nature of International Relations*, edited by Edmund A. Walsh (New York, 1922), 208; Mark T. Gilderhus, *Pan American Visions: Woodrow Wilson in the Western Hemisphere, 1913–1921* (Tucson, 1986), 57; "Some Requisites for the Development of a Closer Commercial Relationship with Central and South America," 2 November 1920, Box 16, *Rowe Papers*, OAS.

24. "Inter-American Problems in the Foreign Policy of the United States," 6 August 1926, Institute of Politics, Williams College, 4th conf., round table no. 4, Box 16; "Relations between the United States and Latin America," 23 February 1911, Box 1; "Inter-American Problems in the Foreign Policy of the United States," 25 August 1926, Institute of Politics, Williams College, 12th conf., round table no. 7, Box 26; all *Rowe Papers*, OAS.

25. Joseph S. Tulchin, *The Aftermath of War: World War I and US Policy toward Latin America* (New York, 1971), 155–205; Rowe to Julius G. Lay, 11 March 1919, 810.51/915, Record Group (RG) 59; Rowe, Latin American Division memorandum, 23

March 1920, RG 59, 817.51/1198, National Archives (NA) of the United States, Washington.

26. Tulchin, 113; Rowe to State Department, 25 February 1916, 411.19 L 22/415, RG 59, NA.

27. "Inter-American Problems," 30 July 1926; "Inter-American Problems," 4 August 1926; "United States and Central America," 6 August 1924; all Box 26, *Rowe Papers*, OAS.

28. "Purpose of the Pan American Union," radio address, 18 February 1932, Box 2, *Rowe Papers*, OAS.

29. Leo S. Rowe, "Columbus Day Radio Address," 12 October 1929, Box 26, *Rowe Papers*, OAS.

30. Sallas, ii–ix; Robert N. Seidel, "Progressive Pan Americanism: Development and United States Policy toward South America, 1906–1931," (Ph.D. diss., Cornell University, 1973), 147; Julius Klein to Herbert Hoover, 20 June 1923, Commerce Papers, Herbert Hoover Presidential Library, West Branch, Iowa. For contemporary accusations of Rowe's naiveté, see correspondence between Edward Duffy (a contributor to *The Nation*) and Oswald Garrison Villard: Duffy to Villard, 2 June 1927, Oswald G. Villard Collection, bMS Am 1323 (3344), Houghton Library, Harvard University, Cambridge, MA.

5

A Greater America? Pan Americanism and the Professional Study of Latin America, 1890–1990

Mark T. Berger

During the nineteenth century, and well into the twentieth, the most influential North American narratives on Latin America represented the United States as civilized, progressive, virtuous, democratic, and developed in contrast to the uncivilized, corrupt, undemocratic, and underdeveloped lands to the south. Since the early 1800s, Latin America has been homogenized and objectified as essentially different from, and in negative opposition to, the United States. However, with the First Conference of American States in 1889–1890, the establishment of the Commercial Bureau of the American Republics, and the appearance of Pan Americanism as a political and intellectual current, an ostensibly more favorable image of an America (North and South) with a common history and destiny also began to gain influence in the United States.[1] Since World War I some version of Pan Americanism has increasingly challenged, but certainly not displaced, those representations of Latin America that emphasize the region's difference from and inferiority to the United States. By the second half of the twentieth century, North and South America were also increasingly represented as having a shared history, heritage, and commitment to democratic values (a trend that has accelerated with the end of the Cold War).

The rise of Pan Americanism in the early twentieth century coincided with the professionalization of the study of Latin America. Pan American ideas have been central to the institutionalization of Latin American studies in North America between the First and Second World Wars. This process has been, and continues to be, linked to a tendency on the part of U.S. historians, political scientists, and policy makers to project distinctly North American ideas about a common past and a common future on the region as a whole. This chapter charts the growing significance of Pan Americanism to the professional study of Latin America during the twentieth century. Pan Americanism, along with Cold War–era modernization and development theories, provides the crucial underpinning for the dominant professional narratives on Latin America and complement the way in which U.S. politicians and policy makers have approached Latin America. Moreover, despite the inclusive character of Pan American ideas, inter-American power relations have ensured that Latin American studies and U.S. policy have exercised dominance over Pan American discourses in the Americas.

Between the late nineteenth century and the 1920s, the United States emerged as the main imperial power in the Caribbean. Many countries in that region saw their economies and political institutions subordinated to the North American economy and the U.S. government. This occurred in the wider context of the U.S. emergence as a great power by 1898 and its subsequent rise to global predominance by the end of World War II. Changes in U.S. foreign policy in Latin America between the early 1920s and the 1940s flowed in part from a shift from underlying Anglo-Saxon racism in the late nineteenth century to a more expansive, but still virulently ethnocentric, civilizing project underpinned by an emerging Pan Americanism. By the beginning of the twentieth century the United States was clearly a rising world power, at the same time that Latin America was increasingly seen as trapped in a condition of unrest and backwardness. Despite the emergence of Pan American ideas about hemispheric cooperation, and the appearance of embryonic elements of an inter-American infrastructure between 1890 and the early 1920s, Pan Americanism was not strongly reflected in U.S. policy in the Caribbean and beyond until the 1930s. Through the 1920s, U.S. foreign policy continued to be more concerned with punishment than with Pan American cooperation and development. By the end of the 1930s, however, Pan American ideas had risen to a position of some prominence, at the same time that Latin American specialists and U.S. policy makers began to articulate an early version of modernization theory, or liberal developmentalism.[2]

Between 1890 and 1940, against the backdrop of Pan Americanism and an emergent liberal developmentalism, the study of Latin America became an academic specialization. The connection was close between the practice of U.S. foreign policy in Latin America and the professional narratives on Latin America. The work of Latin Americanist academics complemented and helped legitimize the U.S. rise to predominance in the Caribbean region and beyond. Many Latin America specialists who came of age around World War I went from academia to spend at least part of their careers at the State Department, other branches of government, or privately funded organizations and foundations. A Latin American specialist who exemplified these links was Leo S. Rowe, a professor of political science at the University of Pennsylvania. Well connected in government circles and clearly in sympathy with U.S. policy in Latin America, he served as president of the American Academy of Political and Social

Science from 1902 to 1930. Rowe was director general of the Pan American Union from 1920 until 1946.[3]

In *The United States and Porto Rico*, Rowe drew on his work for the U.S. government in Puerto Rico; he characterized U.S. expansion into the Caribbean basin as inevitable. Those countries were natural economic dependencies of the United States. Rowe argued that the United States could learn from European colonial powers about how to manage those dependencies. The United States, Rowe continued, would provide the region with prosperity. He emphasized that the recent U.S. experience in the Caribbean pointed to the necessity for "greater elasticity." If the United States showed "a harsh, unbending spirit" toward Caribbean peoples, a "feeling of distrust" in the region would block the U.S. "mission" in the Americas. "The real significance of the extension" of U.S. influence in the Caribbean was not "territorial aggrandizement" but the introduction of U.S. "political ideas and standards."[4] Like other Latin Americanists, Rowe posed questions in terms that reflected U.S. expansion. His career and approach pointed to the emergence of Pan Americanism as a narrative that rested on U.S. assumptions about progress. Rowe also symbolized the close relationship between Latin Americanists and the state. His work fulfilled an important legitimating function as the United States rose to predominance in Latin America.

Some academics predicted more aggressively than did Rowe that Latin America was headed in a direction complementary to the United States. They emphasized similarities between U.S. and Latin American histories. This became known as the Greater American thesis and meshed with Pan Americanism; it allowed North Americans to believe that they understood Latin America and that the United States could guide the region to a common future. Writing in 1932, Wallace Thompson noted that both U.S. and Latin American cultures originated in Europe and that the Americas possessed a common pioneer experience. Their economies would inevitably become more integrated, and there would be a growing political convergence between north and south.[5] The most influential proponent of a Greater America was University of California (Berkeley) historian Herbert Eugene Bolton. A founder of the *Hispanic American Historical Review*, Bolton was a major historian of the Spanish frontier in North America. In 1932 he gave a now famous address to the American Historical Association in which he reasoned that the history of the Americas should be studied as a comprehensive whole. Bolton stressed common colonial origins, European migrations, the exploitation of indigenous peoples, and a shared struggle for political stability and economic progress, among other themes.[6] Bolton's address marked the shift from Anglo-Saxonism to Pan Americanism among academics. Even so, interest in the unitary and/or comparative study of the history of the Americas faded after 1945. A conventional break between U.S. and Latin American histories persisted, and that demarcation lasted in the minds of policy makers and other North Americans. However, the theme of a common history survived in the rhetoric and work of government employees and would reappear among some Latin Americanists after World War II. Greater America meshed with President Franklin D. Roosevelt's Good Neighbor policy, implemented in 1933, and the growing interest of the United States in developing a hemispheric security structure.

A central objective of the Good Neighbor policy was to substitute the punishment of Latin Americans for "uncivilized behavior" with a Pan American policy that emphasized political and economic integration, development, and stabilization under U.S. leadership. Following the proclamation of the Good Neighbor policy, Washington moved to create an inter-American system based on cooperation, which in theory would respect the sovereignty of the American republics. The emerging Pan American system helped the United States to maintain hegemony in the hemisphere. The Good Neighbor policy increasingly came to accept Latin American dictatorships, which protected U.S. business interests and brought political stability without the cost of U.S. military landings. Under the new Pan Americanism of the Good Neighbor policy, the United States became even more interventionist; now, however, diplomats, military attaches, and economic advisers backed by private capital substituted for marines and gunboats.[7]

One key goal of the Good Neighbor policy was to encourage respect for Latin American cultures. In practice, however, the U.S. government appreciation for hemispheric cultures was limited to the use of cultural ties to bolster U.S. influence. In 1935, Assistant Secretary of State Sumner Welles characterized cultural relations as "but another aspect of the policy of the good neighbor."[8] Grandiose rhetoric was followed by a modest U.S.-funded exchange program. Samuel Guy Inman, an ardent Pan Americanist and proponent of cultural ties in the Americas, was employed to guide the program, which saw the exchange of one professor and two students in 1937. By 1938, neither Inman nor Laurence Duggan, chief of the State Department's Division of the American Republics, was satisfied with the program. It had failed to generate a hoped-for interest on the part of U.S. universities to foster their own exchanges. But later in 1938—in response to reports that European countries were offering Latin American governments technical advisers, academics, and student exchanges—the State Department founded the Division of Cultural Relations. Cultural ties were more overtly tied to business with the creation in 1940 of the Office for the Coordination of Commercial and Cultural Relations between the American Republics (its name was later changed to the Office of the Coordinator of Inter-American Affairs [CIAA]). Under the direction of Nelson A. Rockefeller, the CIAA channeled U.S. economic and cultural influence through the hemisphere to counter Axis propaganda and economic incursions. In the process, it became the major employer of Latin American specialists during World War II.[9]

The CIAA soon overshadowed the Division of Cultural Relations. By 1941 the two offices had begun to work together as the Joint Committee on Cultural Relations, through which the State Department tended to set policy while the CIAA delivered funds. By the end of 1941, hundreds of seminars on inter-

American relations had been held across the United States, and Pan American cooperation and understanding were being propagated in the school system through poster-making and essay competitions. Academic research around a Pan American agenda was also mobilized. In the 1930s the Committee on Latin American Studies of the American Council of Learned Societies had made a limited effort to encourage research on Latin America; the Social Science Research Council was more successful late in the decade, as was the Joint Committee on Latin American Studies in the 1940s. The Joint Committee set out "to focus the attention of North American social scientists on Latin American problems of pressing international concern, especially on those questions which are important in the formulation of American public policy."[10]

The United States emerged from World War II as the dominant power, driven by anticommunist globalism and a commitment to an open world economy in which U.S. business would thrive. The Cold War became a context for the emergence of a more interdisciplinary and methodologically sophisticated social science. Discourses on Latin America were shaped by modernization theory. The U.S. civilizing mission to Latin America became an anticommunist modernizing mission. At the same time, professional discourses on Latin America, like U.S. foreign policy, continued to be shaped by ideas on Pan American cooperation and commonality. Cold War Pan Americanism was central, for example, to J. Lloyd Mecham's works. Mecham argued that because the American republics "were born in popular revolt against a foreign sovereign," there existed throughout the Americas "a consciousness of community of origin." Because Latin American countries had adopted U.S.-influenced constitutions, there was a "sense of community of political institutions and objectives" in the Americas. He insisted that U.S. citizens and Latin Americans were both "motivated by deep underlying spiritual forces" that he characterized as a desire for democracy, peace, independence, and improved social, economic, and educational standards. For Mecham, this led to a commonality of interests in the hemisphere on inter-American security.[11]

Growing North American concerns in the early 1960s that the Cuban Revolution would spread to the rest of the hemisphere caused a dramatic shift in U.S. policy and stimulated what historian Jules Benjamin called "the full flowering of liberal developmentalism" in the Alliance for Progress, President John F. Kennedy's massive aid and development program for Latin America.[12] Latin American studies complemented Alliance goals. At the same time, ideas from the Good Neighbor era resurfaced in the Kennedy administration. Adolf A. Berle had served as U.S. ambassador to Brazil in the 1930s and 1940s; Kennedy charged him with leading the task force on Latin America. Present also were prominent developmentalists such as Seymour Martin Lipset and Max Millikan, Puerto Rican politicians and technocrats Teodoro Mososo and Arturo Morales Carrión, and academic Latin Americanists Robert J. Alexander and Arthur Preston Whitaker. Influenced in part by Operation Bootstrap, a 1940s U.S. government initiative in Puerto Rico to reform the rural social order and increase capital investment, the task force submitted its report in January 1961. Berle and his colleagues identified a communist menace in Latin America more severe than the Nazi threat of the 1940s. In addition to increased economic assistance, the report urged a "psychological offensive" to channel "the vast, powerful, disparate North American intellectual effort so that it reaches Latin America and Latin Americans at all levels, giving effective support to the United States social-economic-political system."[13] The Kennedy administration built on the state-led reformism and Pan Americanism of the Good Neighbor era to breathe new life into Republican-style globalism.

Frank Tannenbaum and J. Lloyd Mecham were among a number of Latin American specialists who supported the Alliance, which failed miserably. The Alliance had an unstated goal, in conjunction with a decade-long program of land and economic reform, to protect U.S. business interests in the region. These objectives were contradictory. U.S.-based transnationals worked with landed Latin American oligarchies, in a context of growing U.S. military aid to dictatorial regimes, to maintain the status quo, even as the Alliance for Progress and Kennedy administration rhetoric promised meaningful change. By the end of the 1960s, as Washington tried to manage the challenges to its empire, particularly in Vietnam, U.S. foreign policy in Latin America entered a decade of neglect. At the same time, Latin American studies grew rapidly. During the presidency of Richard Nixon, U.S. policy toward Latin America was characterized by a conservative militarism that pursued Cold War objectives. Jimmy Carter's presidency initially rejected Cold War assumptions in favor of an emphasis on north-south cooperation and a managerial approach to revolution. Reinvigorated liberal professional discourses on Latin America intersected with the managerial foreign policy of the early Carter years.

Many members of the Latin American Studies Association (LASA) were sympathetic to Carter's human rights emphasis.[14] Founded in the turmoil of the 1960s, LASA quickly emerged to challenge the ethics of the academic-government relationship that had shaped the Pan American consensus through the Cold War period; it objected to the close relationship academics had had in the past with U.S. foreign policies that had ignored persistent poverty, dictatorship, and human rights abuses. LASA members quickly found themselves at odds with the Reagan administration in 1981. They challenged the U.S. militarization of Central American conflicts and the U.S. government emphasis on East-West conflict in explaining social unrest in Latin America. Much of the academic work produced in the 1980s countered Reagan administration policies in the region. Abraham Lowenthal emerged as a prominent Reagan critic. His work reflected the influence of Pan American ideas and wider concerns about the direction of U.S. policy. Lowenthal served on LASA's executive council and coauthored a report, *The Americas in 1984: Year for Decisions*, which emphasized that Reagan's Nicaragua policy was counterproductive, as it undermined U.S. prestige, alienated Latin American governments, hardened the position of the revolutionary Nicaraguan Sandinista government, and legitimated Nicaraguan-Cuban-Soviet relations.[15]

In Lowenthal's view there were four major approaches that the United States might consider to further its "core interests" in the Caribbean basin. He favored a "developmental alternative" in which the United States would work with various political and economic approaches with Latin American governments, "even Marxist ones," as long as they posed no "direct security threat." A major assumption of this development approach was reminiscent of an earlier Pan American view: history, geography, and economics would continue to tie Latin America to the United States. This approach focused on "long-term economic and social progress," not short-term political orientation. It differentiated between those nations "ready for significant economic advance" (virtually every country but El Salvador and Nicaragua, in Lowenthal's view) and nations where "civil turmoil" still represented an obstacle to "effective economic progress" in the short term. Lowenthal advocated that the United States provide "free access" to North American markets to all the countries in Central America and the Caribbean (no matter what their foreign policy, ideology, internal political organization, or socioeconomic structure), except El Salvador and Nicaragua, with the only proviso being that they avoid a military alliance with the USSR. The United States would extend foreign aid for the development of human resources and infrastructure in a multilateral rather than a bilateral context.[16]

By the time Lowenthal had published his book-length study and had mapped out his policy alternatives, the Reagan administration had entered its final year. With the election of George Bush as Reagan's successor and the rapprochement with the Soviet Union, a new consensus around the Bush administration's "pragmatic" approach to foreign affairs appeared imminent.[17] After his election, Bush moved quickly to deal with Reagan's Central American legacy. As Washington sought to end its decade-long obsession with Central America, evidence of growing optimism among some Latin American specialists about the future of inter-American relations was provided by Lester D. Langley. A prominent diplomatic historian, he invoked an idealistic vision of a hemispheric partnership that complemented the Pan American partnership articulated by Lowenthal, Robert Pastor, and others. In the late 1980s, Langley lamented that the current generation of scholars was "less persuaded by the power of ideas in the hemispheric experience" than earlier Latin American specialists had been.[18]

Langley's approach to inter-American history represented ideas and culture as an important but neglected axis of history in the Americas. The "United States" and "America," argued Langley, have pursued historical trajectories that have been both "reinforcing" and "contradictory." He argued that harmonious inter-American relations were also impeded by the "crucial differences" that stemmed from the U.S. "belief" in a "just political order and economic opportunity for the individual," in contrast to Latin America's "faith in the centrality of the social order and an apparent resignation to a failed political tradition and an unfair economic system." Langley asserted his "liberal American's faith" that U.S. relations with Latin America would "be better served by negotiation of disputes" and by the "reaffirmation of hemispheric unity."[19]

Langley's work reaffirmed and emphasized the exceptionalism and idealism that runs through the understanding of U.S. history in the United States and continues to legitimate U.S. predominance in Latin America. His approach reflected powerful Pan American ideas about a common history and destiny, which had remained central to the liberal discourses on Latin America. Langley's preoccupation with culture and a vision of hemispheric harmony built around a U.S. model also referred back to the work of earlier Pan Americanists who had emphasized cultural understanding.

In early 1990, despite the dramatic end of the Cold War and the apparent shift in Washington's policy toward Latin America, Abraham Lowenthal found it hard to be optimistic about the future of U.S.–Latin American relations. The region was entering the 1990s in "deep trouble." Economic and social conditions were "desperate in many countries," and political tensions were on the rise. Cuba was "the only country in the Hemisphere openly defying the regional commitment to democracy." In the face of shaky democracies, Central America was "poised uncertainly between the possibility of peace through utter exhaustion, the prospect of renewed and more violent confrontation, or years more of low-level but deadly conflict." At the same time, Washington's apparent recognition that its "preoccupation" with Central America had been "misplaced" meant that it "may finally be ready in the 1990s to redirect its concerns away from Central America." However, Lowenthal believed that the United States might well "revert to pervasive neglect of Latin America" rather than turning "to such problems as drugs, migration, trade and environmental protection" and the task of "building effective partnerships with its neighbors in the Americas."[20]

Some of Lowenthal's concerns were ostensibly addressed by George Bush's Enterprise for the Americas Initiative, launched on June 27, 1990. The Initiative symbolized the triumph of economic and political liberalism in the hemisphere and beyond. It reflected the consolidation of the new North American consensus around Bush's more pragmatic Latin American policy.[21] According to Roger B. Porter, assistant to the president for economic and domestic policy, this was "part of [Bush's] longstanding interest in encouraging democracy and economic growth in Latin America and the Caribbean." He held the Enterprise for the Americas Initiative up as a "turning point" in inter-American relations. In contrast to an earlier watershed, the Alliance for Progress, which had emphasized the "importance of governments," the Enterprise for the Americas Initiative, according to Porter, was focused on markets—particularly with regard to trade, investment, and debt reduction. It would encourage the negotiation of trade agreements toward a hemispheric free trade area and "unlock the potential for domestic and foreign investment and encourage capital flows" while ensuring the provision of extra debt support and debt-service reduction. He characterized the Initiative as a "new approach to building a stronger economic partnership between the United States, Latin America and the Caribbean" and as "a vital tool for Latin leaders in achieving higher standards of living and meeting the challenges of an increasingly inter-related global economy."[22]

The response to the Initiative by many Latin American specialists was cautiously favorable. For example, Sidney Weintraub (a former diplomat and professor of public affairs at the University of Texas) was doubtful that U.S. free trade treaties with countries other than Mexico were likely in the near future; however, he saw an overall trend in that direction. His main criticism was of the U.S. decision to work toward bilateral free trade agreements. Instead, Weintraub argued for subregional free trade blocs in Central America and the Andes. At the end of 1991, Robert Pastor voiced critical but sympathetic support for Bush's policy. He emphasized that Bush's "pragmatic pursuit of the regionalist option" could lead to the realization of "a century-old dream, a democratic community of the Americas." This would "combine the technology, skills, and capital of North America with the market, resources and labor of the south, creating a formidable new economic and democratic giant."[23]

In early 1991, with the cautious support of Weintraub, Pastor, and others, the U.S. Congress approved some debt relief and gave authority for U.S. representatives to negotiate the North American Free Trade Agreement (NAFTA). By mid-1991 the United States had signed fifteen framework trade agreements with various Latin American republics, forming the basis for the eventual expansion of free trade areas throughout the hemisphere. NAFTA came into effect on January 1, 1994. At the end of that year, thirty-four heads of state from the Americas gathered in Miami to sign the Partnership for Development and Prosperity. During the meeting in Miami, the growing trend toward unification in Europe was repeatedly invoked at the same time as the participants set out the goal of negotiating a Western Hemisphere Free Trade Agreement (WHFTA, soon to be renamed the Free Trade Area of the Americas, or FTAA) by the beginning of 2005. However, after the Miami meeting the momentum for hemispheric integration and laissez-faire capitalism faded somewhat. The growing skepticism about hemispheric free trade was coming from various quarters in the United States as much as, if not more than, from Latin America. The apparent decline in support for regional economic integration and unfettered free trade was reflected in President Bill Clinton's failure to get congressional approval for his fast-track initiative, which would have allowed the president to extend NAFTA southward.[24] The political struggle in the United States to bring NAFTA into being was considerable, and, as the sociologist Joe Foweraker has argued, the "political consensus" in the United States precludes the realization of the grandiose WHFTA by 2005 or thereafter.[25] By the time of the second summit of the Americas, which was held in Santiago, Chile, in April 1998, enthusiasm for regional integration had waned somewhat.

At the same time, the FTAA has many supporters among Latin America experts. For example, in a recent book entitled *The Pan-American Dream*, Lawrence Harrison argues that (t)he realization of a genuine Western Hemisphere community will depend on the speed with which the values that make democracy and the free market really work displace the traditional values that largely explain why . . . Latin America lags so far behind Canada and the United States.[26]

Harrison was adamant "that by far the most important factor behind the divergent evolution of the northern and southern parts of the Western hemisphere is cultural values and attitudes with respect . . . to work, frugality, education, merit, community and justice." He contrasts the Anglo-Protestant culture of North America, in which "progress-prone values are emphasized," with Ibero-Catholic culture, where they are given a "lower priority"; Latin America's "chronically poor policies and weak institutions . . . are principally a cultural phenomenon flowing from the traditional Ibero-Catholic system of values and attitudes."[27] Harrison's vision of a Pan American partnership is a particularly stark ethnocentric variation on a wider theme that has continued to be central to the dominant U.S. narratives on Latin America. They rest on the Pan American assumption that the extension throughout the Americas of liberal economic and political ideas and structures will bring prosperity and democracy for everyone and lead to the emergence of a Greater America.

As the twentieth century dawned, the rise of the United States to a position of growing power in the Americas and the increasing significance of Pan American ideas played a key role in the professionalization of the study of Latin America. Through 1940, professional students of Latin America increasingly invoked a shared past and future in the Americas and emphasized the need for inter-American cooperation. At the same time, as U.S. policy in the Americas drew on the Greater America message, U.S. power and influence in Latin America exacerbated differences between north and south. By the second half of the twentieth century, Pan Americanism and influential modernization theories formalized during the Cold War became the key concepts on which professional and popular narratives on Latin America were constructed. Visions of Pan American cooperation and the overall modernizing projects in which professional Latin American specialists have played such an important role complemented the U.S. political and economic approaches to Latin America. Influential ideas about cooperation and modernization emphasized equal participation and mutual benefit. During the 1980s, under the umbrella of the Latin American Studies Association, many scholars broke openly with U.S. government policy in Latin America and the official version of the Pan American ideal. In the early 1990s, but with more caution than Leo S. Rowe or Herbert Bolton, the vision of a Greater America was held up again, in conjunction with Bush- and Clinton-era neoliberal economic policies, as a cultural, political, and economic model to which all inhabitants of the Americas should aspire and as potentially beneficial to all.

NOTES

1. By the end of the 1930s Pan Americanism was generally understood in the United States as "the cooperative activity of the American states in the political, economic or cultural spheres" (Dexter Perkins, "Bringing the Monroe Doctrine Up to Date," *Foreign Affairs* 20. no. 2 (1942): 26. In this chapter, the definition of Pan Americanism is broader: a changing set of ideas, institutions, practices, and movements linked explicitly and implicitly to assumptions about a range of common experiences and aspirations held by peoples and governments in the Americas. Pan American narratives emphasize the commonality of the hemispheric experience in contrast to other parts of the world. They often point to the necessity and even the naturalness of closer cooperation and integration in the region.

2. See James William Park, *Latin American Underdevelopment: A History of Perspectives in the United States 1870–1965* (Baton Rouge, 1995), 46, 62–63, 75–92; Mark T. Berger, "Power and Progress in the Americas: The Discovery of Latin American 'Underdevelopment' and the Cultural Antecedents of Modernization Theory," *Australasian Journal of American Studies* 15. no. 2 (December 1996); Mark T. Berger, *Under Northern Eyes: Latin American Studies and US Hegemony in the Americas 1898–1990* (Bloomington, 1995), 25–47.

3. Richard M. Morse, "The Strange Career of 'Latin American Studies,' " *Annals of the American Academy of Political and Social Science* 356 (November 1964): 111; Roscoe R. Hill, "Leo S. Rowe," *Hispanic American Historical Review* 27, no. 2 (1947): 187–88.

4. Leo S. Rowe, *The United States and Porto Rico: With Special Reference to the Problems Arising out of Our Contact with the Spanish-American Civilization* (New York, 1904), vii, xi-xiv, 10–13, 17–19, 261.

5. Wallace Thompson, *Greater America: An Interpretation of Latin America in Relation to Anglo-Saxon America* (New York, 1932), 214–16, 245–48.

6. Herbert Eugene Bolton, "The Epic of Greater America," *American Historical Review* 38, no. 3 (1933); Charles Gibson, "Latin America and the Americas" in *The Past Before Us: Contemporary Historical Writing in the United States*, edited by Michael Kammen (Ithaca, 1980), 200–201; John F. Bannon, *Herbert Eugene Bolton: The Historian and the Man, 1870–1953* (Tucson, 1978), 110, 182–189, 255–56.

7. Jules Benjamin, "The Framework of US Relations with Latin America in the Twentieth Century: An Interpretive Essay," *Diplomatic History* 11, no. 2 (1987): 100–102.

8. Sumner Welles, *The Roosevelt Administration and Its Dealings with the Republics of the Western Hemisphere* (Washington, 1935), 1, 16; Sumner Welles, *Pan American Cooperation* (Washington, 1935), 2, 7.

9. Benjamin, 102–104.

10. Preston James, "Outline of Research in the Study of Contemporary Culture Patterns in Latin America" cited in Frank A. Ninkovich, *The Diplomacy of Ideas* (Cambridge, England, 1981), 42.

11. J. Lloyd Mecham, *The United States and Inter-American Security* (Austin, 1961), 462–64, 474–75.

12. Benjamin, 107.

13. Adolf A. Berle, cited in Benjamin, 107–8.

14. Richard L. Clinton and R. Kenneth Godwin, "Human Rights and Development: Lessons from Latin America," in *Latin America, the United States and the Inter-American System*, edited by John D. Martz and Lars Schoultz (Boulder, 1980), 235.

15. Morris H. Morley, *Washington, Somoza and the Sandinistas: State and Regime in U.S. Policy toward Nicaragua 1969–1981* (Cambridge, England, 1994), 1–5, 142–43, 159, 308–9; Inter-American Dialogue, *The Americas in 1984: Year for Decisions* (Queenstown, MD, 1984).

16. Abraham F. Lowenthal, *Partners in Conflict: The United States and Latin America* (Baltimore, 1987), 165–70, 187–89, 196–97, 199–200.

17. Robert A. Pastor, "Forging a Hemispheric Bargain: The Bush Opportunity," *Journal of International Affairs* 43. no. 1 (1989): 71–73; Mark T. Berger, "The Limits of Power and the 'Lessons of History': North American Neo-Liberalism and the US Crisis of Empire in Central America," *Australasian Journal of American Studies* 9. no. 1 (July 1990): 57–69.

18. Lester D. Langley, *America and the Americas: The United States in the Western Hemisphere* (Athens, OH, 1989), xiii, 248–50, 291–92.

19. Langley, xvi–xvii, xix–xx, xxii.

20. Abraham F. Lowenthal, *Partners in Conflict: The US and Latin America in the 1990s*, rev. ed. (Baltimore, 1990), 215–16, 218, 220–22.

21. Berger, 154–227.

22. Roger B. Porter, "The Enterprise for the Americas Initiative: A New Approach," *Journal of Interamerican Studies and World Affairs* 32, no. 4 (1990), 1–2, 4–7, 11.

23. Sidney Weintraub, "The New US Initiative toward Latin America," *Journal of Interamerican Studies and World Affairs* 33, no. 1 (1991): 1–2, 12–16; Robert A. Pastor, "The Bush Administration and Latin America: The Pragmatic Style and the Regionalist Option," *Journal of Interamerican Studies and World Affairs* 33, no. 3 (1991): 22–24, 29.

24. Peter H. Smith, "The United States, Regional Integration and the Reshaping of the International Order," in *Cooperation or Rivalry? Regional Integration in the Americas and the Pacific Rim*, edited by Shoji Nishijma and Peter H. Smith (Boulder, 1996) 42–43.

25. Joe Foweraker, "From NAFTA to WHFTA? Prospects for Hemispheric Free Trade" in Nishijima and Smith, 150–52, 164–67.

26. Lawrence E. Harrison, *The Pan-American Dream: Do Latin America's Cultural Values Discourage True Partnership with the United States and Canada?* (New York, 1997), 24.

27. Ibid. 4, 24, 33.

6

Rubén Darío and Literary Anti-Americanism/Anti-Imperialism

Alberto Prieto-Calixto

To Roosevelt

The voice that would reach you, Hunter, must speak
in Biblical tones, or in the poetry of Walt Whitman.
You are primitive and modern, simple and complex;
you are one part George Washington and four parts Nimrod.
You are the United States,
future invader of our naive America
with its Indian blood, an America
that still prays to Christ and still speaks Spanish.

You are a strong, proud model of your race;
you are cultured and able; you oppose Tolstoy.
You are Alexander-Nebuchadnezzar,
breaking horses and murdering tigers.
(You are a Professor of Energy,
as the current lunatics say).

You think that life is a fire,
that progress is an eruption,
that the future is wherever
your bullet strikes.
     No.

The United States is grand and powerful.
Whenever it trembles, a profound shudder
runs down the enormous backbone of the Andes.

If it shouts, the sound is like the roar of a lion.
And Hugo said to Grant: The stars are yours.
(The dawning sun of the Argentine barely shines;
the star of Chile is rising . . .). You are a wealthy country,
joining the cult of Mammon to the cult of Hercules;
while Liberty, lighting the path
to easy conquest, raises her torch in New York.

But our America, which has had poets
since the ancient times of Nezahualcóyotl;
which preserved the footprints of great Bacchus,
and learned the Panic alphabet once,
and consulted the stars; which also knew Atlantis
(whose name comes ringing down to us in Plato)
and lives, since the earliest moments of its life,
in light, in fire, in fragrance, and in love—
The America of grand Moctezuma and the Inca,
the aromatic America of Columbus,
Catholic America, Spanish America,
the America where noble Cuauhtémoc said:
I am not on a bed of roses—this America,
trembling with hurricanes and living of love:
O men with Saxon eyes and barbarous souls,
our America lives. And dreams. And loves. And vibrates.
And it is the daughter of the sun. Be careful.
Spanish America lives!
A thousand cubs of the Spanish lion are roaming free.
Roosevelt, you must become, by God's own will,
the deadly Rifleman and the dreadful Hunter
before you can clutch us in your iron claws.

And though you have everything, you are lacking one thing:
God![1]

At the turn of the twentieth century, Latin America was engulfed in a series of changes through which different communities tried to define an all-encompassing national identity. It is from within this historical context that the literary movement known as Modernismo emerged. The Modernistas—and particularly their leading literary exponent, Rubén Darío (1867–1916)—have been considered evasive and superficial by some; this widely held opinion followed José Enrique Rodó's now famous declaration: "Rubén Darío is not the poet of America." This chapter challenges this critique to show that Modernismo addressed social and political concerns in a Pan Hispanic context, where Darío's idea of Pan Hispanism (a cultural and ideological union of Latin American peoples, apart from the United States) stood in marked contrast to the U.S.-led, business-oriented Pan Americanism. The poetry of Darío reflects his search for aesthetic regeneration, which in turn calls into question political and ideological issues. In the poems "Salutación del optimista" and "A Roosevelt," for example, Darío inveighs against U.S. imperialism and in favor of Latin American independence. Moreover, through Darío's work we can identify an ideological perspective that underscores his liberal character and his deep conviction for freedom, independence, and self-determination for the peoples of the Americas. This analysis will explore the political and ideological aesthetic in Modernismo, an open challenge to U.S.-dominated Pan Americanism.

In 1905, *Cantos de vida y esperanza, Los cisnes y otros poemas* was published for the first time in Madrid. In this collection we find two of the most well known of Darío's poems, "Salutación del optimista" and "A Roosevelt." Their numerous interpretations reflect different and frequently diametrically opposed points of view, from those of Eduardo Arellano and Fiodor Kelin, for whom these poems represent the culmination of an anti-imperial and socialist revolutionary position, to those of critics who called the poems "trumpet blasts" and "out of place."[2] More moderate positions include that of Cathy L. Jrade, for whom Darío's *Azul* (1890) and *Prosas profanas* (1896) show an important political and philosophical conscience hidden behind the apparent frivolity, musicality, and aesthetic play:

As the Modernist poets reflected upon the formation of nation states and the integration of Spanish America into the world economy, they confronted the issue of Spanish American literature. From this perspective, the political impetus of Modernist literature becomes evident.[3]

The exaltation of art in Modernismo implies a rebellion against the social pressure of bourgeois materialism. The renovation of language carries within an ideological charge, because it reveals what is hidden, contradicting the precepts of scientific positivism. The modernista condition presupposes an ideological position, one that is essentially Pan Hispanic. Politics, according to Terry Eagleton, is "the way we organize our social life together, and the power-relations which this involves."[4] Politics impregnate each and every aspect of the human experience. For decades critics have denied the ideological character of Darío's work. Like a planet that revolves around an invisible sun, ideology is made of what is not said—what Pierre Macherey calls an "ideological horizon." The labor of the critic is to offer a reading that discovers the gaps and contradictions in the text, beginning at the surface to locate its problematic aspects. This way of reading becomes relevant upon uncovering the mechanisms by which the ideology is served to define the individual as a social subject willing to accept a particular view of what is: what is good and what is possible. In addition to the ideological character that this renovation of language implies, Hispanic Modernist poetry nourishes itself with the constants of liberty and the search for a national and inter-American identity in contrast to a commerce-based Pan American model and a Spanish-inspired practical Hispanismo.

Throughout Darío's work an ideological tone is set by its liberal character as well as by the profound belief in liberty, independence, and self-determination of the peoples of the Americas. Some have accused the Nicaraguan poet of having neglected to explicitly demonstrate these ideals in his poetry and to help change a political reality of growing U.S. predominance. According to Keith Ellis, "he was far from advocating any methods by which these [liberty, self-determination, and independence] should be achieved,"[5] but this position is untenable. Darío contributed a methodology necessary for achieving political transformation. On some occasions his concepts of liberty and independence became a call to action, a sermon designed to encourage the people of the Americas in an adverse historical moment. This is the case in "Salutación del optimista" and "A Roosevelt," in which Darío takes on U.S. expansionism in Latin America.

Writing in a period of Latin American nation building and political self-definition, Darío cannot help but reflect upon historical and political developments. He cannot turn a deaf ear to poetic responsibility, defined for many Latin American authors by Victor Hugo, which links the poet to the labor of understanding and above all to improving the world. Darío cannot evade his position as "priest," communicator, and transmitter of "the truth," which forces him to remain sincere, to be faithful to himself, and to act with integrity. Political ideas take on relevance in his lyric work. For this reason, we must consider the ideological, historical, and political context in which his work *Cantos de vida y esperanza* appeared in the first decade of the twentieth century.

In the late nineteenth and early twentieth centuries, the theoretical construction of the dialectic civilization focused on barbarism, as articulated by the Argentine writer Domingo Faustino Sarmiento. In his novel *Facundo*, Sarmiento generated dozens of political and literary discourses throughout Latin America at the end of the nineteenth century. The "enlightened" arguments of Andrés Bello and others proposed a path that started from barbarism and ended in civilization. The positivist currents that advocated utilitarianism, materialism, and "progress" relied on the new sciences to improve society. Scientific positivism became the Bible of Latin American politics at the turn of the century. The powerful classes found in these ideas a means to legitimize social injustice. However, signs of a new path also emerged, from civilization to barbarism. Gradually, positive values in "barbarism" were rediscovered. Principal among these was spontaneous strength: the natural, even divine originality that can be corrupted by the outbreak of progress.

Modernismo is, in a way, the fruit of this conflict between civilization and barbarism, the repercussions of that conflict. It reflects the emerging hegemony of the United States and new U.S. cultural influences in Latin America, in part through Pan Americanism. The path of return toward barbarism—understood as that which is indigenous and natural, the essence of America—represents the assumption of a political stance at a time when sentiment in the territories of the former Spanish viceroyalties swayed between admiration and mistrust for the United States, which had been considered a role model in the formation of national identities through the nineteenth century. But the fear of an already palpable imperialism provoked a gradual awareness on the part of the intellectual class to a menacing situation. Corrupt ruling elites watched as poetry, with other art forms, carried the germ of the new consciousness to the populace. In fact, on the eve of the Modernist movement, scientific positivism had exaggerated the importance of economics while relegating what played no part in economic development to a "thematic of the uselessness."[6] That poetry had been reduced to "uselessness" by political and economic elites in Latin America is precisely what made it, more than many other forms of literature or art, able to serve as a vehicle for ideas disagreeable to the establishment.

The Modernist project sought philosophical and aesthetic renewal—the perfection of the spirit and form, the expression of sensitivity, and the essence of the peoples of Latin America. It also aspired to a political and ideological renewal, a rebellion against the social pressure of bourgeois materialism. Modernist poetry was not, as a rule, politically revolutionary, bellicose, and radical, although several important members of the movement exhibited these traits (e.g., José Martí, the Cuban essayist and political leader, and Leopoldo Lugones, the Argentine socialist ideologue). The development of consciousness, particularly in regard to U.S. expansionism, was common among Modernists, who were hardly escapists seeking refuge in ivory towers. Some of the most intense clamor and the most often aired protests against U.S. predominance before 1930 came from the Modernist pen, notably that of Darío.

Several historical events decisively influenced Darío in the writing of "Salutación del optimista" and "A Roosevelt." The first was the Spanish-Cuban-American War of 1898, which brought not only the loss of the last of Spain's colonial possessions in the Americas but also U.S. control over Puerto Rico, the Philippines, and Guam and profound U.S. influence over Cuba. This power shift provoked a reaction among Latin Americans favorable to Spain and hostile toward the United States. The echo of these occurrences is heard in Darío's well-known "El triunfo de Calibán":

No, I cannot, I will not support those silver-toothed buffaloes. They are enemies of mine. They despise those of Latin blood, they are the barbarians. . . . And I have seen them, those Yankees, in their overwhelming cities of iron and stone, and the hours I have spent with them have been in a state of vague distress. . . . No, I will not support them, I am not in favor of the triumph of Calibán.[7]

Primed again five years later by the U.S.-backed separation of Panama from Colombia, Darío wrote the following in the preface to *Cantos de vida y esperanza*:

If in these songs there is politics, it is because it is universal. And if you find verses to a president, it is because they echo a continental clamor. Tomorrow, all of us could be

Yankees (and it is the most likely) at any rate, my protest remains written on the wings of immaculate swans, as illustrious as Jupiter.[8]

In "Salutación del optimista" and "A Roosevelt," an ideological position is defined through the "Latinness"—that is, the Hispanic as well as the indigenous American—as opposed to those in the North, the United States and the Anglo-Saxon. The most remarkable aspect of "Salutación del optimista" is its hopeful tone. Hexameters, fluctuating between thirteen and eighteen syllables, are divided into variable hemistichs. In this way, verses are free, floating, and expanding in successive waves, reproducing in this way the "magic waves of life." This flexibility supports the optimism and acts to counterbalance the loss of faith in the Hispanic world. A melancholy, worried, and pessimistic quality stemming from Spain's "Disaster of '98" is allowed into the poem only to be confronted by the poet. "Forgetfulness," "death," "disgraces," "the pallid indolences," "fatal doubts," "the mouth that predicts eternal disasters," "the eyes that see only disastrous signs," and "the hands that stone the illustrious ruins" are all images in the first part of the poem that represent the disillusioned sadness that rules the souls of Spaniards. However, the poetic voice seeks to raise the spirits of Spain and the Hispanic. Darío wishes to present an affirmation of the existence of "the Hispanic" in spite of the misfortunes of the historical moment. Light is turned into a message of hope, divine eternity, and regenerative energy—"luminous souls," "divine queen of light, Celestial Hope!," and "You will see the sun rise." A political function is clear: it is a call to action. The poem includes many exhortations, developed as a civil sermon, among which one stands out for its vigor:

> Gather, shine, let all these dispersed vigors support one another,
> Let all of them form one sheaf of ecumenical energy
> Blood of fecund Hispania, solid, illustrious races
> Show the pretermit gifts that of old were your triumph.
> Let the old enthusiasms return, return the burning spirit
> that will rain tongues of fire in that epiphany.[9]

The union of these Hispanic forces and their transformation in light—in "ecumenical energy," or, in other words, universal energy—reveals the almost mystical importance of this union, from which would issue a race with a new characteristic: solidity. The union of the Hispanic peoples in a "solid" way is the straightest path toward hope. Once again, the motif of union appears in the last stanza:

> One continent and another, renewing the old lineage,
> united in spirit, in spirit and desires and tongue,
> see the arrival of the moment in which new hymns will be sung.[10]

Two elements in these verses stand out. First, a Pan Hispanic union is predicted and imagined, in sharp contrast to the business-oriented Pan Americanism. Pan Hispanism would spark creative and regenerative forces and operate as a vehicle of the future hope. Second, Darío strikes an almost dogmatic position, a call to action that is nearly strictly political. He does not limit himself to pointing out a problem; he indicates how to correct it. In the preface to *Cantos de vida y esperanza*, Darío had affirmed, "I am not a poet for the masses, but I know I must inescapably go to them."[11] In "Salutación del optimista" the poet calls on the popular classes in all Hispanic nations to reach a true apotheosis, the triumph of horizons illuminated by a dawning future, the hope of and in "the blood of fecund Hispania."

"A Roosevelt" magnifies and makes explicit the political enjoinders of Pan Hispanism. The first part of the poem is dedicated to Theodore Roosevelt, the personification of the United States. The second part deals with the Latin American character:

> You are the United States,
> future invader of our naive America
> with its Indian blood, an America
> that still prays to Christ and still speaks Spanish.[12]

In these verses we see a central characteristic of the poem, the fusion of Spanish and indigenous blood in the "naive America" as opposed to the arrogant United States. The temporal adverb *still* communicates the anguish and fear of those who know that they are threatened by the invasion predicted by the poet's voice.

Tension escalates in the second verse, when Roosevelt is addressed as "hunter," an image strengthened by the comparison with Nimrod, the ancient Babylonian hunter and archetype of tyranny. The allusion to the president's well-known affection for the hunt also suggests an aggressive and expansionist politic. The antitheses "primitive/modern" and "simple/complex" show the difficulties and contradictions, with shadows of hypocrisy, in the character of the American dignitary. The contrasts continue in the second stanza: "you are cultured and able; you oppose Tolstoy." Tolstoy had advocated social reform primarily through agriculture, a perceived strength of Latin America. In opposing Tolstoy, Darío believed, Roosevelt was in opposition to the most important product of Latin America, denying its potential. This criticism was in keeping with those who opposed high U.S. tariffs in the early years of the new century—tariffs that hit hard at Latin American agricultural products—at a time when American political leaders worked through the Pan American Union for improved conditions for American business interests in Latin America.

Nebuchadnezzar and Alexander symbolize imperialism incarnate in Roosevelt. The verses grow progressively shorter. From the fourteen syllables of the opening alexandrines, the rhythm accelerates, to ten and then eight, to finish with the ringing monosyllabic "No," the shortest and strongest adverb. The effect is to create an instructive tone, which concludes with a shout that mixes protest and challenge. Once again, the poem becomes an exhortation to action and offers energy to resist:

> The United States is grand and powerful.
> Whenever it trembles, a profound shudder
> runs down the enormous backbone of the Andes.
> If it shouts, the sound is like the roar of a lion.[13]

The poem identifies a series of values that contrast with the falseness of high U.S. morality and that represent Pan Hispanism. Latin America has had poets since antiquity, "since the ancient times of Nezahualcóyotl." The poet, in his role of priest, has a key function in this presentation. He is charged with preserving the spirituality of his people. Bacchus stands out as deity of wine as well as archetype of pleasure and triumph. The presence of the Muses who taught him Pan's alphabet is suggested. The Muses bring spiritual and sensual inspiration. In "consulted the stars, which also knew Atlantis" there is an allusion to pure idealism, represented by Atlantis, in contrast with the materialism of the north. At the same time, the consultation of the stars carries implicit the search for universal knowledge. The ancestral wisdom is therefore shown to be one of the defining and differentiating characteristics of Latin America. The lines "and lives, since the earliest moments of its life / in light, in fire, in fragrance, and in love" complete this image of an Arcadian Latin America that is happy, sensual, and overflowing with life and in which all kinds of physical and spiritual sensations are mixed. The poet identifies the origins of a culture now threatened by an American business mentality:

> The America of grand Moctezuma and the Inca,
> the aromatic America of Columbus,
> Catholic America, Spanish America,
> the America where noble Cuauhtémoc said:
> I am not on a bed of roses—this America[14]

These origins are the sum of what arrived with Columbus, was there before Columbus, and what came from the clash that Columbus engendered. The common inheritance presents Catholicism, the greatness of Moctezuma, and the heroism of Cuahtémoc as equal symbols of the eternal resistance of the invader. This inheritance still lives: "And dreams. And loves. And vibrates. / And it is the daughter of the sun."

The Modernists' awareness of oppression and isolation gave rise to a compelling political responsibility that took the form of anti-imperialism. Darío was no revolutionary; he was an aesthete. Nevertheless, the exaltation of art, which every Modernist seeks, does not exclude social criticism. The aesthetic quest that aspires to the renewal of language, at the same time and as a consequence of itself, carries an ideological stance that urges a political renewal. Darío's denunciation of U.S. imperialism and his promotion of the independence of the peoples of the Americas appears doubly incisive on ideological and aesthetic levels. In *Cantos de vida y esperanza*, at the maturity of his production, Darío's vision is widened, and his tone more profound. The poet assumes a responsibility to improve the world and to make history. The world in which Darío lived was threatened by U.S. expansionism; his task, as he saw it, consisted of spreading this information and calling on Pan Hispanic ideals to oppose it.

NOTES

1. From *Selected Poems of Rubén Darío* by Rubén Darío, translated by Lysander Kemp. Copyright © 1965, renewed 1993. Reprinted by permission of the University of Texas Press.

2. Jorge Eduardo Arellano, "Rubén Darío: Anti-imperialista," *Casa de las Américas* 133 (1982): 104–8; Fiodor Kelin, "Rubén Darío," in *Estudios sobre Rubén Darío*, edited by Ernesto Mejía Sánchez (Mexico City, 1969), 181–85; Publio González-Rodas, "Rubén Darío y Theodore Roosevelt," *Cuadernos Americanos*, 168 (1970): 185–86.

3. Cathy L. Jrade, "Socio-Political Concerns in the Poetry of Rubén Darío," *Latin American Literary Review* 18 (1990): 47.

4. Terry Eagleton, *Una introducción a la teoria literaria* (Madrid, 1988), 231.

5. Keith Ellis, *Critical Approaches to Rubén Darío* (Toronto, 1974), 44.

6. Alvaro Salvador Jofre, *Rubén Darío y la moral estética* (Granada, 1986), 33.

7. Rubén Darío, *El Modernismo y otros ensayos* (Madrid, 1898), 161.

8. Rubén Darío, *Poesía*, edited by Ángel Rama (Barcelona, 1985), 244.

9. Ibid., 248.

10. Ibid.

11. Darío, *Poesía*, 243.

12. Ibid., 255.

13. Ibid.

14. Ibid., 256.

7

Hispanismo versus Pan Americanism: Spanish Efforts to Counter U.S. Influence in Latin America before 1930

Richard V. Salisbury

Since the early nineteenth-century wars of independence, Spanish America and Spain have been linked by Hispanismo. Proponents of that movement in Spain and the Americas have stressed a common Hispanic community based "on the conviction that through the course of history Spaniards have developed a life-style and culture, a set of characteristics, of traditions, and value judgments that render them distinct from all other peoples."[1] The colonization of America saw the transfer of these "Spanish" characteristics to the developing societies in the New World, bringing peninsular Spaniards and Spanish Americans together in a spiritual and political empire. Independence, however, strained relations between Spain and its former colonies. Spain hesitated to extend diplomatic recognition to the new Spanish American states, at times procrastinating for decades. On several occasions Spain tried unsuccessfully to regain influence and power in the Western Hemisphere through military intervention: in Mexico in 1829, Peru in 1864, and the Dominican Republic between 1861 and 1865. That Spain held control of Cuba and Puerto Rico through the late nineteenth century provided another reason for the animosity and fear that Spanish Americans held for the former mother country.

Spain's catastrophic defeat in 1898 in the Spanish-Cuban-American War, at the hands of the United States, drastically changed the perceptions that Spaniards and Spanish Americans had of each other. Gone forever was the Spanish American concept of Spain as a threatening presence; instead, Spain's pathetic debility was apparent to all. In the aftermath of the Spanish American War, Spanish Americans began to look on Spain with some compassion rather than resentment. In turn, Spaniards began to look to Spanish America as a potential source for their spiritual, economic, and political regeneration. Accordingly, intellectuals on both sides of the Atlantic placed a new emphasis on a greater Hispanic community and worked to promote cultural awareness within this transoceanic *patría*. In Spain, intellectual leaders such as Rafael Altamira, Miguel de Unamuno, Joaquín Costa, and Rafael María de Labra welcomed the Hispanista overtures of Nicaraguan Ruben Darío and Uruguayan José Enrique Rodó, among other Latin Americans. This intellectual approximation marked the birth of a new cultural, or "lyrical," Hispanismo.[2]

Darío visited Spain in 1898 and again in 1905. Through interaction with Spanish intellectual leaders and in his poetry, he helped to create a strong literary bond linking kindred Hispanic spirits in Spain and Latin America. Rodó's seminal 1900 work, *Ariel*, juxtaposed the ethereal and noble Ariel (meant to represent Latin America) with the crass and materialistic Caliban (a metaphor for U.S. power). This vastly popular imagery reinforced the concept of an intellectual union of Hispanic peoples set against an all too obvious foe; in what seemed to be Spain's darkest imperial hour, "Darío and Rodó, and their thousands of Spanish-American enthusiasts, helped to restore confidence to a generation of Spaniards and to arouse them from the pessimism and apathy produced by the disaster." All the same, the approximation between Spain and Spanish America in the post-1898 period would, for the most part, involve "the realm of intangibles," focusing on the production of "lyrical oratory, passionate poetry, and elegant prose" rather than on the creation of meaningful political and economic linkages.[3] Be that as it may, the idealism and confidence that lyrical Hispanismo generated helped to inspire Spaniards to take concrete steps to achieve rapprochement with their trans-Atlantic brethren in the face of a Pan Americanism orchestrated by the United States.

If lyrical Hispanismo called for a reassertion of Spanish intellectual and cultural influence in Spanish America, then a natural corollary of the movement was opposition to non-Hispanic influences in Spanish America. In the years immediately following the Spanish American War, there were a number of official Spanish efforts to promote closer economic and political linkages with the Spanish American nations. Such Spanish policy initiatives reflected a desire to counter the growing economic and political influence of the United States in hemispheric affairs, and it represented a "practical" Hispanismo. Ultimately, however, Pan Americanism would prove insurmountable. Despite Spanish efforts and in contrast to the cultural resurgence generated by lyrical Hispanismo, practical Hispanismo brought no new economic and political influence for Spain in the Americas.

Initially, practical Hispanismo emerged as an alternative to Pan Americanism to which Spanish Americans wary about U.S. hegemony in Latin America might be attracted.[4] U.S. Secretary of State James G. Blaine organized and set the agenda for the 1889–1890 Pan American conference in Washington. Delegates would focus primarily on promoting economic, scientific, and cultural relations between the United States and the nations of Latin America. In light of long-standing economic ties with Europe, Latin Americans were less than enthusiastic in their support for an American customs union and other U.S.-directed economic initiatives brought forward at the meeting. They pressed instead, through the early 1900s, for a more ample Pan Americanism that would include discussion of so-called political questions, including respect for the concept of sovereignty and acceptance of the principle of nonintervention. To this end, Latin Americans consistently promoted U.S. acceptance of the tenets of international juridic equality. One key component of Pan Americanism after 1900 was a U.S. initiative for an end to international trade restrictions; Spanish American officials hoped to take advantage of Latin American rejections of that initiative to create opportunities for new economic ties with Latin America.[5] Latin American resistance to U.S. economic penetration could be buttressed, Spaniards reasoned, through Spanish economic initiatives in the Western Hemisphere. By the same token, the Latin Americans' desire to have the United States acknowledge their concerns in the "political" sphere provided yet another opening to the former mother country; discreet encouragement by Spain might bring Spaniards and Latin Americans closer together. Thus, although U.S.-dominated Pan Americanism was formidable, through practical Hispanismo Spain sought an alternative influence in hemisphere affairs. This latter initiative reached its height in the 1920s.

Early Spanish efforts to counter U.S. influence arose at the Hispano-American Economic and Social Conference, held in Madrid November 10–18, 1900.[6] Spanish and Latin American delegates passed an impressive but nonbinding array of resolutions calling for extended economic, cultural, and juridic linkages between Spain and the Spanish American nations.[7] Inspired by success in Madrid and new diplomatic contacts with the American republics, Spanish policy makers directed their attention to the second Pan American conference (Mexico City, 1901). The Spanish ambassador in Washington warned the Ministry of State that the U.S. government intended to use the conference "to implant and maintain its predominant influence in the Americas." The approximation with Latin Americans won in Madrid was in jeopardy; the United States had as its sole objective the separation of Spain from these Republics, for the purpose of making them "politically and commercially dependent on the United States." The ambassador's most immediate concern was the projected establishment in Washington of an inter-American arbitration tribunal. The Spanish envoy noted that the American republics, "given their own instincts of self preservation," would fight such a proposal. In fact, a U.S.–Latin American impasse might benefit Spain; during the Madrid congress some had suggested the establishment in Madrid of an arbitration tribunal representing Spain and the Latin American nations, a project that might be realized in the event of a Pan American deadlock. Such a denouement, in the ambassador's view, "would constitute a major failure for the United States and for Pan Americanism."[8]

The Ministry of State acted on the dispatches from its envoy in the United States. In a Royal Order of April 18, 1901, sent to all Spanish diplomatic missions in Latin America and based on common ties across the Atlantic of "history, tradition, and blood as well as commercial interest," Madrid instructed its diplomats to prevent the United States from using the Pan American conference as a vehicle for establishing hegemony. Spain urged its envoys to "give all your efforts to see that delegates to the conference were individuals who were supportive of, or at least not contrary to, the policy that we wish to maintain." Spanish envoys were also enjoined to discover the positions of Latin American governments regarding the prospect of a Washington-based arbitration tribunal; they were to prevent the realization of this project. If the United States were successful in this Pan American project, Spanish authorities feared that it would enjoy "definitive hegemony in the Western Hemisphere." The Spanish Ministry of State assumed that battle lines would form over the arbitration tribunal, an issue that would determine "victory or defeat" for the United States—and, potentially, for Spain.[9]

However, Spanish diplomatic authorities had misread U.S. goals; the U.S. delegation to Mexico City carried instructions to oppose the principle of obligatory arbitration.[10] Moreover, Chile, Bolivia, Peru, Venezuela, and Costa Rica had each indicated prior to the conference that obligatory arbitration was not in its national interest. As a result, the question of a tribunal made no headway at the conference.[11] Failure to anticipate U.S. intent, however, in no way diminishes the well-orchestrated Spanish response to the perceived threat. In the years immediately following the Mexico City conference, Spanish diplomats followed up on their promotion of practical Hispanismo. They called on the Ministry of State to encourage Spanish maritime, commercial, and financial interests to establish linkages with Spanish America. Many of these diplomatic initiatives came from Spanish representatives in the Caribbean region, an area especially vulnerable to U.S. economic and political influence. The Spanish commercial sector, as well as Ministry officials, was less than enthusiastic about promoting such linkages. The area's political instability had led all too often in the past to cycles of financial default and reclamation. That financial guarantees from the Caribbean basin states rested on unpredictable agricultural production—which, in the words of an internal Ministry of State memorandum, was more subject to "acts of God" than to those of men—discouraged the Spanish entrepreneurial sector from committing resources to the area and laying a commercial basis for Hispanismo.[12]

Moreover, between 1901 and 1914, Spain did not try to reenter the Pan American fray through efforts to influence Pan American conference debates. Spanish diplomats were largely silent during the 1906 and 1910 Pan American conferences, held in Rio de Janeiro and Buenos Aires, respectively. In the years leading up to World War I, practical Hispanismo languished in unsuccessful bilateral initiatives suggested by Spanish diplomats but often ignored by Madrid. The onset of war led Spanish diplomats to abandon approximation with Spanish America.[13] Spain's preoccupation with the cataclysmic and rapidly shifting course of events in Europe is reflected, at least indirectly, in the dramatic decrease in correspondence between officials in the Ministry of State and their representatives throughout Latin America. As Spain guarded its wartime neutrality, relations with Latin America were shifted to a back burner.

After 1918 the Americas presented Spain with new opportunities and challenges. Adversely affected by the war, England, France, and Germany were no longer in a position to exercise the kind of economic and political influence in the Western Hemisphere that they had exerted before 1914.[14] On the other hand, another competitor for economic and political influence in the region, the United States, now enjoyed a relatively free hand to pursue a postwar economic and political agenda. With the United States looming large and its European neighbors severely weakened, Spain revived practical Hispanismo.

In a June 7, 1919, dispatch from Washington, Spanish Ambassador Juan Riaño made reference to a recent Pan American commercial conference hosted by the United States. The envoy informed the Ministry of State that the United States "in order to cement its hegemony in the new world," was "undertaking a commercial conquest of the Latin American nations."[15] Less than a month later the Spanish minister in Venezuela echoed Riaño's concern: Spain was in danger of being overwhelmed by a version of the Monroe Doctrine that Washington was engaged in applying to its hemispheric financial policy, and it should move to protect its interests in the Western Hemisphere by launching a vigorous commercial offensive. The recent Pan American commercial conference and the upcoming Pan American financial conference set for January 1920 in Washington were, in the envoy's words, "facts of such a nature that did not require commentary."[16] In a subsequent dispatch the minister noted a shift in U.S. hemispheric policy from a "political-political" to a "political-economic" orientation. If Spain did nothing to counteract this U.S. economic offensive, then Spaniards would lose "spiritual and material influence" in the Americas. In response to the growing power of U.S.-branch banks in Latin America, the Spanish minister had already tried to encourage Spanish banks to establish offices in Caracas. These efforts were unsuccessful, prompting the diplomat concerned to observe that "the Spanish businessman continues to travel in a stagecoach . . . while his competitors travel in airplanes."[17]

In January 1920, while the U.S. government hosted the Second Pan American Financial Conference, the French minister in Venezuela sounded out his Spanish colleague on a joint French-Spanish policy for Latin America to counter U.S. power. The Spanish minister reacted positively, believing that Spain might take advantage of the French initiative to carve a role for itself as a mediator between U.S. and European interests.[18] However, Madrid was unable or unwilling to take advantage of this or other proposed leadership initiatives. An economic basis for practical Hispanismo never materialized. Spain's trade with Spanish America during the early twentieth century was never significant. In 1918 Spain sent 4.5 percent of her exports to Spanish America and received 2.5 percent of Spanish America's exports in turn. During the 1920s Spanish exports dipped below 4 percent while imports hovered between 1 and 2 percent.[19] Spain's woefully inadequate internal transportation system, a weak merchant marine, "an anachronistic and underfinanced commercial credit structure," and the long-standing friction between conservative leaders of Spain's core area and commercial leaders of the economically active peripheral regions, such as Vizcaya and Cataluña, all served to impede Spanish economic development—both internal and external. Perhaps more significant, Spain's trade with Europe and the United States was both extensive and lucrative. This enabled Spain to maintain a favorable balance of payments and diminished the necessity "of seeking a major expansion of trade with Spanish America."[20]

Internal conflict and almost endemic political instability also impacted negatively on Spain's efforts to conduct a coherent and sustained foreign policy in Latin America. Moreover, postwar Spanish foreign policies assigned a relatively low priority to Latin America. Spanish interests in Morocco were of paramount importance to the authorities in Madrid, and the second level of foreign policy concern involved Spanish efforts to establish influence in Tangier. Hispanismo was relegated to a distant third on Spain's international agenda. Spain's catastrophic defeat by the Riffs at the 1921 Battle of Anual served to focus an even greater degree of the nation's attention on North Africa, which in turn left official advocacy of Hispanismo in relative insignificance, if not diplomatic limbo, insofar as the Ministry of State was concerned.[21]

Even so, Spain tried to build a forceful, Spanish-led Hispanismo movement. In 1921 Spaniards received what they felt was an important vote of support. The Venezuelan foreign minister came to the United States to dedicate a statue of Simón Bolívar in Central Park. At a Pan American Union banquet, Spanish Ambassador Juan Riaño turned out to be the only European diplomat invited. The Venezuelan foreign minister gave such a warm toast to Spain that Riaño reported that, in more than a decade, "Spain has never been recognized as such in the Pan American Union."[22] In February 1923 the Ministry of State returned to diplomacy within the Pan American Union. Madrid asked Spanish diplomats in the Americas for their opinions and suggestions on the upcoming Fifth Conference of American States, to begin on March 25 in Santiago, Chile. Authorities in Madrid were especially interested in finding out whether this would be an appropriate occasion to "strengthen and tighten our relations with the American Republics." This time Spain's objectives were more nuanced. Though still confronting U.S. power in Latin America, Spanish officials reasoned that they might gain authority by working with the United States in some instances.[23]

At Santiago, Spain sought observer status. Madrid was aided in this effort by the government of El Salvador, for, as the Spanish chargé d'affaires reported, Cecilio Bustamante, the Salvadoran representative to the Santiago Conference, was "very much a friend of Spain." Prior to his departure for Santiago, Bustamante had informed the chargé that Spain should be represented in order to serve "as a counterweight" to the influence of the United States. Accordingly, during the conference organizational meeting, Bustamante requested that the Pan American nations extend an invitation to the Spanish minister in Chile to attend as an observer.[24] Members of both the U.S. and Chilean delegations opposed Spanish participation. Moreover, U.S. Delegation Chief Henry P. Fletcher indicated that an invitation to Spain would have to be followed by invitations to England, Portugal, and France, the other mother countries of the Pan American community. Chile's opposition to Spanish participation, according to most observers, derived from a desire to do nothing at the conference that would go against the wishes of the United States. Chile was afraid that such action might lead to an adverse arbitration decision on the part of Washington in the pending dispute with Peru over Tacna and Arica.[25]

Nonparticipation at Santiago did not mean that Spain was unable to promote its interests at the meeting, but because of U.S. opposition to Spanish observer status, it did mean that the notion of a friendly Spanish-U.S. interaction within Pan Americanism had come to nought. The Spanish minister in Chile maintained close contact throughout the conference with Latin American representatives who led an attack on U.S. interventionism. When the nations of Central America and the Caribbean formed a bloc to resist excessive U.S. influence in Pan American affairs, the Spanish envoy moved quickly to establish rapport with the group. He reported to Madrid on extensive conversations he had held with bloc delegates who professed admiration for Spain and were interested in promoting initiatives at the conference beneficial to their own nations and to Spain.[26] In the Spanish minister's view, the cooperative action taken by the Central American and Caribbean nations at Santiago against "the United States government's policy of absorption" could only serve to enhance his country's own "policy of attraction" to the American republics.[27] Indeed, several months after the conference had adjourned, Cecilio Bustamante reflected on this theme when he told the Spanish chargé in El Salvador that the U.S. delegation at Santiago had viewed the Central American–Caribbean bloc as an instrument, at least in part, of Spanish diplomacy.[28]

Less than two weeks after Bustamante's remarks, a major political change shook Spain. On September 12, 1923, General Miguel Primo de Rivera launched a coup against the parliamentary government. Within a matter of days the Spanish government collapsed and Primo de Rivera's dictatorship began. Many Spaniards, frustrated with seemingly endemic political instability and an apparent lack of direction and success in the conduct of foreign affairs, viewed Primo de Rivera as a leader who would bring about the regeneration of Spain. His immediate agenda, however, would be domestic; for the first several years of his dictatorship, internal pacification and political reorganization would occupy the Spanish strongman almost exclusively. When his government did turn to foreign affairs, Morocco and Tangier remained the nation's primary focus. Although the regime did, during the mid-1920s, undertake to improve relations with Latin America, these efforts were essentially bilateral, resulting in a commercial treaty with Cuba, a loan and the sale of several naval vessels to Argentina, and an arbitration agreement with Chile.[29]

It would be another three years before Spain mounted a new multilateral diplomatic initiative in both the League of Nations and the Pan American Union to revive practical Hispanismo. That effort began in December 1926, in response to a major U.S. Marine invasion of Nicaragua. Spanish diplomats relayed news of widespread Latin American criticism of the United States to Madrid. In Spain, anger over the U.S. invasion was widespread; King Alfonso XIII requested the latest news from Central America and then called on his minister of state, José María de Yanguas, to send him a detailed analysis of the Nicaraguan situation. After an interview with the King, Yanguas moved quickly to develop a new Spanish Hispanista policy for the Americas.[30] Yanguas instructed the Spanish representative in Switzerland to sound out "with reserve and tact" the Latin American members of the Permanent Council of the League of Nations. Would the governments of Chile, Colombia, and El Salvador be willing to make a formal protest to the League against Washington's intervention in Nicaragua? Spain's withdrawal from the League the previous year precluded any direct action by Madrid in the matter.[31] In Paris the Spanish ambassador relayed his government's proposal to José Gustavo Guerrero, the Salvadoran representative to the League of Nations. Guerrero thought that the potential was great for Latin American–European solidarity in the League over U.S. military intervention in Nicaragua. He had yet to receive instructions from his government, however, and France, given its extensive ties with the United States, would probably not support any anti-American action in the League.[32]

An equally limited response from the Chilean representative in Rome prompted Minister of State Yanguas to suspend, at least for the time being, any further efforts to promote his nation's Hispanista agenda. However, in August 1927, the Spanish chargé d'affaires in Mexico reported that the Mexican government was campaigning throughout the region for the formation of a Latin American league to oppose the U.S. policy of "absorption." The chargé believed that such a league would prove an excellent vehicle for the promotion of Spanish approximation with the various Latin American nations. This same line of thought had occurred to others as well; the U.S. ambassador to Mexico had approached the chargé to find out whether or not Spain had received an invitation to participate in the projected league.[33] The possibility that a unified Latin America would look to Madrid for support was underscored when the Mexican undersecretary of foreign relations, Genaro Estrada, suggested that Spain should try to secure observer status at the forthcoming Sixth Conference of American States (Havana, 1928); a Spanish presence at Havana would serve as a "guarantee" for the nations of Spanish America.[34]

Spain sought admission to Havana on less diplomatically aggressive grounds. On September 21 Primo de Rivera instructed his ambassador in Washington to approach the United States about observer status at Havana. The Spanish leader outlined the long and intimate relationship that bound Spain and the American nations together and expressed the desire to make this relationship even closer through participation in the Havana deliberations. Primo de Rivera emphasized as well the cordial relations enjoyed by Spain and the United States; these might also be advanced if Spain could be present officially at Havana.[35] The United States demurred. Secretary of State Frank B. Kellogg informed the minister that the conference was to deal exclusively with American problems; were Spain invited, other former colonial powers would also have to be included. When Spanish diplomats tried to generate a challenge to U.S. reasoning among Latin American governments, there was no groundswell of support.[36]

At the fifth Pan American conference in Santiago (1923), Spain had played a behind-the-scenes diplomatic role in supporting an anti-interventionist Pan Americanism, but at Havana, Spanish diplomacy was not in evidence. By 1928, among Spanish policy makers, practical Hispanismo competed with an emerging interest in developing stronger ties with the United States; as the Spanish government found new value in relations with the United States, a challenge to U.S. influence in Latin America through the Pan American Union became less attractive.

In reviewing Spain's efforts to implement practical Hispanismo in the Americas, the classic admonition of Harold and Margaret Sprout comes to mind: "What matters in making policies . . . is how the policy-maker imagines his environment to be, not how it actually is. Conversely, outcomes, accomplishments, the operational results of policy decisions, depend on conditions as they actually are, not as someone imagines them to be."[37] The perception of many high-ranking Spanish officials was that the moment was right, in the wake of the debacle of 1898, for Spain to pursue a policy of approximation with Spanish America. Spanish diplomats in the Americas supported this initiative and endeavored to promote economic and political links between Spain and various Spanish American countries. As the Sprouts' paradigm suggests, however, Spanish officials were responding to what was essentially an imagined environment. Operating in a highly charged emotional milieu, a phenomenon that owed a great deal to lyrical Hispanismo, these individuals desperately wanted to achieve regeneration for Spain through a program of trans-Atlantic approximation. As the Sprouts indicate, however, results of policy decisions depend on conditions as they actually are, not as someone imagines them to be. Spanish and Latin American realities provided no opening for an effective diplomatic, commercial, and practical Hispanismo.

Spanish impediments to Hispanismo included political instability, preoccupation with North Africa, and the inability of the Spanish commercial sector to respond to purported economic opportunities in Spanish America. In the Western Hemisphere, practical Hispanismo faced the rapidly expanding economic and political influence of the United States and the concomitant rise, by the time of the 1928 Havana conference, of a spirit of a new "Pan American" nationalism in Spanish America that deliberately excluded Spain. Spanish ties of blood, language, and heritage notwithstanding, Pan Americanism as a vehicle for practical Hispanismo before 1930 represents a story of opportunities lost and dreams, perhaps ephemeral, unfulfilled.

NOTES

1. Fredrick B. Pike, *Hispanismo, 1898–1936: Spanish Conservatives and Liberals and Their Relations with Spanish America* (Notre Dame, 1971), 1.

2. Pike, *Hispanismo* 55–64; Fredrick B. Pike, "Spanish–Latin American Relations: Two Centuries of Divergence and a New Beginning," in Howard J. Wiarda, ed., *The Iberian-Latin American Connection; Implications for U.S. Foreign Policy* (Boulder, 1986), 65–69.

3. Pike, *Hispanismo*, 66–69.

4. J. Lloyd Mecham, *The United States and Inter-American Security, 1889–1960* (Austin, 1965), 28–29.

5. Mecham, 48–121.

6. *Congreso social y económico Hispano-Americano reunido en Madrid el año 1900* (Madrid, 1902), 86, 156.

7. Pike, *Hispanismo*, 70.

8. Spanish ambassador in Washington to minister of state, 31 March 1901; Spanish ambassador in Washington to minister of state, 8 April 1901, Conferencias y Congresos, 3192, Foreign Ministry Archives, Madrid, Spain (SFMA).

9. Minister of state to the Spanish missions in Central America, Brazil, Chile, Peru, Colombia, Argentina, Uruguay, Venezuela, and Mexico, 18 April 1901, Conferencias y Congresos, 3192, SFMA.

10. William I. Buchanan, "Latin America and the Mexico Conference," *Annals of the American Academy of Political and Social Science* 22 (July 1903): 52–54; Harold F. Peterson, *Diplomat of the Americas: A Biography of William I. Buchanan* (Albany, 1977), 200–204; Second International Conference of American States, *Report of Delegates of the United States, with Accompanying Papers*, 57th Cong., 1st sess. 1902, S. Doc. 330, 34.

11. Spanish minister in Venezuela to minister of state, 5 June 1901; Spanish ambassador in the United States to minister of state, 5 June 1901; Spanish minister in Costa Rica to minister of state, 8 June 1901; Spanish minister in Chile to minister of state, 15 September 1901; Spanish minister in Mexico to minister of state, 8 November 1901; Spanish minister in Mexico to minister of state, 16 November 1901, all Conferencias y Congresos, 3192, SFMA.

12. Richard V. Salisbury, "The Diplomacy of Hispanismo: Spain, the United States and Central America, 1900–1914," Inter-American Relations Conference, 22–23 September 1994, Jacksonville, FL.

13. Gerie B. Bledsoe, "Spain in the League of Nations, 1920–1931" (Ph.D. dissertation, Florida State University, 1972), 1–9.

14. On British involvement in the Western Hemisphere before World War I, see Richard V. Salisbury, "Great Britain, the United States, and the 1909–1910 Nicaraguan Crisis," *The Americas* 53, no. 3 (January 1997): 379–94.

15. Juan Riaño to the minister of state, 7 June 1919, Conferencias y Congresos, 3191, SFMA.

16. Spanish minister in Venezuela to minister of state, 6 July 1919, Política, USA, 2444, SFMA.

17. Spanish minister in Venezuela to minister of state, 12 September 1919, Política, América, 2298, SFMA.

18. Spanish minister in Venezuela to minister of state, 22 January 1920, Política, América, 2298; Spanish minister in Venezuela to the minister of state, 21 February 1920, Corespondencia, USA, 1487, SFMA.

19. J. Fred Rippy, "Pan-Hispanic Propaganda in Spanish America," *Political Science Quarterly* 37, no. 3 (September 1922): 414; Thomas and Ebba Schoonover, "Statistics for an Understanding of Foreign Intrusions into Central America from the 1820s to 1930," *Anuario de Estudios Centroamericanos* 16, no. 1 (1990): 148–49; Pike, *Hispanismo*, 229.

20. Pike, *Hispanismo*, 216–19, 229–30.

21. Bledsoe, 42–80.

22. Riaño to minister of state, 23 April 1921, Correspondencia, USA, 1487, SFMA.

23. Ministry of State to Spanish representatives in the Americas, 14 February 1923, Congresos y Conferencias, 3191, SFMA.

24. Spanish chargé in El Salvador to minister of state, 27 February 1923; Spanish minister in Chile to minister of state, 29 March 1923, Congresos y Conferencias, 3191, SFMA.

25. Spanish chargé in El Salvador to minister of state, 30 August 1923; Spanish minister in Chile to minister of state, 25 March 1923, Congresos y Conferencias, 3191, SFMA.

26. Spanish minister in Chile to minister of state, 6 April 1923; Spanish minister in Chile to minister of state, 26 April 1923, Congresos y Conferencias, 3191; Spanish minister in Chile to minister of state, 6 May 1923, Correspondencia, Nicaragua, 1661, SFMA.

27. Spanish minister in Chile to minister of state, 23 April 1923, Congresos y Conferencias, 3191, SFMA. See also Richard V. Salisbury, "The Anti-Imperialist Career of Alejandro Alvarado Quirós," *The Hispanic American Historical Review* 57, no. 4 (November 1977): 587–612.

28. Spanish chargé in El Salvador to minister of state, 30 August 1923, Congresos y Conferencias, 3191, SFMA.

29. Bledsoe, 230–244; Pike, *Hispanismo*, 226–27.

30. Internal memorandum, Ministry of State, 5 January 1927; Yanguas to the Marqués de Torres de Mendoza, 10 January 1927, Política, América, 2298, SFMA.

31. Yanguas to the Marqués de la Torrehermosa, 10 January 1927, Política, América, 2298, SFMA; Bledsoe, 296–340.

32. Spanish ambassador in France to Yanguas, 12 January 1927, Política, América, 2298, SFMA.

33. Spanish chargé d'affaires in Mexico City to minister of state, 15 August 1927, Política, 2564, SFMA.

34. Spanish minister in Mexico City to minister of state, 19 August 1927, América, 1964, SFMA.

35. Primo de Rivera to Spanish ambassador in Washington, 21 September 1927, América, 1964, SFMA.

36. Spanish ambassador in Washington to minister of state, 22 October 1927; internal memorandum, Ministry of State, 5 November 1927, América, 1964, SFMA.

37. Harold and Margaret Sprout, *Foundations of International Politics* (Princeton, 1962), 288.

8

In Four Languages But with One Voice: Division and Solidarity within Pan American Feminism, 1923–1933

K. Lynn Stoner

Feminism is no longer viewed as a monolithic ideology that originated in France, England, and the United States and engendered derivative movements throughout the world. Scholarship has clarified that historical and cultural environments throughout the world have defined struggles over women's social roles. Consequently, we know that an array of feminist movements and ideals have emerged over the past 150 years, all agreeing to stop women's subjugation but disagreeing on the definition of subjugation and the means by which to combat it.[1] Less well known is that by 1920, even as differences rendered feminist consensus impossible, international feminists made their first entrees into the apparently all-male confines of diplomacy to argue for women's rights worldwide. Indeed, during the 1920s and 1930s, feminism both fragmented and came together; the unifiers sought global support for women's rights. The formation of the Inter-American Commission of Women within the Pan American Union (PAU), 1923–1933, vividly illustrates the tension between national and international feminist objectives and the "intrusion" of women into the diplomatic domain. This chapter elaborates on the cooperation between Latin American and U.S. feminists to demand permanent representation within the Pan American Union. It contextualizes the harmony of their messages against the discord registered by male delegates to the Sixth Conference of American States in 1928, many of whom were disposed to withdraw their nations from the first multinational diplomatic organization. Finally, it assesses the efficacy of the Inter-American Women's Commission against its promise.

By 1920, Latin and North American feminists had constructed self-defined and distinctive movements. Historians have analyzed the feminism and feminist movements of the late nineteenth and early twentieth centuries.[2] Latin American movements emphasized the rights of mothers, hesitated to attack patriarchy as the main source of social and gender repression, mostly ignored issues of sexuality and birth control, incorporated feminism into broad political and social struggles, and argued for social justice rather than gender equality. By contrast, North American feminists focused more, but not exclusively, on the empowerment of individual women through enfranchisement, new economic opportunities, self-definition, and an equal rights amendment. The Latin American approach to women's rights evolved out of a corporate state tradition in which individuals were categorized according to their membership in groups and were granted rights accordingly. Latin society was ethnically more complex and disunified, which demanded readjustments not only of gender relations but also of class, ethnicity, national identity, and social morality. Latin American feminists emphasized women's rights as mothers, workers, and community builders, but not as men's equals. Differences thus divided Latin and North American feminists—philosophically, politically, culturally, and organizationally.

To date, comparative studies of women's movements have concentrated on the varied discourses of feminism and the deconstruction of feminist movements, both inside and outside national boundaries.[3] For the most part, we discover that there was less room for consensus and more room for pluralism among the world's feminists, but moments of cooperation did occur, and they produced results.[4] Between 1923 and 1933 a Pan American feminist movement organized the first permanent international women's association affiliated with an international diplomatic body to force equal rights legislation on signatory nations through a treaty. Executing such a program required a subversion of regional and cultural differences. Without exaggerating the degree of consensus these women obtained or overstating the homogeneity of the group, I would like to note that Latin and North American feminists joined forces to make gender discrimination a matter of Pan American social justice and to place the debate on the level of international diplomacy and universal morality.

Pan American feminism had a global view, subverted internal schisms, and influenced national and international legislation.[5] The approach here illustrates that inter-American feminists shared motives and a spiritual basis for their alliance. They placed women's issues above nationalist interests, and they sought democratic relations among themselves, with men, and among nations. They were idealistic and moralistic, and they proposed to make governments responsive to social needs in a modern, industrial world. Pan American feminists were drawn together by a faith in the efficacy of state laws to eliminate social injustices.

Hemispheric feminism would have been unthinkable had it not been for a Pan American movement built on cooperation, respect, peace, and progress toward modern concepts of governance. Pan Americanism was an ideal, and it had an organic form, the Pan American Union. Promoters of Pan Americanism regarded American states as interdependent, drawn together by geography, colonial backgrounds, independence struggles, and connected commerce. The Monroe Doctrine (1823) put European powers on notice that they could neither colonize nor invade American nations without brooking a response from the United States. In addition to an interest in mutual defense against European intrusion, economic ties also developed between Latin American and U.S. enterprises, and by the 1870s entrepreneurs and politicians called for standard laws of commerce, technology sharing, and guarantees of protection of foreign corporations and citizens.

In 1889, at the First Conference of American States, North American entrepreneurs looked forward to expanding commerce, guided and protected by diplomatic guarantees. Publicists, reformers, and peace advocates hoped that international law and organization would uphold security, promote peace, and reform social systems in Latin America. Latin Americans, wary of North American imperialism, wanted to use a Pan American forum to deflect U.S. actions that threatened to overpower individual nations. All sought peace, sovereignty, and prosperity for their respective nations through negotiation rather than conflict. This preference for hemispheric cooperation was called "the Western Hemisphere idea" by those who were proud to show that young nations could teach European powers about governance and diplomacy.

High ideals often camouflage profound internal contradictions; Pan Americanism was a mask for troubled inter-American diplomatic relations. The restraint of strong states and the protection of weak ones was more difficult to achieve than to imagine. The ideals of Pan Americanism were violated many times over by U.S. invasions of Latin American countries, imposed treaties that truncated the sovereignty of Latin American states, and unequal economic development. These violations threatened the viability of the Pan American Union and exposed the hypocrisy of U.S. intentions. The imposed Platt Amendment in Cuba (1902); the illegal taking of the Panama Canal (1903); and interventions in Cuba (1906–1909, 1912, 1917), Haiti (1914–1934), the Dominican Republic (1905, 1914–1924), Nicaragua (1912–1925, 1927–1932), and Mexico (1914) alienated even the most pro-U.S. Latin American states. By 1923, when the women's question first emerged at the Fifth inter-American conference in Santiago, Chile, the very notion of a peaceful hemisphere was under attack as Latin American nations tried to expose and limit North American intervention.

Despite its weakened condition in 1923, Pan Americanism offered just the sort of moralistic optimism that international feminists needed. It created an opening for women to argue their mission before a hemispheric audience and within the spirit of cooperation. Pan Americanism promised the pursuit of democracy and social justice. By 1923, the Pan American Union had accepted as part of its mission the guarantee of social welfare, hygiene, education, and health to American citizens. It also placed equal rights and women's representation on Pan American Union delegations on the agenda for the next meeting. Women did not appear suddenly in 1923 to demand women's rights; Latin American women had participated in Pan American scientific congresses since 1898, where they contributed mostly to reports and research in health and medicine, education, child care, and nutrition. At the First International Women's Congress (unaffiliated with the Pan American Union), women from Argentina, Peru, Paraguay, Chile, and Uruguay resolved that women should benefit from divorce legislation and equal pay for equal work. In 1915–1916, the traditional presence of women at Pan American Union meetings stopped, because the spirit of Pan Americanism changed. North American leaders wanted Latin American attention on the Great War and not on social issues. The Pan American Union became a men's agency with a male focus: war. No longer invited to participate, women organized an auxiliary meeting, where they discussed social justice and welfare and planned later meetings to endorse women's rights as a hemispheric problem. The 1922 meeting of inter-American women resolved that suffrage, equal rights, and the reinstatement of women in Pan American Union delegations were the first order of business.

Pan American feminists wanted a hemispheric forum, but they had to answer doubters in their ranks who claimed that U.S. feminists would control events. Most moderate and progressive feminists, however, believed that they could use the spirit of Pan Americanism as well as the institution itself to demand women's rights. Between 1923 and 1933, hemispheric feminists joined forces to organize the Inter-American Commission of Women under the auspices of the Pan American Union. They attempted to legislate an equal rights law through an international treaty. Failing to gain the treaty, they maintained pressure on reluctant nations to give women the vote and to initiate progressive labor and civil laws. They hoped to compel individual nations to accept a new social order through an international mandate.

The Sixth Conference of American States (1928) opened amid hostility and resentment expressed by Latin American leaders toward the United States. Repeated invasions and infractions of Pan American agreements had convinced Latin Americans that the United States was the empire to fear, not Spain, Britain, or France. For thirty years, U.S. arrogance in assuming that invasions of Latin America would morally uplift and economically stimulate a "backward" region deeply offended citizens and officials in Latin America. By 1928, Latin Americans had had enough, and they came to Havana to force limits on U.S. dominance. Fearing diplomatic reprisals, the United States sent President Calvin Coolidge, Secretary of State Charles Evans Hughs, international jurist Dr. James Scott Brown, Pan American Union Secretary Leo S. Rowe, and U.S. Ambassador to Cuba Henry P. Fletcher—all men—to convince Latin Americans of the sincerity of U.S. Pan American intentions. Never before had a sitting U.S. president attended a hemispheric conference outside the United States.

Cuban president Gerardo Machado hosted the conference and was eager to persuade visiting delegates that Cuba adhered to Pan American principles. Although he had just revised the Cuban constitution to outlaw opposition parties and had assumed a second presidential term under the contrivance of constitutional reform, he wanted to cast the image of a democrat. In 1928, Cubans had begun to oppose Machado's quasi-legal assumption of power, and Machado had introduced repressive tactics against dissent. Cuban women had become active against Machado. University women demanded and got membership in the radical student organization, the Directorio Estudiantil (Student Leadership). They were arrested along with their male colleagues for handing out their publication, *Alma Mater*. In demonstrations, young school girls dived beneath police horses to elude policemen dispersing strikes. Machado became increasingly dependent upon U.S. support to secure power. He turned a deaf ear to historic Cuban objections to the Platt Amendment, which guaranteed the legality of U.S. intervention in Cuba, control of the economy, and a permanent military presence.

In light of Machado's repressive tactics and repeated U.S. intervention in Latin America, Pan Americanism seemed a parody of itself when Presidents Gerardo Machado and Calvin Coolidge opened the Sixth Conference of American States with claims of their respect for Pan American principles. President Machado's speech ignored the U.S. aggression issue and his own use of brute force. President Coolidge's oration misrepresented history and the nature of hemispheric relations. He began by saying that Christopher Columbus brought with him the seed of the new republics and the promise of great liberty that until then had not crossed the oceans. He emphasized that the United States was determined to resolve regional differences through negotiation, peace, and the application of the principles of equity and justice. The sovereignty of small nations is respected, he proclaimed. Coolidge completely disregarded that even as he spoke, U.S. troops occupied three Latin American nations, a reality that Latin American delegates had to pretend to forget if they were to enjoy expanding trade opportunities with the most powerful nation in the Western Hemisphere.[6]

Coolidge's only concession on the matter of American aggression came in a call for peaceful hemispheric democracy, the cause that previous presidents had defended through military invasion. Coolidge admitted that at times this goal had been forcefully imposed, and he supported the idea that individual nations could do a better job of democratic reform themselves rather than having other governments impose change. President Coolidge wished to distance his administration from previous interventionist policies and to reassure Latin American delegates of his good intentions, but U.S. occupations of Nicaragua, Haiti, and the Dominican Republic made his speech at best a welcome promise and at worst a political fabrication.

Pan Americanism therefore created a context for hyperbole and moral aloofness that feminists could exploit to their advantage. Male delegates, charged with justifying their existence in the face of notable violations of the spirit of Pan Americanism, spoke loftily of their mission and ignored their failures. Magical realism was one of the few means by which to deal with the painful truth of U.S. domination. All delegates participated in manufacturing claims of hemispheric goodwill, partnership, morality, and respect in order to avoid overt conflict. Cast against obvious distortion, feminists would convincingly demonstrate sincere partnership, concrete means of reform, and a logical, moral defense for their positions. Though outsiders, they would present themselves as genuine practitioners of Pan Americanism and, by contrast, imply that men were not credible representatives of "the Western Hemisphere idea."

In early January 1928, an extraordinary event took place. Feminists from throughout the Western Hemisphere forced their way into celebrations of the Sixth Conference of American States to demand hemispheric women's rights. Nowhere had such a demand been made to a ruling international agency, but it occurred because the Pan American Union espoused principles that complemented women's ideals for social justice in the Americas. In 1923, the Pan American Union went beyond overseeing commercial and diplomatic regulations and undertook social welfare, education, and labor issues. At the Fifth Conference of American States, delegates secured a place on the subsequent agenda for a discussion of women's rights and recommended that women be official delegates to the Sixth Conference. However, female representatives were not invited, so only male delegates would consider gender issues.

Protesting their exclusion, Latin and North American women gathered to make a case for hemispheric women's rights and the need for an international women's organization to serve as a guarantor of women's permanent presence at inter-American meetings. The U.S. National Women's Party, along with feminists from throughout Latin America, came to Cuba to offer a show of force. The party set up headquarters in the Seville Biltmore Hotel on the Prado, the main thoroughfare to the capital building from the seawalk. The Party flew its banner out the windows of the Biltmore and flanked it with the Cuban and U.S. flags. This symbolized that feminist demands would be on equal footing with inter-American deliberations and that the women were unified.

Earlier that month, several Cuban feminist organizations had formally allied themselves with the National Women's Party and hammered out a strategy for the Sixth Inter-American Conference. The Club Femenino de Cuba (Cuban Women's Club), one of Cuba's preeminent organizations, became an affiliate of the National Women's Party. The Partido Demócrata Sufragista (Democratic Suffragist Party) and the Alianza Nacional Feminista (National Feminist Alliance) also pledged their allegiance to a common feminist cause. Together these professional, white women initiated an inter-American women's movement. Members of the Club Femenino attended national conventions of the National Women's Party and reported on Cuban campaigns. U.S. representatives helped Cubans to form other suffragist groups, such as the Partido Sufragista Cubano (Cuban Suffragist Party), and all agreed that the immediate objective was to place women on delegations attending the conference in Havana.[7]

In anticipation of the conference, a coalition of Cuban feminist organizations adopted a resolution declaring women and men equal before the law. On January 15, 1928, one day before the conference opened, the Partido Demócrata Sufragista and the Club Femenino received Jane Norman Smith and Doris Stevens, the two National Women's Party representatives, and adopted a resolution to be presented at the conference that declared all women and men equal. On January 22, Cuban, Latin American and North American feminists met and agreed that the proper strategy for international recognition of women's rights should be a Pan American effort, not a state-by-state campaign.[8] In less than two weeks, the Cubans had circulated a petition through every national women's organization, from feminist groups to the Salvation Army, until they had 5,000 signatures demanding a presence at the conference.[9] Representatives from other Latin American women's associations also participated in the planning sessions. The preliminary meetings stressed unity, a focus on inter-American womanhood, and the rejection of nationalist or classist perspectives. The Pan American feminists were determined not to be driven apart.

On January 28, Cubans celebrated the birthday of their independence hero José Martí. In a demonstration of respect for Martí and sovereignty in the Americas, Cuban national officials and delegates to the Pan American meeting marched the length of Avenida Prado to the statue of Martí in Old Havana. Presidents Gerardo Machado and Calvin Coolidge presented a wreath to the hero and then watched the procession. The Cuban delegation to the conference led the parade, followed by representatives of all twenty-one Latin American countries and the United States. Behind the dignitaries marched 5,000 school children, and following them was an uninvited contingent of more than 700 feminists from throughout the Americas. Marchers walked single file, led by Carmen Tamayo carrying the Cuban flag and followed by Elsie Ross Shields with the U.S. flag; both women were descendants of the seamstresses and designers of their nations' first national flags. Presidents of various Cuban women's organizations and twenty-one women dressed in blue, representing the Latin American republics, followed. Then came a delegation from the National Women's Party of the United States and several hundred Cuban women, some carrying banners with Martí's declarations for freedom and social justice written in Spanish, English, Portuguese, and French.

Feminist unity and the drama with which it was presented won applause from the officials in the stands as well as from the crowd. At Martí's statue, the marchers laid a wreath and released more than 2,000 carrier pigeons with tiny messages quoting Martí on women's rights.[10] This was the first international demonstration of women's rights anywhere. As a result of the effective display of hemispheric unity for women's rights, the president of the conference, Dr. Antonio Bustamante, scheduled an ex-officio address by feminists at the end of a plenary session. Formal delegates were not required to attend, and fully two-thirds left before the women took the floor. Their absence was taken up by the rush of more than 1,000 women, mostly Cubans, who crowded the galleries, stairs, and even the conference room of the Great Hall of the University of Havana, where the conference general assembly was meeting. The feminists' speeches gave important evidence of shared values, goals, and spirit of cooperation.

A listener would have been struck by the breadth and depth of the speeches that emphasized three principal themes of the Pan American women's movement: unity, equality, and permanent representation in the Pan American Union. Unity was a force meant to direct and empower the movement. Equality was the ideal relationship between the sexes and between the women of the Americas. To these ends, feminists wanted a permanent inter-American association as the mechanism for keeping women's issues before the conference delegates. Of the eight speakers, four were Cubans, two were from other countries in Latin America, and two were North Americans. If there were significant differences between North and Latin American feminists, it was in the tone and delivery of the speeches and in the deference paid to male delegates. Latin American feminists were more likely to cajole men, whereas North Americans concentrated on the legal and moral worth of issues without paying too much attention to men's egos. All offered positions that were erudite, elegantly stated, and compelling.

Pan American feminists adopted a number of approaches to convince men to grant their appeals. Dr. Julia Martínez of Cuba opened the session by characterizing women's rights as the most vital problem of the century. Doris Stevens, president of the International Action Committee of the National Women's Party of the United States, echoed the significance of the moment: "We have gathered here on a great historic occasion. This is the first occasion in the history of the world when women have stood before an international body to ask for action, by way of a treaty, for their rights."[11] The absence of the majority of delegates implied that the ex-officio meeting was unimportant. Undeterred, women of the Americas demonstrated that the event was unique and that it addressed an issue as important as the emancipation of slaves. Participants were not beyond appealing to male pride to gain allies. Some Latin American women humbled themselves before the august body of delegates, thanking the conference president for his permission to participate and praising the delegates' superior judgment about women's rights. Women were wily supplicants in search of allies. Acknowledging their disadvantaged position, they became the outsiders addressing the powerful, the weak appealing to the strong. This approach was meant to win advocates by reassuring men that women wanted not to remove them from power but to appeal to their judgment and support for women's rights.

Given the humble posture of some of the speakers, the audience might have anticipated docile, mindless, or simpering addresses, but such was never the case. Every speech that began with concessions to male authority ended with commanding arguments or demands for women's rights. Dr. Angela M. Zaldívar of Cuba began apologetically, but she ended by making men responsible for their exclusive control over democratic processes. The iron fist in the velvet glove approach was intended to elicit support from male delegates while impressing them with women's political acumen. By emphasizing the benefits of emancipated and feminine women, Zaldívar hoped that men would see the advantage of granting women equality through a permanent presence in the Pan

American Union. Conversely, by denying women their rights, men showed their own lack of ability to conduct a fully democratic society.

A subtle competition occurred over whether women or men best represented the principles of Pan American unity. In contrast to the conflicts between male delegates, women showed unity. Because they had never held authority over international policies, they could not be charged with violating the terms of Pan American diplomacy. Their objectives were also different from those of men. Women did not struggle for power over one another, even though they were divided by culture and history. Their objective was to pass laws in their own countries that would give them full rights, and they believed that a hemispheric movement freed them from cultural and historical obstructions at home. In fact, feminists exposed and rejected attempts on the part of their own male delegations to divide women along nationalist lines.

Doris Stevens, for example, exposed her compatriots' strategy at several points in her speech before the Pan American conference; she accused U.S. delegates of claiming that Latin American women were not prepared for equal rights, and she publicly rejected any hint of regional superiority within the Pan American women's coalition. She assailed the North American delegation for ostensibly protecting Latin American women through patronizing, imperialist policies. She parried any attack on global solidarity among women, ridiculed men for not being able to unite under the spirit of Pan Americanism, and assaulted the notion that there could be different codes of conduct for women and men.[12] Stevens' speech offered the most direct and scathing denunciation of U.S. imperialism and its efforts to sabotage Pan Americanism and international feminism. By placing gender ahead of nationalism, regionalism, and U.S. interests, Stevens advanced the spirit of Pan Americanism and feminist unity while demonstrating respect for Latin American feminism. She berated all men for not achieving hemispheric cooperation and suggested that American women could overcome the forces that had torn Pan American ideals apart. For Stevens and Latin American feminists, feminism and Pan Americanism were complementary and aspired to higher purposes than nationalism, making women better defenders of Pan Americanism.

Most speakers followed this line of reasoning. Mona Lee Muñoz Marín, of the National Women's Party in Puerto Rico and a professor at the University of Puerto Rico, was eloquent and philosophical in her association of inter-American feminism with the true spirit of Pan Americanism: men had built "many monuments to Pan Americanism" without achieving "deep and true friendship" free of egotism and imbued with inclusive and mutually beneficial policies. She believed that women could offer "a new definition of Pan Americanism: the unity of purpose that makes us all responsible citizens of the spiritual country of Pan America."[13] Muñoz Marín raised the level of diplomacy to include matters of spiritual recognition and interaction, a truly radical challenge. Other Pan American feminists proposed concrete implementation of Muñoz

Marín's proposal in the form of an equal rights treaty and a hemispheric association of women. Pan American feminists deemphasized their disagreements and convinced themselves that cultural and historical incongruencies could be resolved by having hemispheric equal rights and allowing each nation to institute reforms in a manner appropriate to each locale.

Equal rights were paramount for each female speaker; they would bestow full citizenship on women who had fought for independence in their fledgling countries. By attaching female subjugation to colonialism and showing that women were not dependents but patriots and soldiers, feminists posited that women had completed every requirement for citizenship. The subjugation of women was compared to slavery, an institution that ended in the United States in 1865, in Cuba in 1886, and in Brazil in 1888, all within the memories of older citizens of American states. Feminists exhorted men to rise to the occasion and liberate women, just as Abraham Lincoln and Carlos Manuel de Céspedes of Cuba had done for slaves the century before. They asked men how they could condone maintaining their sisters, mothers, and daughters as chattel, and they made every man responsible for such action.[14]

For all their militance, however, feminists guaranteed that equal rights did not mean a female renunciation of maternity and family. They worked hard to maintain a healthy image of the mother and wife. María Montalvo de Soto Navarro, president of Cuba's National Federation of Women's Associations, insisted that since women's natural virtues had not been sullied by wars, then surely they would not be damaged by having political authority. Doris Stevens carried this argument to its feminist conclusion by insisting that high moral expectations and community action from women and men were the salvation of humanity. The new vision for women was public, moral work and leadership.[15]

In addition to ideals and new images of women, the speakers presented legal arguments on the constitutionality of an equal rights treaty. The issue of how to proceed with legal reforms was addressed by Jane Norman Smith and Doris Stevens. After both speakers had acknowledged that the U.S. Constitution guaranteed all citizens' equal rights but that civil and political codes restricted women's legal action, they advocated constitutional and legal reforms through a hemispheric treaty. They confronted the U.S. position that laws defining women's legal authority should be left to domestic legislation and that a hemispheric treaty could not be binding. Smith and Stevens pointed out that men had been writing international treaties that limited women's domestic freedoms for decades, and they cited aspects of the Public and Private Legal Treaty, currently before the Sixth Conference, that curtailed women's freedoms.

Many of these ideas about liberation and social justice had been expressed by other feminists in other places at other times. The distinctiveness of an inter-American feminist movement came from the unification of Pan Americanism and feminism. Both movements strove for justice beyond what mankind had achieved, and both transcended local traditions and interests to attain regional social justice. Yet advocates of Pan American feminism and Pan Americanism did not intend for national cultures and histories to be lost as people accepted a hemispheric view of America. They believed that national and factional characteristics would be embedded in an inter-American identity. The feminism that Pan Americanism projected advocated regional legal guarantees that promised change within the context of national traditions.

By marshalling support for women's issues through a public demonstration of unity at the Sixth Conference, feminists accomplished moderate gains. They had women's rights redefined in the General Convention to include statements about their political and economic independence. They failed, however, to get an international treaty on equal rights. They did convince conference delegates to create the Inter-American Commission of Women, autonomous within the Union, to oversee the installation of women's rights in every American country. By a unanimous vote, delegates appointed a committee of twenty-one women to study laws relating to women throughout the hemisphere and to make recommendations for change. Doris Stevens chaired the Commission.

Unity among the Pan American feminists did not bring support from male delegates or other feminists. Men's tendencies to disregard women's rights, as well as fragmentary forces within the feminist movement, weakened and discredited Pan American feminism. Although women won a number of important concessions in 1928, individual nations, especially the United States, assumed a slow pace in granting women equal rights. As a rule, men regarded equal rights as a dangerous precedent with unknowable consequences, but Latin American men were more enthusiastic than North American men about granting women equality. Guatemalan, Uruguayan, and Costa Rican delegates had introduced the resolution at the Fifth Conference of American States in 1923, and Guatemalan, Cuban, Argentine, and Salvadoran delegates supported it in 1928.

That Central American nations took the lead on women's rights conformed not so much to what was current in their societies but to their efforts to form a Central American court system and devise both national and international laws for the region. Modernization and the chance to institute sweeping reforms inspired them to think beyond the confines of their societies and toward more perfect justice. In the United States, the argument was bounded by legal procedural considerations. U.S. legislation was a state matter, and an equal rights law, forced onto states by a treaty, would be neither legal nor workable. The United States was not inspired by the aim of social justice but by the politics of forcing women's rights on state legislatures that had already rejected the motion.

In addition to the opposition from influential men, feminists themselves were not in agreement about a hemispheric movement. Although Pan American feminists refused to be driven apart, other feminists—particularly socialist feminists, who despised U.S. domination—identified Jane Smith and Doris Stevens as emissaries of imperialism. Socialists believed that North American feminists would focus attention on civil and political legislation while ignoring the U.S. domination that created economic dependency, dictatorships, racial segregation, and military repression in Latin America. These characteristics of hegemony crippled the lives of working-class and dark-skinned women. Socialist feminists throughout the hemisphere shunned Stevens's invitations to support suffrage and equal rights.[16]

Stevens's purpose was not helped by an uncharacteristic article by Carrie Chapman Catt, president of the International Woman's Suffrage Alliance, who judged Latin American women as "lacking fundamental rationality" and wrote that "South American women are a threat to amicable and peaceful relations between the United States and South America."[17] Catt reflected the nationalist posture that U.S. delegates had hoped for from Stevens—that Latin Americans were not ready for democracy and needed U.S. guidance. Such an insult was hard for any Latin American feminist to swallow, but the Pan Americanists chose to ignore it. Others did not. Mariblanca Sabas Alomá, a radical Cuban feminist and noted journalist, joined Colombian feminists in returning the insult. Sabas Alomá wrote the following:

If only Mrs. Chapman Catt's fears were quickly confirmed. If amicable and peaceful relations between the United States and Latin American republics must continually be based on hateful economic and infamous political penetrations [by the United States] that convert us into docile slaves, as they have done by kicking us and breaking our spirits . . . If "amicable and peaceful relations" means the occupation of Nicaragua [and] the Panama Canal, the dominance of Brazilian rubber harvesters, Cuban sugar, Mexican petroleum, Peruvian gold mines, Chilean salt mints, etc. . . . If "amicable and peaceful relations" means twenty American republics becoming independent [from Spain] only to fall prey to humiliating Yankee imperialism, then, Mrs. Chapman Catt, the women of all Indian-Hispanic America will try by every means possible to destroy diplomatic ties.

    . . . We will be revolutionaries in order to serve justice in the highest sense of the word, to give justice the correct interpretation it now lacks.[18]

Latin American socialist feminists were not the only ones to send disparaging messages about the Inter-American Commission of Women. The United States had been the Commission's most consistent foe. As American involvement in World War II became more and more likely, the United States wanted the Pan American Union to focus more on reciprocal defense treaties while setting aside social reform concerns. Eleanor Roosevelt led a campaign against the Commission in 1938 because she opposed equal rights legislation and disliked Doris Stevens. She even had Stevens removed as the director of the organization. In 1938, at the Eighth Conference of American States in Lima, the United States convinced the delegates to abrogate the Commission's autonomous status and place it under the direction of the General Secretary, who was always a North American man.

Thus, the Commission's ability to define its own issues was curtailed by both women and men. These centrifugal forces threatened the credibility and loyalty of Pan American feminists to a hemispheric solution for discrimination against women. They also weakened their effectiveness.

The Seventh Conference of American States (Montevideo, 1933) tested Pan American feminist unity and diplomatic acuity. Delegations received the report of the Inter-American Commission of Women that assessed political and civil rights governing women in all of the signatory nations.[19] Along with stark proof of women's disadvantaged circumstances, Commission members presented recommendations in the form of resolutions for delegates to pass into international agreements. Three resolutions came to the floor. The first was to make the Inter-American Commission of Women a permanent and autonomous agency within the Pan American Union, with the mandate to continue recommending proposals based on equal rights principles. All nations but three approved the measure. The second concerned the nationality of women whose husbands were from other countries. The law in fourteen American nations determined that the wife's nationality should become that of her husband. Most delegates agreed that a wife's nationality should be her own choice, but they were hesitant to alter the law because The Hague was in the process of ruling that women should have the freedom to choose. Despite confusion over how to write a law when the world court was deciding on the same legislation, the assembly voted in favor of the married woman's right to choose her own nationality. Again the United States abstained.

The third and most difficult issue was an equal rights treaty. The Commission had recommended a hemispheric treaty that would be binding on all members of the Pan American Union to grant women equal rights with men. After deliberations, the subcommittee reviewing the Commission's recommendations declined to call for a vote on the grounds that every nation had different social and cultural contexts that affected the passage of equal rights. Therefore, it should be up to each nation to pass equal rights legislation according to its own circumstances. The Pan American Union did encourage all American republics, "so far as the peculiar circumstances of each country will conveniently permit, to establish the maximum of equality between men and women in all matters pertaining to the possession, enjoyment and exercise of civil and political rights."[20] This resolution of intent passed. Dissenters included Cuba, Ecuador, and Paraguay, each of which called for a binding treaty. The U.S. delegation at first abstained, but it later approved the bill with the reservation that equal rights would have to win congressional approval. The Seventh Conference, then, concluded with substantial but incomplete gains for women.

At subsequent conferences the Women's Commission submitted reports on the progress of women's legal battles and the conditions of women's lives. In Latin America, governments sensitized to women's issues passed maternity laws, equal education guarantees, fair custody of children legislation, property rights, labor laws, and, belatedly, enfranchisement. Cuba passed an equal rights amendment in 1940. The evolution of laws in Latin America reflected a social consciousness that stressed social and civil guarantees over electoral laws. After all, in Latin America democracy was fragile at best and often meaningless. Conversely, in the United States, where elections occurred but social services were left to local government or philanthropy, universal suffrage passed in 1920, and social legislation followed slowly. The United States never achieved the guarantees of equal rights or the maternity and protective legislation extant in Latin America.

As the first international women's association linked to an international diplomatic body, the Inter-American Women's Commission used its weight to influence global rulings on women's rights. It represented the rights of women to their own nationality before The Hague and won. It influenced the wording of the U.N. charter to endorse worldwide equality between women and men. It also joined the Women's Commission of the United Nations, even as it maintained its regional standing in the Organization of American States. The Inter-American Commission of Women was a quiet force behind progressive reforms. It offered the pressure of conscience. By working toward mutual respect, peaceful progress, equity, and accord through covenants and declarations, its members hoped to morally bind governments to carry out the promises they made. The Commission worked to develop a powerful body of opinion and precedent that might eradicate the subjugation of women, but like all things Pan American, setting a standard was the best the Commission could manage. It never developed an enforcement mechanism, and it was not a court of law or a police force.

In the end, the Pan American feminist movement amounted to less than what its members aspired to at the outset. Housed in the Pan American Union building in Washington, like the Pan American movement itself, the Commission was dominated by North American male officials. Commission projects were limited to producing reports on conditions in the Americas and to passing resolutions with no "bite." Commission members had trouble convincing governments and citizens of the Americas to address the roots of women's subjugation: patriarchy, hierarchical relations of dominance, and women's willingness to allow patriarchy to govern them. Under the auspices of the Pan American Union and later the Organization of American States, machismo, poverty, inequitable legal systems, corrupt courts, political intolerance, repression, and U.S. domination continued to limit women's freedom.

Lest our attention be drawn solely to tangible reforms, however, we should also examine the function that Pan American feminism served in directing feminist ideals and the place that it held in the world of multiple feminisms. Pan American feminism offered women a means of transcending regional resistance to women's rights, and it bound together a transcontinental movement. Before 1938, it presented a model of understanding and compromise, and it more nearly fit the tenets of "the Western Hemisphere idea" than did agreements about weights and measures, highway and railroad construction, and air transport. Only the Public and Private International Laws and the debates over hemispheric aggression held the same moral weight, and they achieved fewer reforms.

Our knowledge of feminist history has advanced over the past thirty years from ethnocentric studies of western European and North American movements to cultural and subcultural life studies. Comparative histories invite us to analyze the ways in which culture and experience have influenced people who share a biological identity. We have gone from the histories of leaders to the histories of common women, and we are all the better for it. As our attention has been directed toward the deconstruction of women's history, we have treated unified feminist action lightly or assumed it to be superficial. On the whole, our discussions have ignored regional and global movements, even as they have occurred in our lifetimes. We have lost track of those who had a grand design for the empowerment of women, basically because we have judged them to be naive, imperialistic, or failures. That the Inter-American Commission of Women exists today, albeit in an advisory capacity, and that it has brought women's concerns before what is now the Organization of American States and the United Nations, implies that it has at least raised awareness of women's issues throughout the world. Naive or not, imperialist or not, countercurrent or not, the inter-American feminist movement must be understood as part of the evolution of feminist consciousness.

NOTES

I would like to thank the friends and colleagues who helped with this chapter. Dr. Donna J. Guy offered her notes from Equal Rights, *the National Women's Party journal and provided information from Cuban newspapers about the Sixth International Conference of American States. Lucilia Harrington at the OAS Library photocopied sections from the* Final Acts *of the Sixth Conference. Allison Coudert, Gordon Weiner, Philip Soergel, and Frances P. Stoner read drafts of this paper and offered their advice and criticism.*

1. Paula Baker, "The Domestication of Politics: Women and Political Society, 1780–1920," *American Historical Review* 89, no. 3 (June 1984): 620–47; Nancy F. Cott. *The Grounding of Modern Feminism* (New Haven, 1987); Karen Offen, "Defining Feminism: A Comparative Historical Approach," *Signs: A Journal of Women in Culture and Society* 14, no. 11 (Spring 1988): 119–57, Naomi Black, *Social Feminism* (Ithaca, 1989); Nancy F. Cott. "What's in a Name? The Limits of 'Social Feminism' or Expanding the Vocabulary of Women's History," *Journal of American History* 76 (December 1989): 809–29.

2. See, for example, Sandra McGee Deutsch. "Gender and Sociopolitical Change in Twentieth-Century Latin America," *Hispanic American Historical Review* 71, no. 2 (May 1991): 259–306; June E. Hahner, *Emancipating the Female Sex: The Struggle for Women's Rights in Brazil, 1850–1940* (Durham, 1990); Asunción Lavrin, *Women, Feminism and Social Change in Argentina, Chile, and Uruguay, 1890–1940* (Lincoln, NE, 1995); Ana Macías, *Against All Odds: The Feminist Movement in Mexico to 1940* (Westport, 1982); K. Lynn Stoner, *From the House to the Streets: The Cuban Woman's Movement for Legal Reform 1898–1940* (Durham, 1991).

3. Nancy Hewitt, "Sisterhood in the International Perspective: Thoughts on Teaching Comparative Women's History," *Women's Studies Quarterly* 16 (Spring–Summer 1988): 22–32.

4. Leila Rupp, "Conflict in the International Women's Movement, 1888–1950" (paper presented at the Berkshire Conference of Women Historians, Rutgers University, New Brunswick, N.J., 10 June 1990; Leila Rupp, *Worlds of Women: The Making of an*

International Women's Movement (Princeton, 1997); Paula Pfeffer, "A Whisper in the Assembly of Nations: United States' Participation in the International Movement of Women's Rights from the League of Nations to the United Nations," *Women's Studies International Forum* (1985): 459–71.

5. Francesca Miller, "Latin American Feminism in the Transnational Arena," in *Women, Culture, and Politics in Latin America*, edited by Seminar on Feminism and Culture in Latin America (Berkeley, 1989) 10–26; Francesca Miller, *Latin American Women and the Search for Justice* (Hanover, 1991).

6. Sexta Conferencia Internacional Americana, *Actas de las sesiones plenarias de la Sexta Conferencia Internacional Americana: inaugurada en la Habana, el 16 de enero de 1928* (Havana, 1933), 27–28.

7. "Feminism in Cuba," *Equal Rights*, 18 June 1927, p. 147.

8. "Club Femenino Welcomes Emissaries," *Equal Rights*, 11 February 1928, p. 3.

9. Pilar Houston, "Intimate Glimpses of Havana," *Equal Rights*, 18 February 1928, pp. 13–14.

10. Pilar Houston, "Significant Note in the Tribute to Martí," *Equal Rights*, 11 February 1928, p. 3.

11. República de Cuba, *Diario de la Sexta Conferencia Internacional Americana* (Havana, 1928), 350.

12. República de Cuba, 353.

13. República de Cuba, 355.

14. Speeches by María Montalvo de Soto Navarro (Cuba) and Plintha Más y Gil (Dominican Republic), in República de Cuba, 353–55.

15. República de Cuba, 353.

16. For information about the adversarial relationships between Stevens and the Cuban Left, see Ofelia Domínguez Navarro, *50 años de una vida* (Havana, 1971), 223, 233–35; Stoner, 126.

17. Mariblanca Sabas Alomá, *Feminismo: cuestiones sociales-críticas literarias* (Havana, 1930), 165.

18. Ibid., 166–67.

19. Seventh Inter-American Conference, "Civil and Political Rights of Woman," *Minutes and Antecedents with General Index* C.III.N.5, 28–46.

20. Ibid., 46.

9

The New Pan Americanism in U.S.–Central American Relations, 1933–1954

Thomas M. Leonard

In 1933, U.S. Secretary of State Cordell Hull boldly announced at the Seventh Conference of American States in Montevideo that "no government need fear any intervention on the part of the United States under the Roosevelt administration."[1] This not only pleased Latin Americans in attendance, it also marked the beginning of a new phase in Pan Americanism that would last until 1954. For Central American[2] governments the new policy proved significant; the new noninterventionist Pan Americanism contributed to a lessening of tensions between Washington and the Central American republics, to inter-American cooperation in facing the Great Depression, and to solidarity in meeting the threats posed by World War II and the early Cold War. Despite the friendly spirit implied in the new cooperative Pan Americanism, and the long-standing public face of Pan Americanism as one of friendly interchange, a variety of nation- and region-based objectives guided Central American–U.S. cooperation between 1933 and 1954. For the most part, the new Pan Americanism was held together by a combination of domestic political needs, trade necessities, and wartime strategic concerns rather than by a cooperative ideal. With the intensification of the Cold War in the early 1950s and the U.S.-sponsored invasion of Guatemala in 1954, the new Pan Americanism came to an end.

After 1900, U.S. policy toward Central America stressed political and fiscal stability in order to secure the Panama canal. Policy makers in Washington feared that the constant political turmoil in the five Central American republics might spill over into Panama and that fiscal irresponsibility invited European intervention. The United States responded to the perceived threat. The period from 1900 to 1933 is replete with U.S. military interventions, fiscal reorganization plans, and the withholding of recognition from governments that came to power by extraconstitutional means. Twice the United States attempted to impose its political culture upon the republics. In 1907 and again in 1923, the United States hosted conferences in Washington that identified governments unworthy of recognition, a political form of intervention designed to topple unconstitutional regimes. The latter conference also resulted in an arms limitation agreement designed to curtail Central American military expenditures. At the same time, Central American administrations often welcomed or even invited the interventions for a range of domestic political ends.[3]

Others in Central and South America opposed the U.S. interventions. After 1889, they continually used Pan American conferences as vehicles for promoting equality, respect for the rule of international law, and adherence to the principles of sovereignty and absolute nonintervention in the hemispheric community. At the same time, Washington policy makers orchestrated conference agendas to avoid discussion of political issues and to sidestep the question of nonintervention; economic, scientific, and cultural topics dominated Pan American meetings.[4] Growing U.S. frustration in the 1920s over Washington's failed policy of political stabilization in Central America, and increasing Latin American demands for an end to military intervention, helped to pave the way for President-elect Franklin D. Roosevelt to announce his Good Neighbor policy in March 1933 and for Hull to promise to end U.S. intervention.

The road to the Good Neighbor policy began in the early 1920s as successive chiefs of the State Department's Latin American Division, Francis G. White and Edwin C. Wilson, suggested that it was no longer essential for the United States to interfere in Central American affairs. President-elect Herbert Hoover's goodwill visit to Central and South America in 1928 was followed by J. Reuben Clark's Memorandum on the Monroe Doctrine, which renounced U.S. intervention in Latin American domestic affairs by the terms of the Doctrine. At the same time, and in response to the U.S. failure to bring about democratic rule in Central America, there was strong sentiment in Congress and among the public against a U.S. Marine presence in Nicaragua and the overland pursuit of revolutionary leader Augusto C. Sandino. Assistant Director of the Latin American Division Stokeley W. Morgan put it best when he pointed out that because political parties in power in Central America controlled the electoral process, there was no opportunity for peaceful change in government: for those out of power, revolution was the only means to gain control of government.[5]

Historically, Latin American governments and scholars maintained strong anti-interventionist positions and considered all de facto governments as de jure; governments arising out of a revolutionary process were equal to elected regimes. In his opposition to revolutionary governments and to European intervention in the late nineteenth and early twentieth centuries, the Ecuadoran jurist Carlos Tobar was one of the first to break with this tradition. His argument in favor of collective intervention in the Americas, which would include "the denial of recognition to de facto governments rising out of revolution against [a] constitutional regime," found expression in the 1907 and 1923 Central American treaties.[6] But this view was not in line with contemporary Latin American thought. Opposition to it and to U.S. nonrecognition—particularly President Woodrow Wilson's nonrecognition of the Federico Tinoco government in Costa Rica—drew sharp responses. Latin American scholars such as Chilean Ricardo Montamer Bello, Colombian J. M. Yepes, and Paraguayan Higinio Arbo compared what became known as the Tobar Doctrine to the Holy Alliance, legitimizing illegal governments while inviting foreign intervention. At the same time, Latin American governments expressed increasing opposition to U.S. intervention in the Caribbean region.[7]

At the 1927 meeting of the International Commission of Jurists, Latin American leaders finally engineered a diplomatic response to intervention: a resolution for consideration at the Sixth Conference of American States, scheduled for Havana in 1928. The resolution called for the extension of recognition to governments that demonstrated "effective authority with [the] probability of stability and consolidation," and the "capacity to discharge preexisting international obligations, to contract others and to respect the principles established by international law." At Havana, the Latin American delegates were prepared to accept the resolution, but U.S. Secretary of State Charles Evans Hughes was not. Hughes marshalled support for his position among a majority of delegates, and nonintervention was not adopted.[8]

Changing attitudes in the State Department, continuing Latin American pressures on Washington, the absence of a European threat to the Western Hemisphere, and the need to consolidate American resources during the Great Depression contributed to Roosevelt's Good Neighbor policy and to the association of Pan Americanism with nonintervention. In 1933, the United States accepted the Convention on Rights and Duties of States, which proclaimed that "no state has the right to intervene in the internal or external affairs of another," but because the document did not precisely define the meaning of *intervention*, nonrecognition remained a policy option for Washington.[9] Although the 1936 Inter-American Conference for the Maintenance of Peace was called to deal with rising war clouds in Europe, the Argentines, Brazilians, and Mexicans led a Latin American charge to end any ambiguity over intervention. In light of its recent termination of treaties with Cuba, the Dominican Republic, Haiti, and Panama that had granted intervention privileges to the United States, the U.S. delegation had no difficulty approving the conference protocol that declared "inadmissible the intervention of any [member nation], directly or indirectly, and for whatever reason, in the internal or external affairs of any other." Not only was armed intervention now prohibited, explained Mexican diplomat Roberto Córdoba, but so was any action "which we might call peaceable . . . which has the same effect . . . as political, preventative or repressive interventions." Sumner Welles agreed. The United States expressed its "utter unwillingness to interfere directly or indirectly in the domestic concerns of Latin America." Without specifically mentioning the word, Welles implied that the United States had abandoned intervention for the first time since 1913.[10]

For twenty-one years after the 1933 Montevideo conference, the United States used three criteria to determine the granting of recognition: control of national territory and administrative machinery, including the maintenance of public order; the ability to meet international obligations; and the willing support of the nation's people. During the same period, dictators moved into the presidential palaces across the isthmus—with the exception of Costa Rica, where there was a peaceful transfer of political power after the completion of regularly scheduled elections every four years. In Guatemala and Honduras, respectively, Jorge Ubico and Tiburcio Carías became presidents before 1933. After 1934, both men used extralegal means to extend their presidential terms. In 1935, Ubico held a nationwide plebiscite that prompted the national assembly to amend the constitution to extend his presidential term until 1941. That same year, Carías handpicked a constituent assembly that also amended the constitution, permitting Carías to remain in office until 1943. In keeping with its nonintervention pledge at Montevideo, the United States did little more than register displeasure at the constitutional maneuvering of both dictators.[11]

The case of Maximiliano Hernández Martínez was more severe. On December 5, 1931, four days after a coup d'état ousted Salvadoran President Arturo Araujo, Vice President and War Minister Hernández Martínez proclaimed himself president. Although he was not clearly linked the instigation of the coup, and El Salvador had not ratified Article II of the 1923 Central American Treaty (which provided for the nonrecognition of governments that came to power by coup unless legitimized by a free election), the United States denied recognition to the new regime on the grounds that Hernández Martínez had seized power illegally. Subsequently, Hernández Martínez directed the ruthless suppression of a botched peasant uprising led by the communist Augustín Farabundo Martí. Hernández Martínez used the violence as a reason to extend his presidency to 1935. Although some U.S. policy makers expressed satisfaction at the suppression of communism, Secretary of State Henry L. Stimson refused to extend recognition to the Salvadoran government because the new leader's ascent to power allegedly violated the 1923 Central American Treaty. However, Hernández Martínez did not remain isolated very long. In January 1933, Costa Rica gave the required year's notice to withdraw from the 1923 Central American Treaty. El Salvador immediately followed. A year later, representatives from the Central American countries convened in San José, Costa Rica, where they determined to extend recognition to the Hernández Martínez government. In January 1935 Hernández Martínez gained a still stronger sense of legitimacy when he won the presidential election unopposed. At this point the United States extended recognition.[12]

In Nicaragua, Anastasio Somoza De Bayle's capture of the presidency confirmed U.S. nonintervention and the withholding of recognition from illegal governments. A growing confrontation between National Guard chief Somoza and President Juan B. Sacasa followed the departure of the U.S. Marines from Nicaragua in 1933. As Somoza's presidential ambitions became apparent, the State Department instructed its ministers in Managua, Arthur Bliss Lane, and Boaz Long, to avoid the anticipated political crisis. The advice, however, did not prevent Lane from suggesting to Somoza that the United States would withhold recognition if he seized power. Somoza was unmoved. He correctly anticipated that the United States would do nothing in June 1936, when he placed Brenes Jarquín in the presidential palace, or in January 1937, when Somoza himself took the presidency. Although there was sentiment in the State Department to do "something," everyone understood that a reaction after the fact would be ineffectual.[13] Subsequently, U.S. officials scorned constitutional maneuverings to extend presidential mandates by Carías, Hernández Martínez, and Somoza in 1939 and by Ubico in 1941. Washington policy makers criticized the scuttling of democratic practices but did not discuss withholding recognition or intervening. Each regime satisfied the U.S. criteria for recognition: control of the nation's territory and administrative machinery, an expressed willingness to meet international obligations, and popular support (despite the silencing of political opposition). Nor could the United States point to the 1923 Central American Treaty as a basis for nonrecognition; it made no mention of constitutional maneuvering.[14] The new Pan Americanism meant that the United States would not use intervention to confront extralegal regimes, and it would be hesitant to apply nonrecognition.

The new Pan Americanism was crafted in part by the support given by the Central Americans to U.S. global strategies; that backing advanced domestic policy agendas in Central America, lessened the likelihood of U.S. intervention in the region, and helped build U.S.–Central American relations around economic and strategic ties. By 1933 the world staggered under economic collapse. In the four years since the onset of the Great Depression, U.S. exports to Latin America had fallen 78 percent in value. Imports had dropped 68 percent. Central American agro-export–oriented economies were struck hard. The drop in commodity prices for the region's chief exports, bananas and coffee, could not be offset by volume increases. Each republic defaulted on its public external debt. Reacting to the crisis, and in conjunction with Pan American nonintervention, Cordell Hull envisioned a more liberal trade policy to improve the depression-plagued global economy and to ease political tensions. Many U.S. industrialists and large agriculturists supported Hull's proposals, as did delegates at Montevideo in 1933. There, the Latin American representatives supported Hull's resolution calling for liberalized trade policies. In June 1934 the U.S. Congress passed the Reciprocal Trade Agreements Act, which provided for the use of the unconditional most-favored-nation clause and the principle of active tariff bargaining through reciprocal agreements. It also empowered the president to raise or lower tariff duties by 50 percent and enabled him to move goods on and off the duty-free list.[15]

Central America fit neatly into Hull's scheme. It did not have a competitive industrial sector, and its major exports did not compete with U.S. commodities. U.S. firms stood to benefit from tariff reduction and trade agreements by replacing European firms as suppliers of manufactured goods in the region. Despite economic misfortune in Latin America, the State Department faced a difficult negotiating task with the Central Americans. The latter understood that reciprocity would not be mutually advantageous; the bulk of their primary exports already entered the United States duty-free. In addition, the United States extended most-favored-nation status to other countries that stood to benefit at the expense of Central American nations. Central Americans also resisted Hull's advances in part because they enjoyed a degree of independence as a result of bilateral trade agreements completed with Germany and Italy in the early 1930s; these might be superceded by new accords with the United States. Nevertheless, before the decade ended, all five republics completed reciprocal trade agreements with Washington, largely for political rather than economic reasons.[16]

The reciprocity agreements contributed to defining the new Pan Americanism. Anxious to stimulate commerce through a reduction in trade barriers and to present a picture of hemispheric solidarity, the United States seemed decreasingly concerned about the political intrigues of the isthmian dictators. Central Americans viewed the agreements otherwise. With the exception of Costa Rica, the Central American countries saw reciprocity as a means to forestall U.S. intervention by gaining a recognition for the illicit governments. Economically, the agreements did little for either side. Central America had little to offer in the way of commodities and, with its limited purchasing power, could buy little from the United States. State Department counselor Laurence Duggan correctly observed that "the political achievements of the Good Neighbor policy were not matched in the economic field."[17] By late 1941, all Central American–European trade had been severed.[18] At the same time, the United States undertook several wartime projects to maintain regional economic security.[19] The 1940 Inter-American Coffee Agreement, for example, provided coffee quotas at guaranteed prices for the American republics. Although coffee production did not begin to climb until the 1944–1945 crop, coffee growers were able to count on a guaranteed minimum income. Banana producers and workers did not fare as well. With no equivalent agreement in place, banana production decreased by more than 50 percent by the end of 1944. U.S. wartime programs to secure strategic materials supported Central American production, particularly in abaca (hemp) and rubber, but for the most part the programs benefited multinational giants such as the United Fruit and Standard Fruit Companies.

Nelson Rockefeller's Office of Inter-American Affairs and Institute for Inter-American Affairs undertook several projects that promoted good will between the United States and the Central Americans. They also provided badly needed jobs. The Office of Inter-American Affairs sponsored sanitation and health projects in each of the five republics. In Costa Rica it initiated agricultural experimental stations for long-range projects in crop diversification. The Army Corps of Engineers undertook the Pan American Highway project. Although not completed during the war, it did provide employment for many Central Americans. The U.S. Army recruited approximately 10,000 Salvadoran workers to the Panama Canal Zone to replace military personnel in labor-support roles. Still, these programs did not offset the adverse impacts of the war. Central Americans suffered severe shortages of goods. Although the German U-boat played havoc with Caribbean shipping lanes through the end of 1942, the U.S. War Shipping Board later commandeered all merchant ships in the region to service the trans-Atlantic convoy system to England. Without shipping service for nearly eighteen months, the Central Americans endured a shortage of consumer goods until late 1943. Not only were gasoline, tires, and spare parts nearly unavailable, so too were farm and construction equipment. Shortages contributed significantly to an inflationary spiral, which rose an average of 240 percent across the isthmus by late 1944. Local wages failed to keep apace as Central Americans continued to see few benefits from the economic component of the new Pan Americanism.[20]

Central Americans also cooperated with the United States in regional defense and strategy. U.S. defense planners feared that Central America might become a possible staging area for sabotage and a potential base for military operations against the Panama Canal. Initially, the United States sought to help nations meet their defense needs by assigning military missions to each of the countries willing to modernize and equip their local military. All but Honduras were responsive partners. The first mission, to Nicaragua, began in 1939. A year later missions arrived in El Salvador (to modernize a 6,000-man army) and in Costa Rica (to train a 15,000-man police force). Guatemala and Honduras soon followed, but Presidents Ubico and Carías feared that exposure to U.S. influence might encourage their nations' militaries to act independently.

In confronting the wartime enemy, Washington at first focused on German and Italian colonies as a potential source of political subversion and sabotage. The Germans tended to remain aloof from the locals, but at the same time they played a significant role in national economies, particularly in Guatemala and Costa Rica. After 1941, all five republics cooperated with U.S. projects directed at removing an Axis threat in the region. In January 1942, they participated in the Third Meeting of Consultation of Foreign Ministers at Rio de Janeiro, an important step in the integration of defense priorities into Pan Americanism, where agreement was reached to restrict the activities of Axis nationals. These measures included the registration of all Axis nationals and their descendants; restriction of their movement within each country, including internment if necessary; control of their business activity through the so-called Proclaimed List of Blocked Neutrals (the Black List); censorship of their mail; and supervision of their bank accounts.

Despite U.S. pressure, Central American governments were reluctant to nationalize German-owned properties. Costa Rica, true to its democratic tradition, proved the most uncooperative. Presidents Hernández Martínez and Somoza were reluctant to nationalize German properties in El Salvador and Nicaragua out of fear that it would send a signal to their landowning political opponents. In mid-1943, Somoza devised an elaborate scheme for nationalizing German properties while ensuring that his wealthy political adversaries would lose no land arbitrarily. In Guatemala, President Ubico, also concerned with political opponents, argued that he could not nationalize the German properties because Guatemalans could not efficiently operate them. Only after his overthrow in July 1944 did the new military junta seize German agricultural holdings. President Carías' control over Honduran society was more complete, and the German population there was very small. Because the government sold or otherwise passed on German-owned properties to Carías supporters, there was little public outcry.

By the end of February 1942 the five republics had concluded wartime Lend-Lease agreements with the United States. Material received under the agreements illustrated the U.S. wartime emphasis on securing the Caribbean Sea lanes rather than strengthening the local militaries. Small boats and aircraft for coastal patrols and associated spare parts, along with appropriate ordnance and ammunition, constituted the bulk of supplies to Central America. Only a small token of light arms, tanks, and planes were made available to the five nations; as mandated by the program's Joint Advisory Board, the bulk of this weaponry came after 1942, when the German U-boat threat to the region had ended. Although the State Department grudgingly approved military shipments to Central America as the war drew to its conclusion, the Central American nations received only $4.1 million in lend-lease aid from the program's inception in March 1941 through the end of the war in September 1945–an amount significantly less than that proposed in 1941 and representing less than 10 percent of all Latin American lend-lease aid.[21]

Beginning in 1931, application of the new Pan Americanism had provided for mutual cooperation, but not mutual benefits—economically or strategically— as far as the majority of Central Americans were concerned. In wages and prices, few saw the benefits of stronger Pan American ties. During the Great Depression and World War II, the United States won Central American solidarity; at the same time, and also by the tenets of the new Pan Americanism, the quid pro quo for Central American dictators was an enhanced political legitimacy at home and in the region through closer associations with the United States.

Late in the war, the U.S. War and State Departments outlined sharply different primary objectives for the hemisphere. Whereas the War Department focused on maintaining U.S. strategic and military leadership in Central America, the State Department heightened its interest in democratic rule. In 1944 the War Department brought U.S. troop strength down by nearly 50 percent in Central America. It also prepared a postwar strategy on the assumptions that Washington would maintain adequate armed forces in the region to prevent any large-scale aggression against the Western Hemisphere; that the American republics would continue to provide facilities as required to meet the threat of external aggression; and that regional forces would continue to augment those of the United

States by maintaining internal order and security, providing local defense against isolated attacks, protecting coastal shipping, and assisting the United States in protecting overseas commerce.[22] In contrast, from 1944 to 1947, as the winds of political change swept across the isthmus, the State Department sought the promotion of democracy as a first priority. In an effort to achieve that goal, it used gentle persuasion and attempted to revive a nonrecognion policy. The State Department prevailed over the War Department on the question of a first priority in policy, but it faced Latin American opposition on reimplementing nonrecognition. The War Department, meanwhile, achieved many of its objectives in agreements with Central American nations during military staff conversations in 1945. The Central American governments agreed to organize and train their ground forces according to U.S. guidelines and doctrines, to equip their forces with U.S. weapons, to exchange obsolete and foreign-made equipment for modern U.S. materiel, to send officers to U.S. military service schools, and to cooperate in the defense of the Western Hemisphere. These accords designated each nation's military strength, including the size of its ground and air forces and the types and quantities of military equipment that each was to receive.[23]

The Caribbean Defense Command (CDC) confidently believed that the U.S. Congress would approve a large-scale military assistance program for all Latin America. To do otherwise, CDC Assistant Chief of Staff for G-2 Colonel Howard Eager warned, "would result in a loss of U.S. prestige in the area and have adverse repercussions on future military cooperation." President Harry S. Truman shared the War Department's view that Central America had to be incorporated into U.S. hemispheric defense plans when he introduced legislation in 1946 that would have put in place army postwar defense planning. When Congress failed to pass the legislation, Truman reintroduced it in the spring of 1947. This time he assured the legislators that there would be no Latin American armaments race, that the plan fell within the framework of the Act of Chapultepec, and that there would not be a contest to create a military balance of power in Latin America. Congress remained unimpressed.[24]

State Department officials responsible for Central American policy did not share the administration's enthusiasm for the proposed hemispheric defense plans. They worried that rearming Central America could undermine the search for democratic stability. As early as 1943, Assistant Chief of the American Republics Affairs Division John M. Cabot warned that Hernández Martínez's request for 1,000 submachine guns under Lend-Lease was for "lethal toys [that are] more likely to be used for a very different purpose than they were intended." In early 1945 Acting Secretary of State Joseph C. Grew recognized that Somoza's call for 10,000 rifles to keep communism out of Nicaragua was a hoax. In both instances the State Department understood that the real intention was to suppress internal political opposition. Before bilateral military staff conversations between U.S. officials and their equivalents in the different republics in the spring of 1945, the State Department had implemented a policy of not supplying arms to dictators in Central America. "We cannot be accused either by our own people or by the dictators' victims of supporting or making possible the continuance of dictatorships through supplying arms susceptible of use by a dictator against his own people," Cabot explained.[25]

American diplomats in Central America were equally wary. Ambassadors Hallet Johnson in Costa Rica, Edwin G. Kyle in Guatemala, and Avra Warren in Nicaragua warned against the possible misuse of any military equipment sent to the region. The ambassador to El Salvador, John F. Simmons, cautioned against

a build up in their [Salvadoran] military establishment to a point beyond what many people here may consider to be the normal minimum requirements . . . and that we should always consider the possibility that any military matériel and equipment which we may later ship to this country . . . might be used for political purposes and as a means of maintaining a given government in power . . . [rather] than strengthening our hemispheric defense.[26]

Convinced that military supplies would be used to suppress the political opposition, the State Department refused export licenses for arms shipments to Honduras or Nicaragua through 1947. It also adamantly opposed the sale of bomber planes to the Central American governments for fear that they might be used against civilian populations or to settle border disputes. In Central America, the articulate political opposition reasoned—like the State Department—that increased weaponry only served domestic political purposes. Congress shared this view when it refused to approve the Inter-American Military Cooperation Act.[27] In light of the congressional refusal, and over War Department protests, when the nations of the Western Hemisphere ratified the 1947 Treaty of Rio de Janeiro (the Rio Pact), providing for action by all contracting nations against an armed attack on any American republic, no provision for implementation was included.[28]

Although the Rio Pact contributed markedly to moving Pan Americanism toward a regional collective security system, as the Cold War dawned in 1947 the inter-American defense system remained elusive. Further progress toward collective security was made at the Ninth Conference of American States (Bogotá, 1948). Not until 1951 did the U.S. Congress approve military assistance to Latin America, giving practical legitimacy to the Pan American hemispheric defense strategy. Long before that date, however, the Central American dictators were threatened from within their polities. In 1944, Hernández Martínez and Ubico were ousted from power in El Salvador and Guatemala. A "leftist" candidate, Teodoro Picado, was elected to the Costa Rican presidency. Similar pressures in Nicaragua prompted Somoza to announce that he would step down from the presidency when his term ended in 1947. Only Honduran strongman Carías weathered the storm.

Anticipating these changes, Secretary of State Edward R. Stettinius had cautioned U.S. missions that the projected turmoil would put U.S. noninterference policy to a "sure test."[29] When Generals Andrés Menéndez and Federico Ponce replaced Hernández Martínez in May 1944 and Ubico in July 1944, respectively, the United States quickly extended recognition; each satisfied the three basic State Department criteria established in the 1930s. When Ponce and Menéndez were overthrown within fifteen hours of each other in October 1944, U.S. policy makers were more cautious. The junta that replaced Ponce in Guatemala included two fascist-leaning military officers, but when the embassy in Guatemala City reported that the junta had broad-based popular support, promised to meet international obligations, and would set in motion the machinery for national elections, the State Department extended recognition in early November.[30]

In El Salvador, the Supreme Court ruled that the new junta, led by Colonel Osmín Aguirre Salinas, was illegal. Aguirre, who surrounded himself with military officers holding Nazi ideas, also lacked popular support. Under these circumstances, Secretary Stettinius preferred to "await . . . some regime [that met] the requisites of international law" before extending recognition. Latin Americans followed the U.S. lead on nonrecognition. The exceptions were Nicaragua and Honduras, which recognized Aguirre because he cracked down on revolutionaries plotting in San Salvador against Somoza and Carías.[31]

When Somoza's handpicked successor, Leonardo Argüello, captured the presidency in the fraudulent elections of May 1947, the United States quickly extended recognition on the grounds that Argüello satisfied the requisite criteria. Somoza then replaced Argüello with Benjamin Lacayo Sacasa when the former attempted to remove Somoza as head of the National Guard. Subsequently, Somoza attempted to legitimize the new government with elections in August 1947 that brought his uncle, Victor Ramón y Reyes, to the presidency. Assistant Secretary of State for Latin American Affairs Spruille Braden spoke for Washington when he "just took a stance, that as a matter of fact . . . I would not recognize the Nicaraguan regime" because Somoza had taken over "in a revolutionary way." In the meantime Costa Rica's Picado administration extended recognition to Ramón y Reyes, not in defiance of the US but for its own internal political reasons; Costa Rican electoral laws permitted Nicaraguans residing in the country to vote in national elections, and Picado hoped that resident Nicaraguans might vote for his party's candidate, Rafael Calderón Guardia, in elections scheduled for February 1948.[32]

These and other episodes in Central America that tested nonrecognition policy paved the way for related discussion and debate among the American republics at the 1949 Bogotá conference. Between 1944 and 1949, Washington policy makers viewed the isthmian political turmoil as a struggle for constitutional government and encouraged political change toward this end. In 1945, for example, when rumors abounded in Guatemala City that the military might prevent President-elect Juan José Arévalo from taking office, Secretary of State James F. Byrnes instructed Ambassador Edwin G. Kyle to use his influence to express Washington's will that the constitutional process be followed. To prevent Somoza from maneuvering for his own presidential reelection, Byrnes advised the Nicaraguan strongman in November 1945 that the United States had a warmer friendship toward, and a greater desire to cooperate with, nations whose government rested upon the "freely expressed endorsement of the governed." Central America and Caribbean Affairs Assistant Chief William P. Cochran was more blunt: he told Somoza that his reelection bid was not only illegal but also not in the best interests of the United States.[33]

Fearful that the United States was returning to interventionism under the guise of upholding Latin American constitutions, the Colombian and Mexican delegations sought to deal with nonrecognition at the 1945 Mexico City conference. More interested in establishing hemispheric defense solidarity, the United States brushed the issue aside except for charging the Inter-American Juridical Commission to study the problem. In May 1947, the Commission advanced the hemispheric discussion by recommending that the recognition of de facto governments be determined by individual nations guided by the principles used by the United States in the 1930s and by the demonstrated respect of a new regime for the constitutional liberties of the people.[34]

Within the U.S. State Department, those skeptical of nonintervention eventually swayed U.S. policy. Chief of the Central American and Caribbean Affairs Division John M. Cabot encouraged the continuation of nonintervention and pointed out that U.S. interventions in the past had not produced democracy and had often served merely to increase anti-Americanism. Former Ambassador to El Salvador Frank Corrigan reasoned that nonrecognition was "a useless procedure" that only promoted "a nationalistic reaction in favor [of] a regime which might otherwise crumble of its own might." In July 1947, the Department's Historical Policy Research Division concluded that nonrecognition was "little more than an expression of disapproval" that may have served U.S. interests and protected its nationals, but it was not "conducive to the harmonious development of inter-American relations or of constitutional government" in Central America. The critics had their way. The U.S. delegation to the Bogotá conference was instructed to support a broad statement on recognition that would leave the United States free to choose its course of action; the U.S. delegation readily approved Resolution 25, which denounced nonrecognition as a diplomatic tool.[35]

Application was immediate. The United States recognized Somoza in Nicaragua and the junta of José Figueres in Costa Rica. Always an option by the terms of the Pan Americanism of the 1930s and 1940s, the use of recognition as a policy instrument now appeared to be a dead issue, along with the priority in U.S. policy of constitutional rule in the Central American republics.

Cold War politics also shaped attitudes toward intervention, as U.S.-led inter-American relations drifted further from the new Pan Americanism. In Central America there were growing calls for quality-of-life improvements for the poor. Although local elites and the middle class identified social reformers as communists, U.S. policy makers initially did not. Until 1947 Americans viewed communism in Central America as an internal matter. They understood that although the middle class wanted entry into the political processes that had long been dominated by small numbers of elites, it shared the elites' lack of interest in social and economic reform. Assistant Secretary of State Nelson A. Rockefeller and Desk Officer Allen Dawson observed that until the poor were incorporated into Central American political systems as full participants, constitutionalism could not be achieved and a breeding ground for political discontent would remain. The ongoing need for social and economic reform contributed to the State Department's stance against postwar military aid to Central America.

Beginning in 1947, new officers in the field and in Washington had different experiences. Men such as William Tapley Bennett, Jr., Edward Cale, John Fisher, Raymond Oakley, Richard Patterson, and Milton Wells did not have lengthy Latin American experience. Their views were shaped by the dynamics of the Cold War. They shared the view of Central America's elites that, like communists elsewhere, Central American communists were not primarily concerned with the plight of the poor but merely sought to infiltrate educational, government, and labor institutions for their own objectives. Furthermore, they were linked to the Soviet Union.[36]

Even after 1947, U.S. policy makers found no imminent danger from communists in El Salvador, Honduras, or Nicaragua. In El Salvador the landed oligarchy and their military brethren controlled society. In Honduras and Nicaragua, the dictators Carías and Somoza were still in firm control. In Costa Rica, the election of Picado in 1944 signaled the movement of the political pendulum to the left. Picado won with local communist support and advanced legislation long identified with the local communist party, but he failed to deliver on his reforms because the elite-controlled legislature refused his legislative proposals. Until late 1947, most of his programs were described as "liberal." Thereafter, as the communist party became more isolated from the country's political center, U.S. analysis became less sanguine. Costa Rican leader José Figueres who came to power in 1948, claimed that the 1948 civil war was fought to eliminate communism from the country, a fact that Ambassador Nathaniel Davis found difficult to accept because Figueres' philosophy differed little from that of the communist leader Manuel Mora.

However, Guatemala, not Costa Rica, became the litmus test on communism and intervention.[37] There, Juan José Arévalo became president in 1945, the first civilian to do so since 1931. His reform programs—a labor code, rent control, and social security—were labeled "communist" by the elites but as nothing more than a local "New Deal" by U.S. Ambassador Edwin Kyle. As with Costa Rica, after 1947 the U.S. assessment of Guatemala changed. A 1948 embassy staff report was damning: not only had Arévalo lost sight of his original objectives, he had become like a Marxist. His successor, Jacobo Arbenz, was even further to the left. His campaign promise to control foreign investment in the country was a direct slap at the powerful United Fruit Company (UFCO); his program for land distribution was an anathema to the landed elite. When he nationalized UFCO properties, he was judged no different than communists in the Soviet Union or China. Not only did Guatemalan elites determine that Arbenz had to go, so too did the Eisenhower administration.[38]

In March 1954, U.S. Secretary of State John Foster Dulles went to the Tenth Conference of American States in Caracas with a resolution designed to counter the changes in Guatemala. Latin American diplomats arrived in Caracas looking for massive economic assistance. They did not share Dulles' view that an international communist conspiracy threatened all of Latin America. Dulles' resolution charged that international communism had already penetrated and threatened the sovereignty of every hemispheric nation. Communist control of any American state, Dulles explained, was to be considered a foreign intervention that should be eliminated in accordance with existing treaties, presumably the Rio Pact. Guatemalan Foreign Minister Guillermo Toriello accused the United States of leading a campaign to overthrow his government and of attempting to return to the policies of the big stick and dollar diplomacy. He declared that Pan Americanism had no meaning unless it attacked poverty and social backwardness.

Reportedly, Latin American delegates quietly supported Toriello's indictment of the United States. Only the dictatorships of Nicaragua, the Dominican Republic, El Salvador, Peru, and Venezuela gave unqualified support to Dulles' proposal. Panama and Uruguay tried unsuccessfully to add a condemnation of racial discrimination, respect for human rights, and support for higher standards of living. Argentina and Mexico offered the strongest opposition to the resolution on the grounds that it weakened the principle of nonintervention. In the end the U.S. resolution was approved by seventeen of the twenty republics present. Guatemala cast the sole dissenting vote, Argentina and Mexico abstained. To Dulles, the Caracas resolution meant that the principles of the Monroe Doctrine had become the common policy of the American republics—a Pan Americanization of Monroe's policy and the dismantling of the new Pan Americanism.

Shortly after the Caracas resolution, the United States prepared for the overthrow of Guatemala's Arbenz regime. The pretext was a May 1954 delivery of arms and ammunition from Czechoslovakia. The United States sent emergency arms shipments to Honduras and Nicaragua. On June 18, 1954, in a carefully orchestrated plan and with a ragtag army of 150 CIA-trained Guatemalan expatriots, renegade Colonel Carlos Castillo Armas struck into Guatemala from across the Honduran border. Arbenz was toppled and fled the country six days later. Subsequent U.S. maneuverings within the Organization of American States and the United Nations to block international action in favor of Arbenz put an end to the period of the Good Neighbor policy and whatever contributions it had made to a Pan Americanism organized around nonintervention, improving trade ties, and international diplomatic pressure against military regimes.

The ideals of the new Pan Americanism, which had begun in 1933 with President Franklin D. Roosevelt's announcement of the Good Neighbor policy and the subsequent pledge of nonintervention in Central America's internal affairs, proved fleeting. Self-serving policies quickly sidelined the new Pan Americanism in both Washington and Central America. The reciprocal trade agreements proposed by the United States during the Great Depression were initiated primarily for the benefit of the U.S. economy, not for Pan American ideals. Economic and military necessities prompted the United States to incorporate Central America into its World War II strategies. At the war's end, Washington's desire for a more free and democratic world led to a withholding of military assistance and an attempted return to nonrecognition policy. As U.S. policy hardened toward the Soviet Union, suspicions multiplied about the intentions of Central America's socioeconomic reformers. Suspicion changed to fear in 1954 and led to the U.S.-sponsored invasion of Guatemala.

Over the same two decades, Central American reactions to U.S. policies contributed to the mythology of a new Pan Americanism. In the 1930s, the Costa Ricans were pleased with the Good Neighbor policy and Washington's nonintervention pledge because they reflected a long-standing Costa Rican ambition to remove the U.S. presence from the isthmus. However, Costa Rica was the exception. Elsewhere on the isthmus, the four dictators applied political and economic Good Neighbor policies to guard their power. During World War II, Central Americans were cut off from their primary markets in Europe and in the direct line of defense of the Panama Canal and the Caribbean Sea lanes; because of this, they accepted U.S. economic and military assistance out of necessity, but they refused to cooperate with the United States in the treatment of Axis nationals and their descendants. None of the Central American governments was pleased when the United States abandoned its plans for postwar economic assistance in the region and cut off military assistance. Nor could Presidents Picado and Figueres in Costa Rica or Arévalo and Arbenz in Guatemala be satisfied with Washington's characterization of their governments as communist. As Guatemala's Foreign Minister Guillermo Toriello asked at Caracas in 1954, why didn't the United States understand the legitimate demands of the Central American poor? The collapse of the new Pan Americanism in 1954 set an important precedent for the decade that followed. Inter-American affairs came under the shadow of a looming American military threat.

NOTES

1. Bryce Wood, *The Making of the Good Neighbor Policy* (New York, 1961), 118–119.

2. Central America is defined here as Costa Rica, El Salvador, Guatemala, Honduras, and Nicaragua. Two other Central American countries, Panama and Belize, are treated separately by most historians.

3. For a discussion of the 1907 conference, see U.S. Department of State, *Papers Relating to the Foreign Relations of the United States* (FRUS), 1907, vol. 2 (Washington, 1910), 601–728. For reference to the 1923 conference, see Thomas M. Leonard, *U.S.*

Policy and Arms Limitation in Central America: The Washington Conference of 1923 (Los Angeles, 1982).

4. An excellent analysis of Central America's reaction to U.S. intervention is Richard V. Salisbury's *Anti-Imperialism and International Competition in Central America, 1920–1929* (Wilmington, 1989). See also Kenneth V. Finney, "The Central American Reaction to Herbert Hoover's Policy," (master's thesis, Tulane University, 1969); J. Lloyd Mecham, *The United States and Inter-American Security 1889–1960* (Austin, 1963).

5. J. Ethan Ellis, *Republican Foreign Policy, 1921–1933* (New Brunswick, 1968); Kenneth J. Grieb, *The Latin American Policy of Warren G. Harding* (Fort Worth, 1977); Alexander DeConde, *Herbert Hoover's Latin American Policy* (Stanford, 1951); William Kamman, *Search for Stability: United States Diplomacy toward Nicaragua 1925–1933* (Notre Dame, 1968); J. Reuben Clark, *Memorandum on the Monroe Doctrine* (Washington, 1930); Stokeley W. Morgan, "American Policy and Problems in Central America," lecture to the Foreign Service School, Department of State, January 29, 1926.

6. Carlos Arangua Rivas, *La intervención: doctrina de Monroe, Drago y Tobar* (Santiago, 1924); Ostria Gutiérrez, *La doctrina del no-reconocimiento de la conquista en América* (Rio de Janeiro, 1938).

7. Jesus María Yepes, *La codificación del derecho internacional Americano* (Bogotá, 1927); Higinio Arba, *Derecho internacional convencional* (Asunción, 1928); Louis A. Podesta Costa, *Ensayo sobre las luchas civiles y el derecho internacional* (Buenos Aires, 1926).

8. *Comisión internacional del juriconsultos Americanos*, vol. 4 (Rio de Janeiro, 1927); "Report of Delegates Reeves and Scott," 710.C2/240, 1–6, Record Group (RG) 59, National Archives (NA) of the United States, Washington; *Report of the Delegates of the United States of America to the Sixth International Conference of American States held at Havana, Cuba January 16 to February 20, 1928* (Washington, 1928); "Latin American Conferences, 1922–1928," Papers of Charles Evans Hughes, Library of Congress (LC), Washington; FRUS, 1927, vol. 1, 364–409.

9. *Report of the Delegates of the United States of America to the Seventh International Conference of American States, Montevideo, Uruguay, December 3–26, 1933* (Washington, 1934), 18–19, 167; 710.G/123, 7; 710.11/1876; 710.G International Law/6, RG 59, NA.

10. *Report of the Delegates of the United States of America to the Inter-American Conference for the Maintenance of Peace, Buenos Aires Argentina, December 1–23, 1936* (Washington, 1937), 19, 124–26; Buenos Aires Conference 1936, Papers of Cordell Hull, Reel 35, LC; 710. Peace Non-Intervention/22, RG 59, NA; Sumner Welles, *The Practical Accomplishments of the Buenos Aires Conference* (Washington, 1937), 14.

11. U.S. recognition of Ubico is discussed in 814.00/1192–1248; of Carías in 815.00/4610–4613, RG 59, NA. For an analysis of the Ubico regime, see Kenneth J. Grieb, *Guatemalan Caudillo: The Regime of Jorge Ubico* (Athens, OH, 1979); and of Carías see Rafael Bardales Bueso, *El Fundador de la Paz* (San Pedro Sula, 1989). The U.S. role in Ubico coming to power in 1931 is considered in Kenneth J. Grieb, "American Involvement in the Rise of Jorge Ubico," *Caribbean Studies* 10 (April 1970): 5–21.

12. 816.01/334–412, RG 59, NA; FRUS, 1931, vol. 2, 169–212; FRUS, 1934, vol. 4, 423–56; Kenneth J. Grieb, "The United States and the Rise of General Maximiliano Hernández Martínez," *Journal of Latin American Studies* 3 (November 1971): 151–72; L. H. Woosley, "Recognition of the Government of El Salvador," *American Journal of*

International Law 28, no. 4 (April 1934); 325–29; Thomas P. Anderson, *Matanza: El Salvador's Communist Revolt of 1932* (Lincoln, NE, 1971). Biographies of Hernández Martínez are scarce. One important contribution is Gilberto González y Contreras, *El último caudillo: Ensayo biográfico* (Mexico City, 1946).

13. FRUS, 1935, vol. 4, 814–88; FRUS, 1937, vol. 5, 58–70; William Kamman, "United States Recognition Policy and the Rise of Anastasio Somoza, 1936" (paper presented at the Southern Historical Association Meeting, Memphis, Tennessee, November 1982). See also Knut Walter, *The Regime of Anastasio Somoza, 1936–1956* (Chapel Hill, 1993).

14. 814.00/1351–1363; 815.00/4782; 816.00/1048–1052; 817.00/8710–8711, RG 59, NA.

15. Lloyd Gardner, *Economic Aspects of New Deal Diplomacy* (Madison, 1964), 26–39.

16. Unless otherwise noted, this discussion of trade reciprocity is based on J. M. Letiche, *Reciprocal Trade Agreements in the World Economy* (New York, 1948), 22–28; Dick Steward, *Trade and Hemisphere: The Good Neighbor Policy and Reciprocal Trade* (Columbia, 1975), 219–33 and 270–71; Victor Bulmer-Thomas, *The Political Economy of Central America since 1920* (New York, 1987), 48–67.

17. Laurence Duggan, *The Americas: The Search for Hemispheric Security* (New York, 1947), 212.

18. See Bulmer-Thomas, 87–104.

19. Unless noted otherwise, discussion of U.S. policy toward Central America during World War II is based on Thomas M. Leonard, *The United States, Central America, and World War II*, forthcoming.

20. Stephén G. Rabe, "The Elusive Conference: United States Economic Relations with Latin America, 1942–1952," *Diplomatic History* 2 (Summer 1978): 279–94; Roger Trask, "The Impact of the Cold War on United States–Latin American Relations, 1945–1949," *Diplomatic History* 1 (Summer 1977): 271–84.

21. David Haglund, *Latin America and the Transformation of U.S. Strategic Thought, 1936–1940* (Albuquerque, 1984); Stetson Conn and Byron Fairchild, *Framework of Hemispheric Defense: United States Army in World War II* (Washington, 1960), 172–236, 238–314; Stetson Conn, Rose C. Engelman, and Byron Fairchild, *Guarding the United States and Its Outposts: The United States in World War II* (Washington, 1964), 301–53, 409–21; *Building the Navy's Bases in World War II: History of the Bureau of Yards and Docks and the Civil Engineer Corps, 1940–1946* (Washington, 1947), 11, 35–71; Helger Herwig, *Politics of Frustration: German Naval Policy in the Caribbean* (London, 1983).

22. "Post War Planning," File 8-2.8AV, Caribbean Defense Command, Center for Military History CMH, Washington.

23. Ibid., 31–38; "Bilateral Staff Conversations: Appendix 1, Summary of Staff Conversations With American Republics," File 8-2.8BA, 96–146 and 160–66, Caribbean Defense Command, CMH.

24. Colonel Howard Eager, "Report on South American Trip," 10 May 1945, CDC 092 (BLC), Caribbean Defense Command, NA; "Special Message to Congress Transmitting Bill for Inter-American Military Cooperation, 6 May 1946," *Papers of Harry S. Truman, 1946* (Washington, 1962), 233–235; "Special Message to Congress on Military Arms Standardization with Other American States, 26 May 1947," *Papers of Harry S. Truman, 1947* (Washington, 1963), 255–257; Inter-American Military Cooperation Act,

Hearings Before the House Foreign Affairs Committee, 28 and 29 May 1946, 79th Cong., 2nd sess.; Inter-American Military Cooperation Act, Hearings Before the House Foreign Affairs Committee, 23, 25, 26 June and 2 July 1947, 80th Cong. 1st sess.; Executive Sessions of the Senate Foreign Relations Committee (Historical Series) 80th Cong. 1st and 2nd sess. (1976); and Selected Executive Sessions of the Senate Foreign Relations Committee, 1943–1950, vol. 3, pt. 1 (1976).

25. FRUS, 1943, vol. 6, 309–10; FRUS, 1945, vol. 9, 1321–22; "Justice, Lend-Lease and State," Confidential File, *Roosevelt Papers*, Roosevelt Library.

26. FRUS, 1945, Vol. 9, 884–85, 1062–65, 1081–84, 1205–8.

27. Memorandum, 25 January 1945, Box 10; memorandum, 14 March 1946, Box 11; memorandum, 26 September 1945, Box 11; memorandum, 3 October 1945, Box 11; memorandum, 14 March 1946, Box 11; memorandum, 17 July 1946, Box 12; memorandum, 15 August 1946, Box 12; memorandum, 1 November 1946, Box 12; memorandum, 18 November 1946, Box 12; all Office of American Republic Affairs, RG 59, NA. For a discussion of the military assistance program see Chester T. Pach, Jr., *Arming the Free World: The Origins of the United States Military Assistance Program, 1945–1950* (Chapel Hill, 1991); Stephen G. Rabe, "Inter-American Military Cooperation, 1944–1951," *World Affairs* 137 (Fall 1974): 132–49; Larry D. Givens, "Official United States' Attitudes toward Latin American Military Regimes, 1933–1960," Ph.D. Diss. University of California–Davis, 1970).

28. *Report of the Delegation of the United States of America. Inter-American Conference for the Maintenance of Continental Peace and Security, Quitandinha, Brazil August 15–September 2, 1947* (Washington, 1948); Pan American Union, *Inter-American Conference for the Maintenance of Continental Peace and Security, Rio de Janeiro August 15–September 2, 1947* (Washington, 1947).

29. The overthrow of the Hernández Martínez regime is discussed by Patricia Parkman, *Non-Violent Insurrection in El Salvador: The Fall of Maximiliano Hernández Martínez* (Tucson, 1988). On U.S. recognition policy, see 816.00/13244, 13250, 13277, 6-2844, 469A, RG 59, NA. The recognition of the junta replacing Ubico is discussed in 814.00/7-444, 7-544, 7-1444, 7-1044, RG 59, NA. The recognition of the junta replacing Ponce is discussed in 814.01/1-2444-814.01/11-44, RG 59, NA. For a discussion of Central American politics during the early Cold War years, see Thomas M. Leonard, *The United States and Central America, 1944–1949: Perceptions of Political Dynamics* (Tuscaloosa, 1984).

30. 816.01/10-26-44-816.01/3-2145, RG 59, NA; "Daily Developments, Summary of February 20 and 24, 1945," Box 227, and "Mexico City–Background Material: Salvador," 9 February 1945, Box 280, *Papers of Edward R. Stettinius*, University of Virginia Library, Charlottesville; FRUS 1945, vol. 9, 1065–74.

31. 817.00/8-846-817.00/8-1947; 817.01/6-247-817.01/3-2448, RG 59, NA; Avra Warren to Adolf A. Berle, 19 March 1947, *Papers of Adolf A. Berle*, Franklin D. Roosevelt Presidential Library; Dean Acheson, memorandum, 3 April 1947, *Papers of Harry S. Truman*, Harry S. Truman Presidential Library, Independence, MO., Spruille Braden, 1396, Oral History Project, Butler Library, Columbia University, New York.

32. Diary extracts, March–April 1948, Papers of Nathaniel P. Davis, Truman Library; John P. Bell, *Crisis in Costa Rica 1948* (Austin, 1971); Oscar Aguilar Bulgarelli, *Costa Rica y sus hechos politicos de 1948* (San José, 1970).

33. *Report of the Delegation of the United States of America to the International Conference on Problems of War and Peace, Mexico City, February 21–March 8, 1945*

(Washington, 1945); C. G. Fenwick, "Inter-American Juridical Committee Draft of a Recommendation on the Ecuadoran Project, May 30, 1947," *Papers Relating to the Ninth Inter-American Conference of American States, Recognition of Governments*, RG 59, NA.

34. 711.14/12-44, RG 59, NA; "United States Policy in the Recognition of New Governments (with Particular Reference to Latin America)," July 1947, Research Project No. 39, Division of Historical Policy Research; draft memorandum, "Recognition Policy of American Governments," 9 February 1945, *Papers Relating to the Mexico City Conference, 1945*; Nelson A. Rockefeller, "Position of the United States Delegation at the Mexico City Conference" (n.d.); "Proposed Position on Ecuadoran Proposal Regarding Recognition of Defacto Governments," 12 November 1947, John C. Drier, "Possible Resolution on Recognition of Governments for Consideration at the Bogota Conference," 30 December 1947; "To Establish the Policy of the Department Regarding Recognition of New Governments," 15 March 1948, Report 24, Policy Planning Staff; William Dawson, "Governing Board Approves by Substantial Majority Report of Special Committee Favoring Nicaraguan Participation at Bogota," 9 March 1948; letters to William P. Cochran, 19 July 1944 and 20 July 1945, *Papers of Frank P. Corrigan*, Roosevelt Library; FRUS 1948, 99–108, 523–30.

35. FRUS, 1946, vol. 9, 86–110, 955–68.

36. See Leonard.

37. Two recent excellent analyses of Guatemala during this time period are Piero Gleijeses, *Shattered Hope: The Guatemalan Revolution and the United States, 1944–1954* (Princeton, 1991); Jim Handy, *Revolution in the Countryside: Rural Conflict and Agrarian Reform in Guatemala 1944–1954* (Chapel Hill, 1994).

38. Richard H. Immerman, *The CIA in Guatemala: The Foreign Policy of Intervention* (Austin, 1984), provides an excellent discussion of the formulation of U.S. policy that led to the invasion of Guatemala.

10

"Its Most Destructive Agents": Pan American Environmentalism in the Early Twentieth Century

David Sheinin

After 1890, in the minds of Latin American and U.S. politicians, diplomats, business leaders, and academics, Pan Americanism came to represent a set of U.S.-guided projects and plans aimed at bringing democracy, political stability, economic growth, and development to Latin America. Most were connected to the Washington-based Pan American Union, directed at enhancing conditions for U.S. commerce and finance in Latin America, and excoriated as U.S. imperialism by Latin American critics like Argentine politician Manuel Ugarte and Salvadoran diplomat Gustavo Guerrero. All were infused with a set of cultural assumptions around race, ethnicity, civilization, and national competence. Indeed, as a collection of models for progress, Pan Americanism not only depended on a shared belief among American leaders and Latin American elites on how progress would be achieved in political and economic terms, it also drew on a shared confidence that Latin American "backwardness" could be attributed to inherent cultural, ethnic, and racial weaknesses that severely restricted—but did not eliminate entirely—the possibility for civilization and progress on an American model.[1]

As the historian Mark T. Berger makes clear in his chapter in this volume, political and economic Pan Americanism were directly informed by American cultural assumptions about civilization and progress through the career crossovers of many Latin America specialists in academia who also worked for the U.S. State Department and other branches of government, as they carried back and forth their ideas on inherent cultural traits and behaviors in North and South America. Cultural Pan Americanism also fostered other bureaucracies and projects beyond the economic and political structures at the core of the Pan American Union, and these were often infused with beliefs about the inability of Latin Americans to run their countries well and the need for U.S. tutelage. There were exceptions to the pattern of U.S. and Latin American elite condescension toward the majority of Latin Americans in the formation of Pan American cultural structures. During the 1920s and 1930s, for example, Latin American elite and middle-class women used the Pan American Union as a forum to voice feminist positions on the education of women, the abolition of gender-based constitutional and legal restrictions, and the full equality of civil status for women.[2] The creation of the Inter-American Institute of the Indian in Mexico City in 1941, under the umbrella of the Pan American Union, came in part at the initiative of U.S. social worker John Collier, who decried how the United States treated Native peoples and held up progressive Mexican policies on Indian education, community development, and other areas as a modern standard for the United States and the Americas.[3]

Even so, Collier's context for favoring Mexican policy came in a distinctly Pan American context; in fostering educational and community conditions in which Native peoples could prosper, the Mexican government was doing a better job in this instance than the United States was in bringing progress and economic growth to aboriginal peoples. At the same time, the Pan American Union became a forum for U.S. archaeologists who were celebrating the remnants of a rich indigenous past in Latin America and seeking ways to protect it in stark contrast to the "disorder" of early twentieth-century Latin America, the Aztec, Incan, and other empires of the past seemed models of efficiency, science, and progress. For some U.S. academics it was a sad irony that "backward" societies of the present were unable to protect this rich archaeological heritage. Pan Americanism, then, explained aboriginal peoples both as potential citizens and as historical and scientific specimens. In founding the Pan American Institute of Geography and History in 1928, U.S. and Latin American elites also reinforced the cultural order of Pan Americanism; the historical writing sponsored by the Institute highlighted independence struggles, the stories of key political leaders, and cases of historical uplift, in contrast to the uncivilized disorder that U.S. and Latin American elites hoped to overcome.

One notable area where scientific advances in the United States fused with the Pan American cultural hierarchy was in environmental preservation. Writing in the mid-1930s, U.S. biologist Waldo LaSalle Schmitt expressed the emerging anxieties of many U.S. environmentalists. He argued that the "most destructive agents" of the giant tortoises on the Galápagos Islands were the "native inhabitants" of the islands. If the tortoises were saved from these enemies, their numbers might again be "counted in the hundreds instead of on the fingers of one hand."[4] For dozens of scientists, bureaucrats, and political leaders in the United States, Latin American disorder extended to wildlife. Thanks to scientific knowledge and "superior" organization, the United States came to believe that it could save the Latin American environment just as it planned to save Latin American polities from disorder and destruction. Like political Pan Americanism, environmental Pan Americanism reflected assumptions about inefficiencies and cultural weaknesses in Latin America. Moreover, like those advocating political Pan Americanism, proponents of environmental Pan Americanism had an ulterior motive: access. Where U.S. politicians sought open access for U.S. business through Pan Americanism, U.S. scientists saw Pan American environmentalism as a way to preserve specimens for their scientific research and access to those specimens in both the United States and Latin America.

Questions of environmental degradation had arisen in several contexts within the Pan American Union as early as the first years of the century, but it was not until 1940 that representatives of the American republics reached agreement on a draft convention for nature protection and wildlife preservation. In 1916, Great Britain (for Canada) and the United States had signed a Migratory Bird Treaty. A similar agreement in 1937 between Mexico and the United States served as a partial basis for the 1940 Draft Convention on Nature Protection and Wild Life Preservation in the Western Hemisphere, the first comprehensive inter-American agreement that set out provisions for the preservation of hundreds of species of flora and fauna. The agreement was one of several indicators of the growing strength of the United States within the Pan American movement and, more importantly, the ability of the United States to establish policy direction for the Pan American Union. It also marked the resurgence of the U.S. conservation movement during the 1930s, after two decades of comparative weakness, and a heightened sense of crisis in Latin America, after generations of environmental decay. Furthermore, the Convention suggested the importance of cultural and scientific concerns within Pan Americanism. As in the arena of inter-American strategic planning, U.S. cultural and scientific influences in the Pan American Union increased on the eve of World War II and were reflected in the 1940 Convention.[5]

Mandated in 1938 by delegates to the Eighth Pan American Conference (Lima) to reach an inter-American accord on the preservation of wildlife, a committee of scientific and other experts from seventeen countries began work almost immediately, tabulating species to be preserved and identifying means of conservation. The U.S. representative on the committee was Dr. Alexander Wetmore, assistant secretary of the Smithsonian Institution. When completed in early 1940, the Draft Convention had the unanimous backing of those who worked on it and, in an unusually aggressive vote of confidence in its efficacy, contained an article that provided for the convention to enter into force only three months after five ratifications had been deposited in the Pan American Union. The fifth ratification came from Haiti on January 31, 1942 (preceded by El Salvador, Guatemala, the United States, and Venezuela). The committee of experts acted on their mandate "to protect and preserve in their natural habitat representatives of all species and genera of their native flora and fauna, including migratory birds in sufficient numbers and over areas extensive enough to assure them from becoming extinct through any agency within man's control." The committee also recognized as its task the protection of scenery of "extraordinary beauty, unusual and striking geologic formations, regions and natural objects of aesthetic, historic or scientific value, and areas characterized by primitive conditions."[6]

Working from earlier international agreements[7] as well as equivalent designations in the United States, the committee distinguished among national parks, national reserves, nature monuments, and strict wilderness reserves. As in the United States, these distinctions were not entirely clear. The term *national park* referred to an area in which "superlative scenery, flora and fauna of national significance" would be preserved and protected. Parks were meant as preserves for public enjoyment and in which citizens might benefit as a result of government control of the land. *National reserves* were implicitly commercial designations; they were to be regions designated for "conservation and utilization of natural resources under government control." Here, protection of wildlife would be afforded only insofar as consistent with the primary natural resource utilization objective of the reserve. *Nature monuments* were entirely in keeping with equivalent designations in the United States. They might be regions, objects, or living species of "aesthetic, historic or scientific interest." Monuments were to receive strict protection as inviolate, except for authorized scientific work or government inspection. *Strict wilderness reserves* warranted the highest level of protection. These would be regions under government control characterized by what the experts called "primitive conditions of flora, fauna, transportation and habitation." There would be no motorized transportation in this final category of preserve.

Urgency governed the terms of the Convention and paralleled a generalized sense of urgency within the Pan American Union on the eve of the U.S. entry into World War II. The committee of experts recognized the rapid degradation that had taken place over the preceding decades in several Latin American states, particularly those that had undergone swift industrialization. In Argentina, for example, there was widespread ecological devastation in the two generations before the Pan American wildlife initiative. Between 1906 and 1915 in the province of Santiago del Estero alone, rapid commercial integration of the region into national and international markets for sugar, wood, and other products had led to widespread deforestation. In Mendoza, olive trees cultivated for 200 years had disappeared. In San Juan, scientists believed that excessive tree harvesting had had an impact on the climate. In addition to Convention provisions for unusually rapid implementation, the document urged that contracting governments explore right away the possibility of establishing preserves in each of the four preservation categories. If establishing preserves proved impossible immediately, governments were to quickly identify suitable areas for future designation as parks.[8]

Scientific investigation was a key objective of the Convention and was specifically highlighted in the agreement. Though prohibited from national parks, hunting would be allowed for what the Convention described as duly authorized scientific work. Scientists would also be allowed access to the otherwise inviolate wilderness reserves. Where governments were called upon to cooperate among themselves in promoting the Convention, they were also urged by the experts to assist scientists engaged in fieldwork. Far more significant as an act of preservation, Pan American Union member countries designated hundreds of species of plants and animals as protected by the terms of the Convention. That U.S. officials viewed the crisis in Latin America as distinct from the situation in the United States is evident in the scant ten species they placed on the list, including the manatee, the whooping crane, and the Puerto Rican parrot; this was clearly meant to be a document designed to regulate wildlife in Latin America, not the United States.

Though based on an encyclopedic compendium of extinct and nearly extinct species in the Americas, the provisions of the Convention were much more straightforward than the patchwork of thousands of laws and decrees that governed wildlife preservation through the hemisphere. In fact, strict federal control of wildlife preservation, with reference to the Pan American accord, was a principal objective of the committee of experts. The simplicity of the Convention inherently challenged the inefficacy of the tangled existing preservation rules in many countries. Ruins in the Parque Nacional Desierto de los Leones (Cuajimilpa), for example, Mexico's first national park (1917), came under the jurisdiction of the Secretaría de Comunicación y Obras Públicas, while the park itself was overseen by the Secretaría de Fomento.[9] In Argentina, hunting fell within the scope of both federal and provincial jurisdictions. In some provinces it was regulated by law, in others by decree, and in still others by the Rural Code. In contrast, Panama had no legislation to regulate hunting or protect wildlife. In Colombia there were only minimal restrictions of any sort on hunting. A 1927 decree allowed the free importation of hunting guns, and no permits were required for gun ownership. The result was a rapid decline in alligators, iguanas, and other species in the years leading up to the Convention. In Guatemala, wildlife-related legislation covered fauna that might be killed at any time for a broad range of reasons: ferocious mammals (as a threat to livestock), the zopilote (a carrier of anthrax), the taltuza (an agricultural pest), and a range of poisonous snakes.[10]

In the Dominican Republic and Cuba, partly as a result of U.S. influences, wildlife preservation was comparatively well developed. In the former, hunting was prohibited in places where game birds nested, slept, or bred. A 1936 decree created a consultative commission on national fauna in Cuba, which, in addition to government bureaucrats, included a zoology professor at the University of Havana and a member of the National Academy of Sciences. Other progressive measures included a 1936 decree designating that 75 percent of funds derived from permits to export live game go to a Special Fauna Fund for the acquisition of new species of fauna as well as specimens to improve Cuba's existing species; the impetus for this provision was to improve agriculture. A second 1936 decree protected the famous Zapata Swamp as a forest reserve for the perpetuation of wildlife.[11] In Colombia, forest reservations were set up on the basis of their economic importance, with no reference to scenic beauty or important flora. Although Nahuel Huapi National Park in Argentina was inaugurated for its natural beauties, and the Lanin National Park was established for its picturesque landscapes, the Los Glaciares National Park was founded to give tourists access to glaciers in southern Argentina. In Bolivia, in keeping with the conception of a "national monument," officials linked the preservation of historically significant archaeological ruins to that of important species. The Bolivian government estimated that unless immediate action were taken, many fauna—including vicuñas, guanacos, and chinchillas—would die out in fewer than ten years.[12]

In the Brazilian state of São Paulo, the rapid destruction of forests after 1900 came as a result of increased coffee production as well as the slash-and-burn agriculture of settlers on previously uncultivated lands. In 1911, the state established a forestry service that maintained tree nurseries for experimentation and distribution of saplings. Nevertheless it had no police power to prevent environmental destruction and no preservation program. In Pernambuco state, a shortage of foreign coal brought on by World War I led to a run on local forests for fuel by railroads, sugar mills, and textile factories. There was no government supervision of this dissipation of forests,[13] but by the late 1920s Brazil's regulations for forest protection were the most advanced in Latin America. Unlike the laws of most countries, Brazilian legislation served as an important model for the Convention. Brazil's 1934 Forest Code declared that all forests were of national interest. It affirmed that in the case of the alienation of lands deemed to be of general interest to the nation, state, or municipality, respective governments would have the opportunity to reacquire such lands at any future time of sale. Lands covered by forests were exempted from all taxes. Moreover, forest designations for the purpose of preservation were highly refined. "Protective forests," for example, maintained courses of water, prevented erosion, strengthened military defenses, enhanced public health, protected places of natural beauty, and provided a refuge for rare specimens of indigenous fauna. Such forests were to be permanently preserved and inalienable. In dry regions of northeastern Brazil, a variety of activities was prohibited, including the use of wood from trees that had not reached full development, the felling of evergreens, and the cutting of the main shoot and the three newest leaves of palm trees.[14]

In contrast to Brazil, Uruguay faced a crisis on the eve of the Convention. On March 13, 1939, the Uruguayan executive sent a message to the General Assembly requesting the transfer of 200,000 pesos from a "workingmen's dwellings" fund to reforestation work. Trees remained on scarcely 3 percent of Uruguay's surface area, and 10 percent of that represented plantations. Uruguayan leaders viewed the crisis as economic and nationalist, not environmental. The trees that remained were "not even good enough for fence rails," according to the executive request. More forests would be essential in reducing lumber imports for building construction, fruit boxes, vehicle bodies, and other essential items.[15]

Although many Latin Americans had destroyed natural habitats, U.S. and other corporations also played a key role in environmental degradation before the 1940 Convention. The context for the U.S. role in Latin American environmental damage came in U.S. visions of Latin American flora and fauna as an exploitable resource. The U.S. Department of Agriculture, for example, described Latin America as one of the most abundant sources of wood, one that the United States might absorb in large volume without detriment to domestic wood production. Before 1930, timber production in the United States had not kept up with demand. Business leaders and Department of Agriculture bureaucrats sought opportunities throughout Latin America, including areas where deforestation and environmental damage had already been severe. Some understood the danger. In 1913, U.S. Department of Agriculture forestry official C. D. Mell called the exploitation of timber in tropical America even more wasteful than it was in the United States. He argued that it was almost as important to the United States to have timber preserved in Latin America as in the United States, but forest devastation persisted.

The far-reaching destruction of flora and fauna in Cuba during the Spanish-American-Cuban War continued, though not as quickly, in the first decade of the twentieth century. Mahogany, cedar, and yellow pine were cut and burned by both the United States and Cuba on a large scale every year to make way for new sugarcane and tobacco cultivation. By 1907, practically all of Havana and Matanzas provinces had been deforested. Even so, in 1914, one Department of Agriculture official described a Cuban paradise for lumbering: "Timber of every imaginable degree of hardness and for every conceivable use may be found in the Bayano region. Its variety and profusion are almost bewildering." Despite widespread concern in Brazil over damage to forests, in 1929 Interstate Trust and Banking Company official Elish Norton reported that conditions for logging and lumbering in Brazil were outstanding, that Brazil was "almost entirely covered by virgin forests," and that there were "millions and millions" of trees, "many very beautiful when prepared for use." He urged the United States to seriously consider augmenting lumber operations in Brazil, partly because U.S. woods were being depleted.[16]

U.S. lumber contractors in Latin America undertook no reforestation or preservation projects but acted on the favorable reports of resource availability. Honduran interest in the Convention and the passage of legislation in 1939 by the Honduran Congress on soil and forest conservation underlined a need to control, but not limit foreign logging companies. By the terms of a 1927 contract, an American firm paid $11.00 to the government for each mahogany tree cut and $5.00 per cedar tree. Although there were no maximum values established, the contractor agreed to fell an annual minimum of 725 mahogany trees; there were no reforestation provisions in the contract, and the company left a deposit of $20,000 with the government. In neighboring Belize, for more than two centuries there had been profitable exploitation of mahogany and cedar forests on the coast and along many rivers in the territory. Through continual harvesting and virtually no reforestation, forests near the water had been entirely destroyed. U.S. firms pressed into the Belize interior in search of new hardwood forests. One contractor invested nearly $100,000 in tractors manufactured in the United States; during the mahogany cutting season of 1923 alone, the company planned to extract five million feet of wood using some seventy tractors.[17]

The Convention framers had no intention of eliminating the commercial exploitation of wildlife; there was no initiative to bring Pan American environmentalism into conflict with political Pan Americanism. Like other Pan American treaties and instruments, the Draft Convention on Nature Protection and Wild Life Preservation in the Western Hemisphere functioned as no more than a guideline, except where member countries moved specifically to act on its provisions. In 1942, for example, U.S. scientists continued to express concern over the threat to "American" (i.e., "U.S.") migratory birds during their South and Central American travels. In offering so few species on its list of fauna to be protected by the Convention, the United States intended the provisions of the agreement to apply in the first instance to the Latin American republics. In part, the United States planned to bring order and control to aspects of wildlife preservation in Latin America that touched U.S. wildlife preservation. The Smithsonian Institution strongly backed the explicit references to migratory bird preservation in the Convention, expressing the concerns of U.S. naturalists for the safety of migratory birds that left the United States in winter for Central or South America. Although Smithsonian scientists applauded the constructive efforts for international preservation in the accord, they also valued the advantages the Convention promised for U.S. scientists likely to work in Latin America in the future. In fact, Smithsonian scientists spearheaded the inter-American agreement.[18]

A long history of Smithsonian Institution research in the Americas, and collaboration with Latin American scientists, informed an excited interest in the accord among Smithsonian and other U.S. officials. Expeditions to Cuba, Haiti, and Trinidad in the early 1900s had mapped marine geology and methodically identified dozens of species of flora and fauna. A 1906 biological survey of the Caribbean by Edward Alphonso Goldman and Edward W. Nelson generated 17,400 specimens of mammals and 12,400 specimens of birds; 354 of these were described as new, and still more were assigned new scientific names. All specimens were deposited at the Smithsonian. In the 1920s, the work of U.S. National Herbarium scientist Agnes Chase in Brazil helped to establish the practice of a systematic inter-American exchange of botanical specimens as a core procedure in U.S. scientific research. When the Eighth International Conference of American States set in place an inter-American plan for a wildlife preservation convention, the United States created the Inter-Departmental Committee on Cooperation with the American Republics; the Smithsonian was put in charge of this program for the "conservation of flora and fauna in the New World on an international basis." The connection between the Smithsonian and nascent U.S. government environmental policy went further still. With the backing of Ecuadorian officials, curator of marine invertebrates Waldo Schmitt began planning a biological conservation laboratory on the Galapagos Islands in the late 1930s. Schmitt knew the islands well, having accompanied President Franklin D. Roosevelt on his well-publicized 1938 tour of the Galapagos (a visit that had helped to convince the president of a need for a comprehensive inter-American agreement on preservation). Schmitt travelled twice to the islands in 1941–1942 and selected a sight for the research station before World War II derailed the project.[19]

As a U.S. Bureau of Biological Survey biologist, Convention architect Alexander Wetmore spent 1911 in Puerto Rico studying ornithology; he later traveled through South America for two years analyzing bird migration between continents. This work helped to focus his long-standing attention to the problem of protecting birds migrating through different countries, a concern that helped to drive the preparation of the 1940 Draft Convention. Although the possibilities for field research were more limited for U.S. scientists during the Great Depression and World War II, as assistant secretary of the Smithsonian (1925–1945), Wetmore nevertheless pressed forward in his Latin American research, making short research trips to Colombia, Haiti, the Dominican Republic, Mexico, and elsewhere.[20]

Though perhaps well intentioned, many U.S. government wildlife initiatives in Latin America destroyed existing species. In the interest of wilderness conservation, combined with commercial advantage in Latin America, the U.S. Fish and Wildlife Service shipped millions of fish and fish eggs to Latin America before 1940. In 1910, one consignment of smallmouth bass went to a lake in Brazil on behalf of the São Paulo Tramway Light and Power Company while eggs from U.S. species of trout and salmon were shipped to Argentina to help foster a nascent fishing and tourist trade based on the enjoyment of the outdoors. U.S. scientists hoped to re-create "wilderness" in Latin America by introducing fish and other animal species from the United States that figured prominently in fishing and other nature diversions. As a consequence of these foreign species introductions, dozens of local species were destroyed before 1940. Though never explicitly stated in planning for the 1940 agreement, the cataloguing of protected species would have the potential to protect local fish and other species from damaging foreign species shipments.[21]

U.S. officials and scientists were explicitly motivated to complete the 1940 Convention as a means of ending what they believed were abuses of wildlife in Latin America. In 1926, E. A. Goldman, chief of game and bird reservations of the Biological Survey, reported critically that Mexicans in Toluca and Puebla continued to practice a colonial-era method for the slaughter of ducks that risked eliminating their numbers entirely; more than 100 guns, and sometimes more than 200, were set out side-by-side in long formations called "armadas" or "baterias." All were fired at once when the ducks were overhead, and dozens of ducks died in an instant. The result was a gradual reduction in duck numbers through the valley of Mexico. In a second case concerning Mexico, the United States believed that "California's" fish stocks were being depleted when they entered Mexican waters and that Mexican authorities were powerless to make changes.[22]

Planning for the 1940 Draft Convention came out of these and other U.S. initiatives and concerns, particularly President Franklin Roosevelt's suggestion that an international arrangement be reached covering the Galapagos Islands under the leadership of the Pan American Union. Implicit to Roosevelt's plan was the notion that Ecuador could not look after the islands' flora and fauna. A Pan American "trust" would preserve unique species in the Galapagos and would mean the purchase of the islands from Ecuador. The Galapagos project was held up in the White House by the Peruvian-Ecuadorian boundary dispute, which made it diplomatically unfeasible for the United States to enter into an agreement with Ecuador in which the latter would receive several million dollars in compensation—funds that might be seen in Peru and elsewhere in Latin America as money for arms purchases.[23]

In the implementation of the Convention, U.S. bureaucrats and scientists placed themselves in positions of authority. In 1943, the State Department agreed to fund the newly created Nature Protection Section of the Pan American Union for a period of three years to carry out the provisions of the Convention on Wild Life. More than a third of the funds were to cover the salary of a biologist who would oversee implementation in Latin America; according to the State Department:

because of the advanced development of such work in the United States, the biologist would be a North American—and he would . . . present to influential, intelligent and stable elements in the other American Republics some of our proudest accomplishments, in fields that have a strong interest and appeal to our neighbors south of the Rio Grande.[24]

Though concerned principally with the science and administration of wildlife, the Convention was an essentially Pan American document in its emphasis on U.S. leadership, recent precedent in U.S. scientific and cultural advancement, and U.S. government designs on influencing "intelligent and stable elements" in Latin America with policy alternatives that would bring order to the region and normalize inter-American relations. From 1910 through the 1920s, the conservation movement had weakened somewhat as a result of negative public associations of federal power with preservation. However, thanks in part to a renewed popularity for government intervention during the depression years of the 1930s, conservation reemerged as a core component of New Deal–era interventionist federal programs and helped to inspire the Pan American Convention a few years later. The founding of the Soil Erosion Service in 1933 and the passage of the Taylor Grazing Act in 1934 reasserted government control over land use. The Taylor Act withdrew the remaining public lands from settlement and ended the long-standing federal policy of turning public lands over to private ownership as a matter of course. The government drive for environmental renewal extended to Puerto Rico. U.S. officials saw forestry initiatives and a lumber industry as an environmental imperative and also as a means for social and economic advance in an impoverished region.[25]

Two generations of national parks designations, which included the opening of Yellowstone in 1872 and the Grand Canyon in 1908, also fueled the Pan American Convention as well as the creation of national parks in several Latin American countries. Concern over declining species of rare plants and animals did not constitute the core basis for national parks in the United States; of more importance was the effort to define a national identity in natural beauty. This is evident as well in the Pan American Convention language on parks, which makes reference to "superlative scenery" and "national significance," and in the definition of nature monuments as areas of aesthetic or historic interest. At the same time, the 1930s marked a period unprecedented in the influence of scientific thinking on the creation of U.S. national parks; this was evident in the weight of the Department of the Interior, Smithsonian Institution, and other scientists in the drafting of the Pan American Convention. To an extent far greater than earlier national parks designations, the Great Smoky Mountains National Park (1934) and the Shenandoah National Park (1935) were justified on the basis of botanical richness and came in the aftermath of extensive scientific analysis of the bioregions concerned.[26]

As late as 1931, wildlife preservation still stressed commercial and social objectives over environmental ones. In his report for the year ending on June 30, 1931, Bureau of Biological Survey Chief Paul G. Redington highlighted the government purchase of park land as a means of relieving landowners of pressure and controlling pests to agriculture. Acquisitions of land for bird refuges were directed at regions where droughts had severely reduced bird numbers, but also where land held low productive value and where landowners would otherwise have little opportunity for sale. Redington noted that this strategy had already helped somewhat to relieve unfavorable economic conditions in the United States. Redington called attention to the Bureau's economic functions, including its leadership in the control of "injurious" forms of wildlife and its research on fur farming, rabbit raising, and the reindeer industry. As the decade wore on, the Bureau and other government agencies, though still concerned about the plight of farmers and the dangers of injurious animals, deemphasized the commercial and the human components of preservation and turned increasingly to preservation for preservation's sake.[27]

In the decade before the Pan American Convention, the U.S. government bought vast expanses of land to establish parks and preserves, including what would become Shenandoah National Park, as well as wildlife refuges in the areas hardest hit by the dust bowl. Government officials joined a public chorus demanding still greater environmental protections and raising the specter of environmental degradation as a consequence of government projects. In 1936, Bureau of Biological Survey chief Ira N. Gabrielson gave a speech lamenting that with the exception of provisions for migratory birds under international treaty obligations, there was no "definite Federal recognition of wildlife as a national resource." No government program preserved wildlife, although there were national forestry, irrigation, flood control, and other programs. Meanwhile, the national highway and agriculture programs made the preservation of species more precarious; in the latter case, more efficient cultivation meant the destruction of windbreaks, hedges, and patches of underbrush. Gabrielson also pointed out that there was no national program of wildlife cooperation between Washington and the states, and that while the federal government controlled more than fifteen million acres in national parks and monuments set aside for spectacular scenic or historic value (and run primarily from that standpoint), no more than four million acres had been preserved primarily for wildlife. Though by no means its primary purpose, U.S. compliance with the Convention was tantamount to the government program for wildlife protection that Gabrielson and others sought.[28]

In addition to mounting public concern for preservation and federal government authority in the protection of wildlife, the strength of the relatively new science of ecology helped to fuel the 1940 Convention. In the late nineteenth and early twentieth centuries, specimen collection for natural history museums emphasized classification, examination of dead specimens, and recording proportions. The study of live animal behavior was a separate discipline, undertaken at zoological gardens. At the time of the Convention, there was an important change taking place in the nature of scientific inquiry. Investigators were becoming less preoccupied with bringing large animals back to "civilization" for study (a problem explored, for example, in the film *King Kong*, released in 1933); scientists began working increasingly in animals' natural habitats. The Pan American Convention was meant in part to facilitate that transformation in the scientific world by making research in Latin American parks and reserves more open to U.S. naturalists. In another trend underlined by the Convention, scientists had begun to explore the interdependence of all plant and animal life. In the 1920s and 1930s, the U.S. National Park Service—as well as federal authorities in Cuba, Mexico, and a handful of other Latin American countries— still slaughtered coyotes, wolves, and other predators in projects designed to preserve their prey. There was little attention to the larger impact of these killings, not only on park populations of deer and other prey but also on the plants now consumed in much larger quantities by the animals spared from wolf or coyote attack. The Convention emphasis on cataloguing nature reflected a reorientation of U.S. preservation objectives around the larger objectives of environmental preservation beyond the problem of predators and their prey.[29]

In the creation of comprehensive new international standards for wildlife preservation, there was little attention to cultural alternatives in Latin America as to what might define parks, monuments, or preserves. There was no reference to Indian spiritual conceptions of land, nature, or landscape in the Convention. Moreover, intrinsic to the U.S. scientific orientation of the Convention language, which was drafted around advances in ecology, and to the research conducted by the committee of experts in preparation for the Convention was a distancing of indigenous peoples from the designation of wildlife preserves. The Pan American Union had, in fact, recognized Latin America's distinct indigenous cultures in the past. In the 1920s and 1930s, it had designated as historically important several archaeological sites. However, like the Convention on Nature Protection and Wild Life Preservation, this was less a recognition of traditional Native cultures in Latin America than a reflection of American scientific (in this case archaeological) advances that, in turn, held up great civilizations of the past. As in other Pan American venues, the Convention imagined Latin America and Latin Americans not so much as they were or wished to be seen, but through U.S. perceptions and definitions of the region.[30]

In most Latin American countries, recognition of an indigenous vision of parks or wildlife preservation remained decades away. In Argentina, a 1934 decree authorized the capture of vicuñas by Native peoples for the purpose of domestication. This, and dozens of other Latin American provisions specifically directed at aboriginal people, was now subject to classification systems designated through the Pan American Union and associated national scientific bodies. In Brazil, the 1917 civil code declared Native peoples legally "incapable," a childlike status common in the jurisprudence of several nations. The 1937 constitution continued to permit the Brazilian government to deny property rights to Native peoples, issuing colonial-era usufruct permits in their place. This confirmed both a weak legal position for aboriginal peoples and a marginal, "uncivilized" status. Not only was there little opportunity for Native peoples to exercise their views on wildlife preservation at national or international levels, but the Brazilian government specifically challenged Native land claims, and other requests for distinct aboriginal rights, at the eighth Pan American conference by putting forward a motion that rejected the designation of identifiable ethnic minorities in Latin America. In many countries, the 1930s marked a consolidation of central government authority over indigenous communities. Many Argentines believed that the frontier regions of Formosa and Chaco were still under threat of Indian attack as late as the early 1930s. In 1927, the Chilean government abruptly ended special land rights accorded to Araucanians in a deliberate effort to erase their integrity as a community. The Pan American Convention provisions for the creation of park lands and preserves further jeopardized inherent and treaty-based indigenous land rights and cultural sovereignty across the Americas.[31]

The Convention on Nature Protection represented one of several U.S. Pan American initiatives in the late 1930s and early 1940s designed to break down the operations of the Pan American Union into more technically based meetings and bureaucracies. In a compartmentalized Pan Americanism, U.S. authorities hoped to exert more direct influence on the Pan American Union, but in a manner that stressed problem solving as well as practical, immediate solutions. The key imperative in U.S. Pan American policy at this time was World War II and the need to shore up security in the Americas. Beginning in 1939, the Pan American Union launched a series of Meetings of Ministers of Foreign

Affairs. Less unwieldy than the larger inter-American meetings, the foreign ministers meetings were more focused around U.S.-directed strategic initiatives. Often more informal as well, they tackled specific problems requiring immediate attention and prompt decisions. The result of the first such meeting was the General Declaration of Neutrality and the establishment of a security zone in the Western Hemisphere. The second foreign ministers meeting came at the same time that the Convention on Nature Protection was released, in July 1940. In Havana, ministers responded to the threat that European possessions in the Americas might be transferred to new European powers as a result of wartime upheaval. In 1940, the Inter-American Institute on Indian Affairs was created, encompassing all matters relating to Native populations. In 1939, the Inter-American Financial and Economic Advisory Committee was created. Like the Convention on Nature Protection and the Pan American Conferences of Foreign Ministers, the Financial and Economic Advisory Committee was meant as a quick-response body, designed to solve problems efficiently and in a manner that previous Pan American bureaucracies had proved unable to do. Also in 1939, technical and scientific progress in the United States was recognized in the creation of the Inter-American Radio Office. Environmentalism, then, was only one new area of Pan American concern in the 1930s and early 1940s that accented pragmatism, scientific problem solving, and U.S. direction.

The 1940 Convention never achieved the success its planners envisioned. It proved impossible for the Pan American Union to monitor adherence to the pact. International law proved ineffectual in regulating illegal threats to wildlife and parks. At the same time, the Convention did achieve some goals. It helped to entrench preservation policy in many countries, served as a starting point for the international classification of endangered species in the Americas, and contributed to the exchange of scientific information on wildlife and parks. In the United States, it prompted an accelerated interest in domestic and inter-American preservation; a proposed advisory group for the Inter-American Conference on Conservation of Renewable Natural Resources in 1948 included the American Farm Economic Association, the American Fisheries Society, the National Audubon Society, the National Grange, and more than forty other groups. In addition, the National Parks Association used the Convention to buttress complaints against Congress for weak protection of national parks from mining interests.

The Convention also represented a new Pan Americanism in the 1930s and 1940s that was characterized by renewed U.S. efforts to influence the direction of Pan American policy, the compartmentalization of Pan American Union activities, and the growing technical orientation of the body. Finally, it helped initiate an accelerated inter-American interest in environmental issues during the Cold War period, beginning with the transfer of the Barro Colorado island research station in Panama to the Smithsonian Institution in 1946 for use by scientists from throughout the Americas.[32]

NOTES

1. Ricardo D. Salvatore, "The Enterprise of Knowledge: Representational Machines of Informal Empire," in *Close Encounters of Empire: Writing the Cultural History of U.S.–Latin American Relations*, edited by Gilbert M. Joseph, Catherine C. LeGrand, and Ricardo D. Salvatore (Durham, 1998), 68–104; Amy Kaplan, "Black and Blue on San Juan Hill," in *Cultures of United States Imperialism*, edited by Amy Kaplan and Donald E. Pease (Durham, 1993), 219–36. See also K. Lynn Stoner's chapter in this collection.

2. See K. Lynn Stoner, *From the House to the Streets: The Cuban Woman's Movement for Legal Reform, 1898–1940* (Durham, 1991); Francesca Miller, "The International Relations of Women of the Americas, 1890–1928," *The Americas* 43, no. 2 (October 1986): 171–82.

3. Helen Delpar, *The Enormous Vogue of Things Mexican: Cultural Relations between the United States and Mexico, 1920–1935* (Tuscaloosa, 1992), 120–24.

4. Waldo L. Schmitt, "Reptiles," n.d., Box 86, RU 7231, Waldo LaSalle Schmitt Papers, 1907–1977, Smithsonian Institution Archives SI, Washington; George Hugh Banning, "Hancock Expedition of 1933 to the Galápagos Islands: General Report," *Bulletin of the Zoological Society of San Diego*, no. 10 (May 1933), 1–30.

5. Leo S. Rowe, director general, Pan American Union, to U.S. secretary of state, 26 January 1940, 710.H Wild Life/65; Alexander Wetmore, assistant secretary, Smithsonian Institution, to Charles M. Barnes, chief, Treaty Division, Department of State, 15 August 1941, 710.H Wild Life/135, Record Group 59 (RG 59), National Archives NA of the United States, Washington; "American Republics Sign Convention on Nature Protection," *Press News from the Pan American Union*, 12 October 1940; José L. Colom, "Pan American Policy for Nature Protection," *The National Parks Bulletin* (February 1941): 5; "The United States has entered. . . ." n.d., Box 99, *Alexander Wetmore Papers*, SI.

6. Leo S. Rowe, *Report of the Committee of Experts on Nature Protection and Wild Life Preservation in the American Republics* (Washington, 1940); memorandum, Department of State, "Meeting of the Governing Board of the Pan American Union, June 5, 1940," 710.H Wild Life/89; memorandum, Division of American Republics, Department of State, "Draft Convention for Nature Protection and Wild Life Preservation," 27 May 1940, 710.H Wild Life/87; memorandum, Division of International Conferences, Department of State, 6 June 1940, RG 59, NA; Leo S. Rowe, *Convention and Documentary Material on Nature Protection and Wild Life Preservation in the Western Hemisphere* (Washington, 1943); "Proclamation of Convention on Nature Protection and Wild Life Preservation in the Western Hemisphere," 30 April 1942, Department of State press release no. 189.

7. See, for example, John C. Phillips, "Brief Report of the Accomplishments of *The Conference on the Fauna and Flora of Africa*, 1933," 2 December 1933, Box 99, *Wetmore Papers*, SI.

8. Leo S. Rowe, *Convention and Documentary Material on Nature Protection and Wild Life Preservation in the Western Hemisphere* (Washington, 1943); Antonio Elio Brailovsky, *La ecología y el futuro de la argentina* (Buenos Aires, 1992), 68–73; Olivier Dollfus, *Territorios andinos: reto y memoria* (Lima, 1991), 23–24; Antonio Elio Brailovsky, *Memoria verde: historia ecológica de la Argentina* (Buenos Aires, 1991), 196; S. T. Davis, "Forestry in the Argentine Republic," 5 February 1908, Box 92, Research

Compilation Files, 1897–1935, Forest Research Divisions, Department of Agriculture, RG 95, NA.

9. Decreto, 15 de noviembre de 1917, *Boletín Oficial de la Secretaría de Fomento* (Mexico), no. 8, November 1917, 639–40.

10. Leo S. Rowe, *Documentary Material on Nature Protection and Wild Life Preservation in Latin America*, vol. 1, pt. 1 (Washington, 1940), 7, 37–39; Antonio Elio Brailovsky and Dina Foguelman, *Memoria verde: historia ecológica de la Argentina* (Buenos Aires, 1991), 206–9.

11. Rowe, *Documentary Material*, 60–61, 75–78.

12. Leo S. Rowe, *Documentary Material on Nature Protection and Wild Life Preservation in Latin America*, vol. 2, pt. 1 (Washington, 1940), 6–12; Arthur Posnansky, inspector ad-hon. del Museo Nacional, *Un "Parque Nacional en Bolivia"* (La Paz, 1937).

13. C. R. Cameron, U.S. consul, São Paulo, "Paraná Legislation Affecting Pine Lumber Production," no. 233, 26 April 1929; Cameron, "Sao Paulo Forestry Service," no. 73, 27 December 1927; Nathaniel P. Davis, U.S. consul, Pernambuco, Brazil, "Forest Conservation in Alagoas, Brazil," 19 December 1927; E. Kitchel Farrand, U.S. vice consul, Porto Alegre, Brazil, "Lumber Industry in the State of Rio Grande do Sul," 11 February 1926; all Forestry Reports, Foreign Agricultural Service, Department of Agriculture, Box 25, Entry 3, RG 166, NA.

14. Leo S. Rowe, *Documentary Material*, vol. 2, pt. 2, 3.

15. Augustin W. Ferrin, U.S. consul, Montevideo, "Reforestation Plans in Uruguay," 27 March 1939, Box 27, Entry 3, RG 166; "El apostol del monte artificial," *El Plata* (Montevideo), 5 August 1922.

16. "Field Explorations and Laboratory Tests of South and Central American Hardwoods," 25 February 1924, Box 186; Elish Norton, Interstate Trust and Banking Co., New Orleans, to Lynn H. Dinkins, president, Interstate Trust and Banking Co., 22 April 1929, Box 92; H. N. Whitford, School of Forestry, Yale University, to Raphael Zon, U.S. Forest Service, 17 October 1918, Box 92; "Panama Woods," 1914; F. S. Earle, president, Cuban Horticultural Society, to Gifford Pinchot, chief forester of the United States, 25 April 1907, Box 91; C. D. Mell, "The Need of Forestry in Tropical America," 1913, Box 91; all Research Compilation Files, 1897–1935, Forest Research Divisions, Agriculture Department, RG 95, NA.

17. John D. Erwin to secretary of state, no. 593, 14 February 1939; Richard Ford, U.S. consul, Tegucigalpa, "Mahogany Contract Awarded American Firm in Honduras," 11 April 1927; William Wallace Early, U.S. consul, Belize, "Growing Use of Tractors in Mahogany Forests of British Honduras," 28 April 1923; all Forestry Reports, Foreign Agricultural Service, Department of Agriculture, Box 25, Entry 3, RG 166, NA; "Ley de Bosques," *La Gaceta* (Tegucigalpa), 13 February 1939.

18. C. G. Abbot, secretary, Smithsonian Institution, to R. Walton Moore, counselor, Department of State, 28 June 1940, 710.H Wild Life/96; A. Wetmore to secretary of state, 27 January 1941, 710.H Wild Life/118; memorandum, Division of American Republics, Department of State, 10 July 1942, RG 59, NA; International Committee for Bird Preservation, Pan American Section, "Bird Migration in the Western Hemisphere," 1942 (unpublished pamphlet).

19. *Expeditions: 150 Years of Smithsonian Research in Latin America* (Washington, 1996), 16–21; Edward Alphonso Goldman, *Biological Investigations in Mexico*, Smithsonian Inst. Pub. 4017 (Washington, 1951); George Hugh Banning, "Hancock Expedition of 1933 to the Galápagos Islands: General Report," *Bulletin of the Zoological Society*

of San Diego, no. 10 (May 1933): 1–30; "Velero Brings Big Cargo of Rare Animals," (San Diego), *Evening Tribune*, 22 February 1935, "Visiting Scientist, Here From Galapagos Islands, Leaves Reptilian Curio," *Monterey* (Calif.) *Peninsula Herald*, 7 March 1935; Waldo L. Schmitt, "The Galapagos Islands One Hundred Years After Darwin," *Nature Magazine* 26, no. 5 (November 1935): 265–71, 312, 315; "F.D.'s Ship Headed for Galapagos Island," *Washington News*, 22 July 1938; " 'Scientist' Roosevelt's Catch to Enrich National Museum," *Washington Post*, 13 August 1938.

20. *Expeditions* 21–23; Alexander Wetmore and Bradshaw H. Swales, *The Birds of Haiti and the Dominican Republic*, Smithsonian Inst. Bull. 155 (Washington, 1931).

21. I. Dunlop, acting commissioner, Bureau of Fisheries, Department of Commerce and Labor, to W. P. Plummer, 9 August 1910; Huntington Wilson, assistant secretary of state, to secretary of commerce and labor, 25 January 1910; José Leon Suarez, Zoología y Policía Veterinaria, Division de Ganadería, secretaría de agricultura, Argentina, to George M. Bowers, commissioner, U.S. Bureau of Fisheries, 2 March 1910; Epifanio Portela to U.S. secretary of state, 28 December 1909; Suarez to Bowers, 14 August 1909; all Records of the U.S. Fish and Wildlife Service, Box 1, Entry 120, RG 22; "Argentine Fish Culture: Its Beginnings," *Standard* (Buenos Aires) 25 January 1909.

22. E. A. Goldman, "Observations Concerning Waterfowl in Mexico, with Special Reference to Migratory Species," 1926, Box 4, Entry 146, Division of Wildlife Refuges, Fish and Wildlife Service, RG 22, NA; Leighton Hope, "Reported Conference on Fishing on the Pacific Coast to Be Held at San Diego, California," 24 April 1926, Records Concerning Relations with Mexico, Box 1, Division of Wildlife Refuges, Fish and Wildlife Service, RG 22, NA.

23. Sumner Welles to Lawrence Duggan, 26 April 1940, 710.H Wild Life/173, RG 59, NA.

24. Division of Science and Education, Department of State, Project Authorization, n.d. [1943], 710.H Wild Life/176, RG 59, NA.

25. William Beinart and Peter Coates, *Environment and History: The Taming of Nature in the USA and South Africa* (New York, 1995), 64–66; L. S. Murphy, "Points Bearing on a Porto Rico Forest Policy," n.d. [1934]; R. Murray Bruner, chief of Porto Rico Forest Service, "The Relation of Forestry to Economic Progress in Porto Rico," n.d. [1934]; all Box 200, Research Compilation Files, 1897–1935, Agriculture Department, RG 95, NA.

26. Beinart and Coates, 75, 76; Alfred Runte, *National Parks: The American Experience* (Lincoln, NE, 1979), 11.

27. Department of Agriculture, "Redington Makes Report on Wild-Life Administration," press release, 25 November 1931.

28. Ira N. Gabrielson, "A National Program for Wildlife Restoration," speech delivered at the American Wildlife Conference, Washington, 7 February 1936, and Harry B. Hawes, "The Four Vital Factors of Wildlife Conservation," address delivered before the North American Wildlife Conference, 3–7 February 1936, Fish and Wildlife Service, Division of Wildlife Refuges, Box 19, Entry 146, RG 22, NA; Department of Agriculture, "Biological Survey Chief Hails National Movement for Wild Life," press release, 25 January 1934.

29. Aldo Leopold, *A Sand County Almanac* (New York, 1949), 130–35; Thomas R. Dunlap, *Saving America's Wildlife: Ecology and the American Mind, 1850–1990* (Princeton, 1988); Susan Flader, *Thinking Like a Mountain: Aldo Leopold and the Evolution of*

an Ecological Attitude toward Deer, Wolves and Forests (Columbia, 1974); Frank Thone, "Americas Unite to Save Wildlife," (Cleveland) *Everyweek Magazine*, 15 June 1941.

30. Judith K. Kenny, "Climate, Race, and Imperial Authority: The Symbolic Landscape of the British Hill Station in India," *Annals of the Association of American Geographers*, 85, 4 (1995): 694–714; T. Barnes and J. Duncan, *Writing Worlds: Discourse, Text and Metaphor in the Representation of Landscape* (London: 1992); H. Bhabha, *The Location of Culture* (London, 1994).

31. Claudia Menezes, "Estado y minorías etnicas en Brasil," *América Indígena* 49 (1989): 158; Roque Roldán Ortega, "Notas sobre la legalidad en la tenencia de la tierra y el manejo de los recursos naturales de territorios indígenas en regiones de selva tropical de varios paises suramericanos," in *Derechos territoriales indígenas y ecologia en selvas tropicales del América*, edited by Martha Cárdenas, Hernán Darío Correa, and Mauricio Gómez Barón (Bogotá, 1992), 47–48; Leo S. Rowe, *Documentary Material*, vol. 1, pt. 1, 7; Daniel W. Gade, "Landscape, System, and Identity in the Post-Conquest Andes," *Annals of the Association of American Geographers*, 82, no. 3 (1992): 460–67.

32. Division of International Conference, U.S. Department of State, "Proposed Members of the Advisory Group," 7 September 1948, Box 100, *Alexander Wetmore Papers*, SI; "Nature Protection and Wildlife Preservation," *Science*, 20 June 1941.

11

Pan American Shift: Oswaldo Aranha and the Demise of the Brazilian-American Alliance

W. Michael Weis

This chapter examines the evolution of Oswaldo Aranha's thinking on Pan Americanism and his influence on Brazilian foreign policy during the age of Getulio Vargas (1930–1964). Whereas most works on Pan Americanism necessarily deal with ideology, trade, security, and inter-American cooperation, the role of individuals at key moments—James G. Blaine, Sumner Welles, and Aranha, among others—has been decisive yet often ignored. By examining the evolution of Aranha's ideas and writings, we might better understand the evolution of Pan Americanism, as well as the reasons for the weakening of the "special relationship" between the United States and Brazil, a long-standing alliance that served as a cornerstone of a functional Pan Americanism.

In most works on Brazilian history between 1930 and 1964, Oswaldo Aranha receives a great deal of praise as the architect of the 1930 Revolution, which saw Vargas come to power, and as the latter's chief lieutenant. The historian Joseph Love calls Aranha "second only to Vargas in his place in national history."[1] For thirty years the charming, handsome, eloquent, and cosmopolitan *gaucho* (a native of Rio Grande do Sul) served Brazil in a variety of important posts. A man of vision and brilliance, an imaginative and resourceful administrator, Aranha possessed tremendous energy and ambition. Although he never attained the presidency, Aranha played a key role in the centralization of power, the beginning of import-substitution industrialization during the 1930s, and Brazil's supplanting of Argentina as the predominant power in South America.[2]

Despite significant domestic accomplishments, Aranha is best known as one of the great Brazilian statesmen of the twentieth century and a strong proponent of Pan Americanism. Aranha's Pan Americanism went through several phases over his long career. From the outset and through his career, Aranha was a strong economic nationalist committed to rapid economic development and industrialization. His experience as ambassador to the United States (1934–1937) turned him into a Pan Americanist. While Pan Americanism dovetailed with traditional Brazilian foreign policy, Aranha's conversion came about as a result of Franklin D. Roosevelt's Good Neighbor policy, which recast Pan Americanism in a manner that complemented the U.S. renunciation of military intervention and its willingness to accommodate economic nationalism in Latin America.

World War II changed Aranha's Pan Americanism. Even before Pearl Harbor, Aranha drifted from the rhetoric of the Good Neighbor to more forceful arguments in favor of an inter-American defense shield. As the main architect of the Brazilian-American alliance during World War II, Aranha's efforts on behalf of hemispheric solidarity during the height of Good Neighbor Pan Americanism paid rich dividends for both the United States and Brazil. A new, post–Good Neighbor Pan Americanism, championed by Aranha, was organized around mutual security and collective defense. It was defined by the multilateral adoption of the Rio Pact (Inter-American Treaty of Reciprocal Assistance) in 1947 and the creation of the Organization of American States (OAS) in 1948. At the dawn of the Cold War, Aranha continued to speak out strongly for inter-American unity.

Gradually, though, his Pan Americanism shifted again. He and many other Brazilians became disillusioned with Cold War Pan Americanism and the United States. To Brazilians, 1950s U.S. globalism meant the abandonment of the alliance with Brazil. At the same time, many became uneasy over the U.S.-led anticommunist crusade in Latin America and the reversal of Roosevelt's pledge of nonintervention and tolerance for economic nationalism. Aranha went so far as to announce the demise of Pan Americanism.[3] The evolution in Aranha's thinking coincided with Brazil's frantic attempt to maintain its alliance with the United States. By the mid-1950s Aranha forcefully argued for a more nationalist, internationalist, and independent foreign policy. World War II and the Cold War had shaped Aranha's thinking, as had his postings to the United Nations (1947 and 1957) and to the Brazilian Finance Ministry in the second Vargas government (1950–1954). Aranha's change from Pan Americanist to internationalist mirrored Brazil's course after 1955. Like Aranha, Brazilians gradually and reluctantly accepted the ruin of the American alliance and the waning of the inter-American system—first under Juscelino Kubitschek's Operation Pan America after 1957, and later during a period of independent (and sometimes anti-U.S.) foreign policy of Presidents Janio Quadros and Joao Goulart in the early 1960s.

There is little agreement among scholars on the definition of Pan Americanism. According to Thomas L. Karnes, it is "more easily traced than defined." Pan Americanism has been described variously as a movement, a cause, a sentiment, a dream, a hoax, a myth, an illusion, and a device to spread or contain U.S. hegemony. In fact, each of these characterizations has some element of truth. A standard definition is that Pan Americanism was the belief that the peoples of the Western Hemisphere have a special relationship that sets them apart from the rest of the world. It arises from common historical experience and destiny. Although most scholars differentiate between Pan Americanism and the Monroe Doctrine, the two are intimately connected. Pan Americanism has cultural, social, political, strategic, and even spiritual connotations, but it—and its institutional manifestations, particularly the Pan American Union (PAU) and OAS—largely served to legitimize and regularize U.S. hegemony. Because of this, Pan Americanism was never popular in Latin America, with the exception of Brazil.[4]

Before 1950, Pan Americanism functioned in practice as a result of the close cooperation of the two hemispheric giants, Brazil and the United States. For the first half of the twentieth century the United States and Brazil had what authors have called a "special relationship" or an "unwritten alliance."[5] The alliance was at the core of Pan Americanism; indeed, to Brazilian leaders Pan Americanism represented the maintenance of the special relationship. The alliance of the first half-century was based on compatible goals and mutual assistance. Close relations began in 1889, the year of the overthrow of the Brazilian monarchy, the promulgation of the Brazilian Republic, and the first Pan American conference in Washington, sponsored primarily by U.S. Secretary of State James G. Blaine. Brazilian-American amity steadily improved; by 1900, a mutually advantageous alliance was in place, largely due to the efforts of José Maria da Silva Paranhos, Jr., the baron of Rio Branco, Brazil's foreign minister from 1902 to 1912. For Brazil, friendship and cooperation with the United States became the primary means to achieve foreign policy objectives. In return, Brazil received preferential treatment in U.S. Latin American policy. Examples of bilateral cooperation include Brazilian support for Panamanian independence and the Roosevelt Corollary to the Monroe Doctrine. In return, the United States admitted most Brazilian goods duty-free, including coffee, rubber, and cacao, the three principal Brazilian exports of the early twentieth century. In addition, the United States supported the Brazilian position in territorial disputes with Bolivia and Argentina.[6] Brazil's elite diplomatic corps added theoretical justification for the alliance through support for Pan Americanism. Rio Branco and Joaquim Nabuco, who served long terms as foreign ministers to Washington, assiduously courted United States officials, especially Secretary of State Elihu Root, to make Rio de Janeiro the site of the third Pan American conference in 1906.[7]

Rio Branco's successors transformed his tactical alliance into a strategic objective. The evolving special relationship continued throughout the major crises of the early twentieth century. Brazil became the only major Latin American nation to declare war on Germany in World War I, and it resigned from the League of Nations shortly after the United States refusal to enter the war. The alliance with the United States helped to advance Brazilian foreign policy goals: the neutralization of Argentine designs of regional leadership; securing an assured market and price stability for exports (an especially important goal given the export orientation and the boom-bust cycles of the economy); and the desire for increased Brazilian power, prestige, and status.

Since the late nineteenth century, the United States has been the largest market for Brazilian goods and Brazil's major supplier. Both nations welcomed this trade and worked to build equivalent strength in bilateral political relationships. For most of the twentieth century, their economies were complementary: the United States was heavily industry-based while Brazil was more agriculturally grounded. With the exception of cotton, Brazil's tropical exports did not compete with U.S. agriculture. Another significant ingredient in cementing the bilateral relationship was a shared sense of separateness from Spanish America. Both nations embraced Pan Americanism in part because they recognized that they were not trusted by their sister republics. Their size and sense of cultural separateness encouraged mutual support in inter-American forums. This cooperation became the glue of the alliance that remained in place on the eve of the Revolution of 1930, which catapulted Oswaldo Aranha into power.

Aranha was born in 1894 into one of Rio Grande do Sul's leading families. He was both more nationalist and cosmopolitan than many of the other *gaucho* leaders in the "Generation of 1930," partly because he was educated in Rio de Janeiro at the Colegio Militar and the Faculdade de Ciencias Juridicas e Socaias. He also attended the Ecole des Hautes Etudes in Paris, returning home at the outbreak of World War I. With a law degree in hand, Aranha entered *riograndese* politics. He backed a strong central government and executive to promote industrialization and minimize class conflict. A forceful democrat later on, during the 1920s Aranha's positivism and noblesse oblige attracted him to Italian fascism.

The Great Depression disrupted markets and caused domestic upheavals in the United States and Brazil. Coupled with a global ideological struggle, it marked the most severe test to date for the alliance. Brazil was without credit or foreign investment. Its exports suffered from extremely low prices, which decimated the nation's foreign exchange supply and import capacity. This exacerbated a political crisis in Brazil and provided a major impetus to the Revolution of 1930. A series of unsuccessful rebellions in the 1920s had exposed widespread dissatisfaction with government corruption, a lack of progress, and the political domination of Brazil by the states of São Paulo and Minas Gerais. The economic crisis prompted the breakdown of the *paulista-mineiro* alliance when Brazilian President Washington Luis, a *paulista*, sidestepped the norm of designating a *mineiro* successor and imposed fellow *paulista*, Julio Prestes, as his successor. The decision drove Minas Gerais and Rio Grande do Sul into opposition. These states united with Paraiba under the leadership of Getulio Vargas and the Liberal Alliance. In 1930, Aranha was a prominent conspirator in Vargas's service, purchasing arms from Czechoslovakia, serving as Vargas's emissary between the government and rebel officers (*tenentes*), and serving as acting governor in Rio Grande do Sul. Washington Luis's fraudulent election victory and the murder of vice-presidential candidate Joao Pessoa catalyzed the revolution. On October 3, troops led by Aranha, Jose Antonio Flores da Cunha, and Pedro Aurelio de Goes Monteiro captured the commander of the Third Army and began marching north. Faced with the prospect of a bloody civil war, the army deposed the president and handed power to Vargas on October 31, 1930.[8]

Over the next fifteen years Vargas skillfully maneuvered through the labyrinth of Brazilian politics and global ideological competition as provisional president (1930–1934) with tremendous arbitrary powers, constitutional president (1934–1937), and dictator (1937–1945). Aranha served as minister of Justice and Internal Affairs during the Revolution's retribution and definition phase, placing emphasis on the centralization of power. Within a year, Vargas shifted Aranha to the Ministry of Finance to impose fiscal austerity by balancing the budget, consolidating the national debt, and promoting industrialization through government investment and national planning. Aranha proved to be a bold and imaginative finance minister. He encouraged the development of the northeast and Amazon regions, burning surplus coffee to keep prices high, instituting tariff reform, and suspending international debt payments. Finally, when a *paulista* revolt forced Vargas to accept the Constituent Assembly, which would draft a new democratic constitution, Aranha led the pro-Vargas forces that secured Getulio's election but weakened his executive power. For this latter infraction, in 1934 Aranha was banished to the United States as ambassador.[9]

Though demoted, Aranha proved ideal for the U.S. post. The outgoing finance minister knew Brazilian economic policy as well as anyone. His flamboyance, charm, and wit equally suited him. As ideological storm clouds threatened around the globe, Aranha learned his diplomacy in crisis. He quickly resolved to maintain Rio Branco's tradition of close relations with the United States in order to assure free access for Brazilian products to American markets, and to maintain U.S. support for Brazil's strategic and economic position of strength in South America. Although his diplomacy was always rooted firmly in strong nationalism, in Washington Aranha became an international statesman. Unable to speak English and largely ignorant of the United States when he arrived there, he returned to Brazil fluent in English and as a strong believer in democracy. The transformation was rapid. On the basis of a cross-country car trip and initial dealings with U.S. citizens, Aranha's pro-U.S. attitudes were confirmed and reinforced. He became convinced that Brazil's economic recovery would require close cooperation with Washington. His dispatches to Rio de Janeiro praised the United States almost excessively, as a "land without equal, colossal, a spectacle of grandeur and beauty, and seething with activity." U.S. wealth convinced Aranha of the wisdom of democracy and capitalism.[10]

The administration of President Franklin D. Roosevelt brought an unusual continuity to U.S. foreign policy, especially in the hemisphere. The dynamic president was active in policy making, and his policies were executed ably by Secretary of State Cordell Hull (1933–1944) and Assistant/Undersecretary of

State Sumner Welles (1934–1943). Characterized as the Good Neighbor policy—suggesting friendly political and diplomatic ties—Roosevelt's first priority in the hemisphere was, nevertheless, to develop markets for U.S. products whose sales had suffered during the Depression. The necessary components for an effective Good Neighbor were the renunciation of intervention, first offered at the Montevideo conference in 1933, and the elimination of trade barriers through the Reciprocal Trade Agreements. Aranha favored these efforts, arguing that Vargas's industrialization goals were not antagonistic to Hull's Reciprocal Trade Agreements, although he lobbied for a preferential agreement with Washington as a still better alternative for Brazil. Brazil became the second nation (after Cuba) to sign a trade accord with the United States.[11] To open Latin American markets, the Roosevelt administration also created an Export-Import Bank (EXIM) and made limited accommodations to the region's growing economic nationalism. Roosevelt's second priority in Latin America was to maintain the alliance with Brazil. He thus eagerly embraced Vargas and Aranha, and he even made two trips to Brazil. In 1936 FDR claimed that Vargas had instituted the "South American New Deal." Vargas was flattered by this attention, telling Ambassador Jefferson Caffery, "As long as I am in office the United States can count on my sympathy and cooperation. I have entire confidence in the goodwill and good intentions of President Roosevelt. I know Brazil will get a fair deal at his hands." In their 1943 meeting at Natal, after the Casablanca Conference, Vargas left his son's deathbed to talk with Roosevelt.[12]

Although as ambassador Aranha was the highest-paid official in the Brazilian government, Vargas monitored him closely—even opening all his mail—while ignoring him at times and keeping him in the dark about events in Brazil. As a result, the establishment of the fascist-inspired *Estado Novo* in November 1937 surprised and embittered the ambassador, who only a week before had made a speech in Cleveland denouncing dictatorships. Aranha had also assured U.S. officials that Vargas would relinquish power to an electoral victor at the end of his mandate. Although he defended Vargas from the condemnation of the U.S. press, Aranha resigned in anger immediately following the coup.[13]

Not wanting to drive his chief lieutenant into opposition, Vargas maneuvered Aranha back into government as foreign minister in February 1938. Aranha's appointment as foreign minister pleased the United States; it seemed a signal that, despite Vargas's flirtation with fascism in domestic politics and the suspension of foreign debt payments, Brazil did not intend to alter its foreign policy. Because he was perceived as pro–United States, Aranha's presence was decisive. At the time, key elements in the Brazilian Armed Forces, especially War Minister Eurico Gaspar Dutra and Army Chief of Staff Goes Monteiro, championed Nazi Germany. Although the United States and Brazil were diplomatic allies and economic partners, their alliance did not extend into the military sphere until World War II. Before then, France and Germany were the principal suppliers and models for Brazilian military organization and tactics. Admiration and sympathy for Nazi Germany concerned American policy makers, but, being unable to supply the armaments Brazil required, the United States could not compete effectively until after Hitler invaded Poland. Even a special mission to Brazil headed by U.S. Army Chief of Staff George C. Marshall in 1939 accomplished little except to generate a measure of goodwill.[14]

After Aranha became foreign minister, Brazilian–U.S. relations steadily improved, reaching a high point during World War II. U.S. policy makers, especially Summer Welles, were aware of Brazil's influence as well as its sense of alienation from Spanish-speaking nations, and thus they consulted with the Brazilians before taking any important actions affecting the hemisphere. The United States began supporting Vargas to keep Brazil loyal to U.S. foreign policy objectives, particularly in the face of growing diplomatic conflicts with Argentina. The United States supplied Aranha with information designed to persuade Vargas of an ultimate Allied victory. Throughout this period, Aranha publicly extolled the benefits of Pan Americanism, now that U.S. interventionism was at an end, to persuade Vargas in favor of the Allied wartime cause and to score points against Dutra and Goes Monteiro.[15] At the same time, Aranha was no hireling of the United States. He refused to restrict a bartering agreement with Germany that was prejudicial to the United States but desperately needed by exchange-poor Brazil.[16]

As he used Pan Americanism to win policy battles within Brazil, Aranha also used the Nazi threat to extract promises from the United States to supply arms. Still, the foreign minister was committed to closer relations and aided the United States immeasurably at the Lima (Eighth) conference in December 1938, where Aranha voiced propositions on behalf of the United States in order to achieve the "Declaration of Lima," which called for hemispheric solidarity against the Axis. Aranha considered the conference a milestone in inter-American relations and a step toward multilateralizing, or Pan Americanizing, the Monroe Doctrine.[17] In February 1939, Hull invited the chancellor to Washington to iron out difficulties caused by Brazil's German trade and its default on international debts. Aranha skillfully sold Brazil in the U.S. press. He publicly invited American farmers and unemployed skilled workers to come to Brazil as colonizers. At the mission's conclusion, the U.S. press announced a great "Aranha victory": the glib diplomat had cajoled $120 million from the United States in return for agreeing to resume debt payments. At the end of the day, Aranha received only $20 million, but he won assurances of new arms deliveries, secured the invitation of General Goes Monteiro to the United States, and invited General George Marshall to Brazil to help determine Brazil's defense needs. Yet despite these successes, Vargas allowed Brazilian newspapers to characterize the Aranha mission as a sellout; Vargas wished both to deflect praise from his friend and keep his options open in regard to the coming war.[18]

During the war, U.S. strategists feared an Axis invasion of Brazil's northeast, only 1,200 miles from German-held Dakar. Brazil worried about the growing closeness between the Axis and its own arch-rival, Argentina. In 1940, Brazil became the first Latin nation to sign a military staff agreement with the United

States and, even before Pearl Harbor, Brazilian-American naval cooperation increased as Brazil opened its ports to U.S. vessels.[19] Brazil became crucial to the United States; the alliance that Aranha and Welles had sought became reality. In January 1942, the political wisdom of the Good Neighbor bore fruit at the important third Pan American conference of foreign ministers, called to consider severing relations with the Axis. U.S. officials chose Rio de Janeiro so that Aranha would preside over the conference. Aranha was able to use his influence to achieve a unanimous declaration recommending the breaking of relations with the Axis and the creation of the Inter-American Defense Board, an act of solidarity unimaginable in the big-stick era of U.S. foreign policy two decades before. According to Sumner Welles:

Dr. Aranha . . . is one of the most brilliant statesmen [in] the New World. . . . An orator of rare eloquence and extraordinary intuition, whose mind works with unexcelled rapidity, he holds an unswerving conviction that Brazilian-American amity is a necessary keystone of practical Pan-Americanism.[20]

At the dramatic closing of the conference, Aranha announced that Brazil had broken relations with Italy and Germany. By August, Brazil had declared war on Germany.[21]

Early in 1942 the United States and Brazil cemented their special relationship under the hemispheric security umbrella. The United States began immediate shipment of lend-lease equipment to Brazil. By the end of the war, Brazil had received $361.4 million in lend-lease equipment, 73 percent of the total sent to Latin America. The massive infusion of U.S. equipment resulted in Brazil replacing Argentina as the dominant military power in South America.[22] In May 1942, a secret treaty permitted the United States to construct and operate naval and air bases in Brazil's northeast. It also established two joint commissions— the Joint Brazil–United States Defense Commission (JBUSDC, Washington) and the Joint Brazil–United States Military Commission (JBUSMC, Rio de Janeiro)—to oversee lend-lease and newly created training missions. Unique to the region, the joint commissions were symbols of the special relationship and became models for the future Inter-American Defense Board.[23]

Brazil's main contribution to the war was to supply an "Arsenal for Democracy" with many of the materials that U.S. factories and armed forces needed for victory. In addition to commodities long marketed in the United States, such as coffee and cacao, Brazil sent large quantities of rubber, manganese, quartz (radios, gun sights, precision instruments), tantalite (radar, condensers), diamonds (machine tools), iron, hardwoods, corn, and cotton—all at fixed prices. An agreement in February 1942 guaranteed the United States 100 percent of Brazil's strategic materials at noncompetitive prices. Brazilian exports of these minerals rose from $3 million in 1938 to $44 million in 1942.[24] Brazil's importance to the war effort was strategic and psychological as well as material. Bordering nearly every South American nation and endowed with several deep water ports along its long coast, Brazil's entrance into the war aided Allied naval efforts in the Atlantic and helped to shield other South American nations from Axis invasion. Brazil's northeastern bulge became "the trampoline to victory," the point of embarkation to provision the Russian, East Asian, and African fronts. In addition, a 30,000-strong Brazilian Expeditionary Force fought in Italy, the only Latin American ground troops to see action.[25]

Brazil's contributions to the war effort did not go unrewarded. The United States sent the country large amounts of equipment, capital, and technicians through such agencies as the Institute for Inter-American Affairs, which contributed to sanitation, farming improvements, and rural health services.[26] Perhaps the best example of the special treatment given to Brazil during the war was the Cooke Mission (1942–1943). Roosevelt sent his close friend Morris Cooke and gave him a free hand to recommend anything that he and his 125 experts deemed necessary to encourage Brazilian economic development. Working with Brazilian experts, the Cooke Mission offered Brazil its first systematic analysis of Brazilian resources and needs. No other Latin American nation was visited by an equivalent mission. Brazil also received special treatment in material allocations. In 1942, the United States sent 15,000 tons of rail to all of Latin America; Brazil acquired 13,000 tons. The United States also provided $150 million to develop Brazil's strategic materials. Welles and FDR even supported a $45 million EXIM bank loan to build a government-owned steel industry in Brazil during the war, despite scarce resources. Situated at Volta Redonda and built with U.S. capital and technicians, Latin America's first steel industry became a symbol of inter-American cooperation, U.S. accommodation of economic nationalism, and Brazil's "coming of age."[27]

Nevertheless, Brazilian participation in the "war for democracy" created problems for the Vargas regime. In August 1943, Aranha called for immediate elections and a return to democracy, reasoning that Vargas would either retire or win easily. Aranha's old nemesis, War Minister Eurico Dutra, convinced Vargas that the time was not right either for an election or retirement. To force his patron's hand, Aranha joined the pro-U.S. Society of the Friends of America and became its vice president. In August 1944, Vargas closed the organization. This insult resulted in the immediate resignation of the foreign minister and drove Aranha into opposition for the first time in his career. The resignation negatively affected Brazilian foreign policy by breaking down lines of communication with the United States at the very moment that U.S. policy had begun to move away from Good Neighbor nonintervention and toward a more aggressive postwar policy. Historian Frank McCann claims that had he stayed in power, Aranha would have recognized the shift in U.S. policy sooner and better protected Brazilian interests than the policy makers who replaced him.[28]

For the remainder of the war, Aranha practiced law. Though out of government, he hoped to lead the Brazilian delegation to the peace conference. When Vargas finally called for elections in 1945, Aranha supported Eduardo Gomes's Uniao Democratico Nacional (UDN) instead of Vargas's candidate, Eurico Dutra of the Partido Social Democratico (PSD). Dutra's election appeared to have temporarily ended Aranha's political career. The two had long been at odds within the cabinet, and, as a member of the UDN, Aranha was part of the minority opposition. In February 1947, while attending a forum on international relations in the United States, the Brazilian delegate to the United Nations, Pedro Leao Velloso Neto (who replaced Aranha as foreign minister), suddenly died. With Brazil due to chair the Security Council in a few days, Dutra asked Aranha to serve as a temporary replacement. For the next year, Brazil's most able statesman became its UN representative. Within two months, he was elected almost unanimously as president of the UN General Assembly. Aranha chaired the sessions concerning the creation of the state of Israel, had a street named after him in Tel Aviv, and was nominated for the Nobel Peace Prize.

After the war U.S.-Brazilian relations began to stagnate and deteriorate. Faced with worldwide interests and responsibilities, the United States abandoned the Good Neighbor policy. To Aranha and many Brazilians, this seemed to be an abandonment of Pan Americanism, even though during the war, U.S.-Brazilian strategic and defense ties had been at the core of a shift in Pan Americanism toward a defensive alliance. As Latin America ceased to be the focus of U.S. foreign policy, the new Cold War Pan Americanism led U.S. officials to expect continued Brazilian adherence to U.S. policies. Throughout the Dutra years, Brazil remained an important supporter of the United States in the United Nations, especially on Cold War and colonial issues; between 1946 and 1960 only Nicaragua, led by the dictator Anastasio Somoza, voted more consistently with the United States than did Brazil. While pursuing their own interests, Brazilian officials did their best to be supportive of the United States, not for sentimental reasons but from the realization that only the United States could provide the capital and technology Brazil needed. U.S. goodwill was crucial to securing the economic and strategic interests of Brazil. Brazil also felt a sense of obligation to support the cause of Christian democracy during the Cold War.

The Cold War initially strengthened Aranha's Pan Americanism, mainly because he was stridently anticommunist. However, his Pan Americanism was evolving toward a more internationalist vision, which dominated his writings. In U.S. magazines such as *The Rotarian, Education*, and *Vital Speeches*, Aranha called the Americas a "continental commonwealth" that would lead the rest of the world to peace and democracy. According to Aranha, the Americas were bound by common ideals and a common mission in history. The Americas were the "backbone of the planet," where East met West. The Americas had transformed the world, ushering in a new era of concern and hope for humanity. The duty of the Americas was to solve world problems by providing examples of specific solutions, which the Americas had shown was possible through the Pan American conferences. Aranha also claimed that the Americas had only recently taken the ultimate steps, by banishing war within the hemisphere and implementing collective security from outside aggression with the Inter-American Treaty of Reciprocal Assistance (Rio Treaty) of 1947.[29]

In the prestigious journal *Foreign Affairs*, Aranha favored and defended the

Rio Treaty and other regional arrangements as necessary for the success of the United Nations, the "last hope of the world." Lacking force, the moral authority of the United Nations required many regional defense systems to maintain peace, an idea proposed by Roosevelt at the Tehran Conference. Thus, Aranha favored the strengthening of the inter-American system, to defend the American way of life as well as to instruct the rest of the world. The Rio Treaty established the Americas as the dominant military and economic force in the world and made war against and within the Americas impossible. He also defended as necessary the creation of the OAS and its various councils.[30]

To his critics, Aranha's ideas showed naive beliefs in the goodness of the United States as well as some misconceptions about the inter-American system. In part, this explains his lack of popularity among Brazilian nationalists. They also show the development of a political philosopher. His year at the United Nations, along with the emerging Cold War and the dissolution of the Grand Alliance, initiated the final phase in the transformation of Aranha from nationalist to Pan Americanist to internationalist. Aranha admonished the world to strengthen the United Nations as the only way to establish world peace. "Peace is one and indivisible—nations which work outside the United Nations work for war, not peace. . . . Ours is not only a pact among nations but a pact with the destinies of nations."[31] Neither North Americans nor Brazilian nationalists were ever comfortable with this globalist vision. Though a defender of the harsher anticommunist inter-American system, Aranha's vision of a brotherhood of nations was reminiscent of a worldview that Washington had abandoned: Good Neighbor–era Pan Americanism.

Getulio Vargas regained the presidency in 1950 by taking advantage of an economic crisis and promising to be more effective in securing assistance from the United States government and in curbing the excesses of U.S. corporations. Having endorsed the UDN during the campaign, Aranha refused offers from Vargas to serve as ambassador to the United States. He chose, instead, the role of unofficial adviser. Vargas assumed the presidency amid international and domestic economic crisis. In Korea, China's intervention and General Douglas MacArthur's ignominious retreat intensified Washington's efforts to secure international support. The United States turned to its erstwhile ally, even as Brazil faced a severe economic downturn at home. Early in 1951 the Truman administration asked Brazil to send troops to Korea, promising in return a large aid package. Along with most nationalists Aranha opposed Brazilian participation in the war, but he urged accommodation with Washington in other ways. Aranha saw Korea as a prelude to a wider war, and he urged Vargas to offer to send a division to Germany, a potentially decisive front in any future war. Vargas turned down this suggestion but took Aranha's counsel on other questions. He sent no troops to Korea but agreed to participate in the First Point Four Program, the Joint U.S.-Brazil Economic Development Commission to more effectively exploit Brazilian minerals. Vargas also signed the Military Assistance Pact with the United States and sought North American development assistance.

After Dwight D. Eisenhower was elected president in 1952, Aranha believed that the new administration's approach to Brazil and Latin America would reflect Aranha's own internationalism. However, Eisenhower proved no more willing to resuscitate Good Neighbor Pan Americanism than had Harry S. Truman before him. Bilateral relations deteriorated in conjunction with uncertain economic conditions in Brazil. Reelected to the presidency in 1950, Getulio Vargas returned Aranha to the cabinet three years later; with the Korean War winding down and the Brazilian economy in crisis, the Finance Ministry emerged as the most important post in the cabinet. Aranha, the old troubleshooter, returned to his familiar role and the post he had held twenty years previously. This time, however, Aranha secured Vargas's promise to back him fully. These as well as other changes reflected the weakness of Vargas's position and his desire for conciliation with the UDN, to which Aranha belonged. Vargas's selection of Aranha showed both his desire to maintain close relations with the United States and his exasperation with Brazil's economic failures.[32]

Made into a virtual economic czar, Aranha began work on repairing Brazil's finances. He aimed for a practical Pan Americanism that would mean U.S. financial backing for the ailing Brazilian economy. Given control over the Bank of Brazil's credit policy as well as the Finance Ministry, he began an emergency program of import and credit restrictions, to reduce both inflation and the balance of payments crisis. The finance minister also sent two economists, Quartim Barbosa and Egydio Camara Souza, to the United States to try to extend the payment schedule on the EXIM $300 million loan and to provide some breathing space for the government. At the same time, Aranha sent similar negotiating missions to England, France, and West Germany.[33] Barbosa and Souza arrived in mid-July. Ambassador Joao Salles joined the team and began a series of meetings with officials from EXIM, the World Bank, and the State and Treasury Departments. The U.S. delegates expressed misgivings about the genuineness of and political support for Aranha's austerity plan. U.S. officials were also bothered by rising coffee prices and an uncertain Brazilian petroleum policy, both of which threatened Aranha's success. Despite these problems, on July 30, 1953, EXIM announced it would release $204 million to Brazil that it had held against concerns over repayment.[34]

Although the EXIM announcement hailed the agreement as another example of Brazilian-U.S. cooperation, Brazilians failed to see U.S. largess; both Britain and Germany had extended Brazilian debt repayment periods for nine years, whereas EXIM had offered only an additional year. As Aranha wryly noted: "We got the worst settlement from our best friend."[35] In October 1953, he unveiled a plan that created a multiple exchange system with a sliding exchange rate scale based on Brazilian industrial needs. This forced importers to purchase dollars at exchange auctions (an ingenious, if unorthodox, attempt to increase government revenues while hiding a devaluation of the cruzeiro). In addition, both imports and exports that earned foreign exchange would receive cruzeiro bonuses. Aranha acknowledged the necessity of continuing the current rate of industrial growth despite a balance of payments crisis. He also asked Congress to consider an excess profits tax, to increase tax rates on all profits over 12 percent of capital investment to 50 percent. The plan won the approval of U.S. and International Monetary Fund economists. Still, the finance minister warned potential U.S. investors: "We welcome [U.S.] investment that will be governed here and not govern us. We need them badly, but we are not asking for them. You don't invite into your house people who ask for guarantees to enter, guarantees to stay and guarantees to leave."[36]

A more visible and dramatic confrontation between the United States and Brazil involved coffee, a crop crucial to many Latin American nations. Shortly after the 1953 frost destroyed much of the crop, coffee prices in the United States increased rapidly, from a 1952 average of 52 cents to 97 cents per pound in April 1954. So sharp an increase during a recession and in an election year prompted a U.S. Senate investigation headed by Guy Gillette (R.-Iowa). Aranha angrily blamed the price rise on speculators at the New York Coffee Exchange. Senator Margaret Smith blamed communists. Eisenhower believed neither claim. Ambassador James Scott Kemper assured the president that the blame lay in New York, not Rio, a position subsequently affirmed by Department of Agriculture and Federal Trade Commission reports.[37] The smaller crop meant that Brazil needed a higher price to earn the same dollar exchange. On June 3, Vargas decreed an export floor price of 87 cents, 10 cents below the actual price. The move was disastrous, giving immediate credibility to Gillette's charge of Brazilian market manipulation and prompting coffee brokers to boycott Brazil, which further aggravated Brazil's balance-of-payment difficulties. While Brazil had a coffee shortage, new milder African blends were abundant, and U.S. consumers lowered their consumption, causing coffee prices to fall below 87 cents by July. Between June and September, Brazil lost approximately $100 million in anticipated revenues.[38]

Vargas and Aranha refused to remove the price floor–setting decree, although they did lower the price by devaluing the cruzeiro. The government also began purchasing and stockpiling coffee stocks in an effort to force the price up and subsidize farmers. A defiant Aranha declared the "campaign against us is unjust if not stupid," and "to abandon the defense of coffee is to abandon the Brazilian worker and economy." Aranha's good friend, journalist Drew Pearson, advised listeners to "ask your grocer for the good neighbor coffee," stressed Brazil's friendship, and cautioned that the United States had to choose between supporting Africa or Latin America. An American expert warned of a world coffee glut by 1955, and "unless Brazil moves coffee the cruzeiro will be destroyed and Brazil bankrupt."[39]

Despite his anger with the Americans over coffee, loans, and other economic issues, at the Tenth Conference of American States (Caracas, 1954) Aranha continued to push for hemispheric solidarity. Anxious for a strong anticommunist declaration to isolate left-leaning Guatemala, State Department officials speculated—and Vargas hinted—that Brazil would form an anti-American bloc with Mexico, Argentina, and Guatemala to oppose John Foster Dulles's "Declaration of Caracas." The bloc would push instead for a resolution against intervention. Only the strong opposition of conference delegate and Brazilian military commander Marshall Mascarenhas de Morais, War Minister General Zenóbio da Costa, and Aranha prevented Vargas from taking a more belligerent course. At Caracas, Brazil assumed a traditional role as arbitrator between the Spanish American republics and the United States. In June, at the UN Security Council, after the U.S.-backed invasion of Guatemalan, Brazil proved to be a staunch supporter of the United States. Guatemalan authorities tried to bring a complaint against U.S. intervention to the United Nations. Washington, in turn, maneuvered to keep all diplomatic conflicts within the OAS, which it was better able to control than the United Nations. Brazil upheld the U.S. stand by affirming the central place of regional multilateral bodies in the resolution of disputes, as Aranha had done six years before in his *Foreign Affairs* article.[40]

Notwithstanding Brazil's position on Guatemala, relations with the United States continued to deteriorate, even as Brazil became engulfed in economic crisis and political intrigue. A 100 percent increase in the minimum wage pushed through by Labor Minister Joao Goulart sabotaged Aranha's economic plans, stimulating inflation and mobilizing opposition to the government in the middle class and the military. In May and June, news of government scandals broke, suggesting widespread corruption. At the same time, some accused Vargas of plotting to create a nuclear industry and of negotiating with Juan Perón to form an anti-American alliance. Shortly afterward, U.S. officials refused a request for an $80 million gold-backed Federal Reserve loan. As the crisis escalated, on August 24 Vargas committed suicide, blaming "a subterranean campaign of international groups joined with national groups."[41]

Soon after, Aranha retired from politics. His health began to fail and he made fewer public appearances, although he continued to write and comment on policy. Vargas's suicide had a profound effect on his thinking. There is no doubting his bitterness; the United States promised but withheld aid, refused to invest in Brazil but demanded the right to invest in the petroleum and power industries, and helped to create, but refused to assist in alleviating, Brazil's economic distress. Brazil had been a good ally, but the Eisenhower administration had consistently discriminated against it. Aranha never again trusted the United States.

The Eisenhower administration reciprocated Aranha's distrust. Commenting on an interview Aranha gave *Imprensa Popular* in the aftermath of the Geneva Conference between Eisenhower and Khrushchev, U.S. Ambassador James Dunn noted that Aranha's comments followed the "true communist line."[42] This was nonsense. Aranha remained committed to nationalism and internationalism. He hailed Geneva as a "victory of the idea of peace." He also expressed increased solidarity with the Third World, arguing that the "old colonial order, founded on force, must give way to freedom, independence, equality and prosperity of all peoples." Changes toward this end would require adjustments in both Pan Americanism and Brazil's foreign policy. According to Aranha, "Pan

Americanism will now have to make increased concessions to world organization." Brazilian foreign policy would have to move toward greater support for the independent action of international economic and political organizations, "in which we have been followers rather than responsible participants."[43]

As always, Aranha had tremendous faith in Brazil's future. In an interview with *O Estado de São Paulo*, he said: "Brazil will be one of the great leaders by the end of the century and will make contributions to the new human order that will not be surpassed by any other peoples, even those who today appear more advanced and powerful."[44] However, Aranha's new advocacy of reestablishing Brazilian ties with the Soviet bloc (broken in 1947) and the admission of the People's Republic of China to the United Nations underscored U.S. Embassy fears of his so-called "communism" and "super nationalism." In the *Revista Brasileira de Politica Internacional* and again in a speech to the *Escola Superior de Guerra* (ESG), Aranha reasoned that Brazil's future as a world power demanded relations with the Soviet Union. Although he remained anticommunist, Aranha believed that the absence of relations with the two communist powers was a source of insecurity.[45]

During the Kubitschek presidency (1956–1961), Aranha continued to be close to the government despite not holding an official position. Juscelino Kubitschek de Oliveira desperately sought close relations with the United States because his ambitious "fifty years' progress in five years" industrialization program required large amounts of foreign capital. Yet despite Kubitschek's easing of restrictions on foreign investment and his blanket support of U.S. positions in the world arena, Brazilian-American relations did not improve. U.S. aid did not increase. By 1957, prominent diplomats, including José Sette Camara Filho and Joao Carlos Muniz, advocated Latin American unity in order to negotiate more effectively with the United States. In a series of newspaper interviews, Hermes Lima, a former UN delegate and deputy, declared that the "OAS is a beautiful idea, but has never functioned" and blamed the US for the "deterioration in U.S.-Brazilian relations [that] constitutes a threat to continental unity." Aranha supported these views and added that Brazil was too great a power to follow U.S. leadership without a "heightened" regard for its own interests.[46]

In this atmosphere, Kubitschek named Aranha head of Brazil's UN delegation in 1957. Aranha's international vision became still more ample; for instance, he predicted a more important role for the Arab world: "It would seem that the grim privilege of casting the lot for war or peace lies in the hands of those who command the newly developed sources of energy." Aranha called disarmament a moral imperative, urged the Word Bank to increase its lending operations for development, and called for increased reliance on the United Nations.[47] While publicly extolling Pan Americanism, in a series of letters to Kubitschek, Aranha was less sanguine. He alerted the president that the United States was too preoccupied with *Sputnik* and the increased danger it represented, as well as to the recent crises in the Middle East, to give much attention or much sympathy to

Brazil. He also urged Kubitschek to reconsider Brazil's long-standing support for colonial powers in favor of the newly emerging independent nations in Africa and Asia.[48]

In April and May 1958, Vice President Richard Nixon embarked on a goodwill tour of Latin America. He was confronted by a series of hostile crowds and riots. Kubitschek saw the crisis as an opportunity to write to Eisenhower and urge a thorough revision of policies "for the furtherance of Pan American ideals in all of their implications." In order to give substance to "Operation Pan America" (OPA), as his initiative became popularly known, Kubitschek created the Special Commission to Study the Formulation of New Methods of Economic Cooperation. This blue-ribbon committee included Aranha as well as several other well-known foreign policy leaders. The Commission took an active role in supplying its chair, Augusto Federico Schmidt, with arguments on behalf of an Inter-American Development Bank, a Latin American common market, and commodity agreements. The Eisenhower administration never enthusiastically supported OPA, but the discussions eventually led to the Alliance for Progress.[49]

Although Kubitschek used the language and administrative apparatus of Pan Americanism for the initiative, OPA represented a break from Brazil's traditional role as mediator between the United States and Spanish America. Indeed, OPA sought to mobilize Spanish America against the United States to force major changes in U.S. foreign economic policy and to force the United States to make Latin American development a priority in strengthening hemispheric solidarity. According to Kubitschek, "Pan Americanism has advanced miles in the field of principles, but it has advanced only a few inches in the field of economic accomplishment." The failure of OPA to gain the support of Eisenhower officials embittered Kubitschek and led to continued deterioration of the relationship.[50]

In the last year of his life, Aranha collaborated with the author Amilcar Alencastre on a book that contained his current thinking on international affairs. Published posthumously in 1961, *Oswaldo Aranha: O Mundo Afro-Asiatico e a Paz* is a survey of the postwar world and Brazil's place in it. Always the nationalist, Aranha argued persuasively for an independent foreign policy based on Brazil's self-interest. This new policy would not be anti–United States but prodevelopment, propeace and internationalist. Brazil would champion the causes of disarmament, decolonization, and a more equitable distribution of global resources in order to assist development. The globalization of Pan Americanism meant an enlargement of Brazil's traditional role as mediator between the United States and Spanish America; now that mediatory role would take into account newly independent nations and the Soviet bloc.[51]

Aranha died in 1960, just as the maneuvering for presidential elections was beginning. Mentioned as a possible vice-presidential candidate for the Partido Social Democratico (PSD) Partido Trabalhista Brasileiro (PTB) alliance, he did not live to see Janio Quadros, the UDN candidate, embrace his ideas—without perhaps appreciating their subtlety or having the skill required to implement a new independent foreign policy. Quadros won in a landslide and almost immediately embarked on a path that led to confrontation with the United States, the accelerated decline of bilateral relations, and U.S. backing for the military *golpe* of March 31, 1964, which ushered in more than two decades of military rule. By the early 1960s, a key axis of early-twentieth-century Pan Americanism had been broken; Brazil and the United States had become hemispheric rivals.

In many ways, the development of Brazilian foreign policy after World War II mirrored the thinking of Aranha. In the 1930s, Good Neighbor Pan Americanism had set standards that Aranha had followed: an end to military intervention and a foreign policy focus on Latin America that placed special emphasis on Brazil. At the end of the war, Aranha stood for Pan American ideals and Western Hemisphere unity. At the same time, the United States exchanged Good Neighbor Pan Americanism for a globalist and interventionist version of the Monroe Doctrine. Despite Aranha's unease over the policy shift, Brazil did not immediately abandon the special relationship with the United States that had been a cornerstone of Pan Americanism; nor did Aranha. Unlike Aranha, however, Brazil gradually adopted an internationalist stance that distanced the country from U.S.-led Pan Americanism. In the face of growing economic problems in the 1950s, Aranha and other Brazilian leaders concluded that the United States and the Cold War had become obstacles to Brazil's economic development. Once a diplomatic imperative for Brazil, U.S. leadership—and with it, U.S.-led Pan Americanism—was shunned, questioned, and eventually challenged by the late 1950s.

NOTES

1. Joseph Love, *Rio Grande do Sul and Brazilian Regionalism, 1882–1930* (Stanford, 1971), 219.

2. Although Aranha surfaces as an important figure in many works dealing with the 1930–1960 period, there is still no major biography of him in English. At present, the only biography is Theodore Berson, "A Political Biography of Dr. Oswaldo Aranha of Brazil, 1930–1937" (Ph.D. Dissertation, New York University, 1971). There are several works in Portuguese, including the recent Aspasia Camargo, Joao Hermes Pereira de Araujo, and Mario Henrique Simonsen, *Oswaldo Aranha: A Estrela da Revolucao* (São Paulo, 1996) and Stanley Hilton, *Oswaldo Aranha: Uma Biografia* (Rio de Janeiro, 1994).

3. To be sure, Aranha was not the only observer to announce the demise of Pan Americanism. In the 1950s historian Arthur Whitaker and economist Simon G. Hanson both bemoaned its end. See Arthur P. Whitaker, *The Western Hemisphere Idea: Its Rise and Decline*, (Ithaca, 1954); Simon G. Hanson, "The End of the Good Neighbor Policy," *Inter-American Economic Affairs* 7, no. 2 (Autumn 1953): 3–49.

4. Arthur P. Whitaker, *The Western Hemisphere Idea* (Ithaca, 1954), 1–8; Joseph Byrne Lockey, *Essays in Pan-Americanism* (Berkeley, 1939), 1–21; Mark T. Gilderhus, *Pan American Visions: Woodrow Wilson in the Western Hemisphere, 1913–1921* (Tucson, 1986), 1–12.

5. E. Bradford Burns, *The Unwritten Alliance: Rio Branco and Brazilian-American*

Relations (New York, 1966); John W. F. Dulles, "Post Dictatorship Brazil, 1945–1964," in *New Perspectives in Brazil*, edited by Eric N. Baklanoff (Nashville, 1966), 21–24. Hilton and most others write of "the special relationship," while Burns uses "unwritten alliance" to describe the same lengthy U.S.-Brazil partnership.

6. Walter LaFeber, *The New Empire: An Interpretation of American Expansion, 1860–1898* (Ithaca, 1963), 210–18, 236–43; Lawrence F. Hill, *Diplomatic Relations between the United States and Brazil* (Durham, 1932), 270–81; Joseph Smith, *Unequal Giants: Diplomatic Relations between the United States and Brazil, 1889–1930* (Pittsburgh, 1991), 3–70; Steven C. Topik, *Trade and Gunboats: The United States and Brazil in the Age of Empire* (Stanford, 1996).

7. Some ambivalence toward Pan Americanism existed within the Brazilian intelligentsia. For example, the diplomat Manoel de Oliveira Lima, *Pan-Americanismo: Monroe, Bolivar, Roosevelt*, (Paris, 1908), voiced concern over U.S. interventionism. He advocated making the Monroe Doctrine multilateral (under a Pan American banner)— exactly Aranha's position a half century later. See also Smith, 52–62.

8. John W. F. Dulles, *Vargas of Brazil* (Austin, 1967), 73–75; Love, 232.

9. Stanley E. Hilton, *Brazil and the Great Powers, 1930–1939: Politics of Trade Rivalry* (Austin, 1975), 32–35; Berson, 145–68, 197–208; Dulles, *Vargas*, 127–130; Peter Flynn, *Brazil: A Political Analysis* (Boulder, 1978), 67–68.

10. Hilton, 51, 75–78; Robert M. Levine, *The Vargas Regime: The Critical Years* (New York, 1970), 33; Frank D. McCann, *The Brazilian-American Alliance* (Princeton, 1973), 51–52.

11. Hull to Gibson, 20 June 1934, Wilson to Hull, 31 October 1934, *Foreign Relations of the United States* (hereafter FRUS), *1934*, vol. 4, 544–552. For an examination of the Good Neighbor policy see Bryce Wood, *The Good Neighbor Policy* (New York, 1961), and David Green, *The Containment of Latin America: A History of the Myths and Realities of the Good Neighbor Policy* (Chicago, 1971).

12. McCann, 306–12; Dulles, *Vargas*, 211–19.

13. McCann, 51–61.

14. Frederick M. Nunn, *Yesterday's Soldiers: European Military Professionalism in South America, 1890–1940* (Lincoln, NE, 1983); McCann, 123–47; Hilton, 203–224; John Child, *Unequal Alliance: The Inter-American Military System, 1938–1978* (Boulder, 1980), 48–52; Gerson Moura, *Autonomia na Dependencia: A Política Externa Brasileira de 1935 a 1942* (Rio de Janeiro, 1980), 105–42.

15. Oswaldo Aranha, *A Revolucao e a America* (Rio de Janeiro, 1941).

16. McCann, 65–68; Hilton, 175; Caffery to Hull, 27 January 1938, 27 February 1938, 13 May 1938, and Hull to Caffery, 28 February 1938, FRUS, 1938, vol. 5, 384, 410–415; Welles to Caffery, 22 May 1941, FRUS, 1941, vol. 6, 494.

17. Gordon Connell-Smith, *The Inter-American System*, (London, 1966), 104–9; McCann, 118–22.

18. Hilton, 203–5; McCann, 123–33; "Solidarity Salesman," *Newsweek*, 20 February 1939; "Brazil's Bid," *Newsweek*, 27 February 1939; "Aranha Victory," *Newsweek*, 20 March 1939.

19. McCann, 201–12; Child, 52–53; FRUS, 1941, vol. 6, 538–42.

20. Summer Welles, *The Time for Decision* (New York, 1944), 415.

21. FRUS, 1942, vol. 6, 73–74, 128–29; Dulles, *Vargas*, 222–24; Welles, 210–26; J. Lloyd Mecham, *The United States and Inter-American Security, 1889–1960* (Austin, 1961), 209–13.

22. McCann, 283; Child, 48–49, 54–55; Gary W. Frank, *Struggle for Hegemony in South America: Argentina, Brazil and the United States during the Second World War* (Coral Gables, 1979), 9–16, 80–89. Stetson Conn and Byron Fairchild, *The Framework of Hemispheric Defense* (Washington, 1960), 194–200.

23. Child, 53–54; McCann, 267–275; (Ret.) Maj. General Richard Steinbach to author, 11 October 1984.

24. "Brazil Has Started!" *Rotarian*, January, 1948, Dulles, *Vargas*, 220, 225–27; Green, 117.

25. McCann, 242–46, 259–81; Child, 54–55; Dulles, *Vargas*, 225–43.

26. Claude C. Erb, "Prelude to Point Four: The Institute of Inter-American Affairs," *Diplomatic History* 9, no. 3 (Summer 1985): 249–70.

27. FRUS, 1941, vol. 6, 73–74, 128–29; McCann, 242–46, 259–83, 385–87; Welles, 210–26; Green, 179.

28. "Aranha's Resignation, *The Inter-American*, 10 October, 1944; "Vargas on the Defensive," *The Nation*, 2 September 1944; McCann, 336–40.

29. Oswaldo Aranha, "Land of Light and Liberty," *Rotarian*, December 1942; Oswaldo Aranha, "The Americas Are Learning," *Rotarian*, January 1948, pp. 8–11, 51.

30. Oswaldo Aranha, "Regional Systems and the Future of the U.N.," *Foreign Affairs* 26, no. 3 (April 1948): 415–20.

31. Oswaldo Aranha, "The Aftermath of War: A Spiritual Struggle Emerges," *Vital Speeches* 13, no. 24 (1 October 1947): 763–64; Dulles, *Vargas* 9.

32. Author interview with Cleantho de Paiva Leite, 6 May 1986; Green to State Department, no. 17, 3 July 1953, 732.00, Record Group (RG) 59, National Archives (NA) of the United States, Washington.

33. "Brazil to Tighten Imports Curb as Easing of U.S. Loan Is Sought," *New York Times*, 17 July 1953; Terrill to State, no. 265, 21 August 1953, 832.00, RG 59, NA; Bouças to Aranha, 14 July 1953, and "Cooperaçao Economico entre os Estados Unidos e Brasil," 18 July 1953, *Aranha Papers*, Fundacao Getulio Vargas (FGV), Centro de Pesquisas de Historia Contemporanea, Rio de Janeiro, Brazil.

34. "Comércio Exterior Brasil-Estados Unidos, 1953," Garrido Torres to Aranha, 15 June 1953, and "Relatório," OA 53 08 06/4, *Aranha Papers*, FGV; Export-Import Bank of Washington, press release, 30 July 1953.

35. *New York Herald Tribune*, 28 September 1953; Hanson, 25–30; Muniz to Aranha, 20 November 1953, *Aranha Papers*, FGV.

36. Thomas E. Skidmore, *Politics in Brazil, 1930–1964.* (New York, 1967), 112–18, 367; Terrill to State, no. 642, 13 November 1953; Terrill to State, no. 673, 20 November 1953, 732.00, RG 59, NA; "Brakes on Brazil," *Business Week*, 10 October 1953.

37. Skidmore, 123; Luiz Alberto Bandeira, *Presenca dos Estados Unidos do Brasil* (Rio de Janeiro, 1973), 360–61; Terrill to State, no. 942, 29 January 1954; Terrill to State, no. 967, 5 February 1954, 732.00, RG 59, NA; Robert H. Ferrell, *Eisenhower Diaries*, 10 February 1954, p. 275; *Hanson's Latin American Letter* 7 August 1954; Cabot to Smith, 12 February 1954, FRUS, 1952–1954, vol. 4, 293–98; Guilherme Araujo to Aranha, 28 December 1954, *Aranha Papers*, FGV; Rao to Vargas, 3 March 1954, *Vargas Papers*, FGV.

38. Skidmore, 135–36; Carvalho to Souza Dantas, 27 July 1954; Drew Pearson to J.C. Muniz, 12 July 1954; Drew Pearson, *Washington Merry-Go-Round*, 12 July 1954, all *Aranha Papers*, FGV.

39. Pearson, 12 July 1954, and Aranha address at the Brazilian Institute of Coffee,

19 July 1954, *Aranha Papers*, FGV; Terrill to State, no. 68, 23 July 1954, 732.00, RG 59, NA.

40. R.P. Terrill to State, no. 660, 17 February 1954; Terrill to W.T. Bennett, 19 February 1954; W.T. Briggs to W.C. Trimble and G.H. Owen, 23 July 1954; 320.OAS, RG 59, NA; author interview with Cleantho de Paiva Leite, 6 May 1986.

41. Skidmore, 122–142; W. Michael Weis, *Cold Warriors & Coups D'etat: Brazilian-American Relations, 1945–1964* (Albuquerque, 1993), 77–79.

42. Dunn to State, no. 91, 28 July 1955, 732.00, RG 59, NA.

43. Briggs to State, no. 137, 4 August 1955, 732.00, RG 59, NA; *Imprensa Popular*, 27 July 1955.

44. Skidmore, 367.

45. Oswaldo Aranha, "Relacoes Diplomaticas com a Uniao Sovietica," *Revista Brasileira de Politica Internacional*, June 1958, pp. 18–28; "O Bloco Sovietico no Panoramo Mundial," speech to ESG, OA 58.00.00, *Aranha Papers*, FGV.

46. José Sette Camara Filho, lecture at ESG, May 1958, ESG print C1-45-58; Joao Carlos Muniz, lecture at ESG, May 1958, ESG print C-50-58; *Ultima Hora*, 28 April 1958; *Ultima Hora*, 5 May 1958; Oswaldo Aranha to Kubitschek, 9 December 1957, *Aranha Papers*, FGV. See also *Imprensa Popular*, 27 July 1957; Briggs to State, no. 137, 4 August 1955, 732.00, RG 59, NA; Weis, 89–112.

47. "Assembly's General Debate Surveyed," *United Nations Review*, January 1958, p. 11; Aranha speech to UN in *Revista Brasileira de Politica Internacional* (March 1958), 120–124; "Aranha Predicts Peace in Mideast," *New York Times*, 10 November 1957.

48. Aranha to Kubitschek, 9 December 1957, OA 57.12.9; Aranha to Kubitschek, nd, OA 57.00.00/2, *Aranha Papers*, FGV.

49. Weis, 113–139; Marvin Zahniser and W. Michael Weis, "A Diplomatic Pearl Harbor? Richard Nixon's Goodwill Mission to Latin America in 1958," *Diplomatic History* 13, no. 2 (Spring 1989): 163–90; Stephen G. Rabe, *Eisenhower and Latin America* (Chapel Hill, 1988), 100–16.

50. Weis, 115–39.

51. Amilcar Alencastre, *Oswaldo Aranha: O Mundo Afro-Asiatico e a Paz* (Rio de Janeiro, 1961).

12

The Theory and Practice of Inter-American Literature: An Historical Overview

Earl E. Fitz

A fast-growing and intellectually engaging area of contemporary literary schol-arship, inter-American literature is flourishing even as it struggles to define itself as an academic discipline. Deeply controversial in its conceptualization, critical assumptions, and methodologies, the study of the literature(s) of the Americas integrates different languages, cultures, and historical experiences. Some of the latter—relating, for example, to racism, genocide, political intervention and eco-nomic exploitation—remain deeply divisive within and across national bound-aries. However, for all the very real differences between the American states, their many similarities point to a common, Pan American experience that is explored in the literary analysis of narratives, poems, dramas, and essays—and in this chapter.

Inter-American literary study may date from the pre-Colombian period, when cultural communications may have followed well-developed inter-American trade routes. To be sure, it reaches back to the earliest colonial past when, for example (in what seems to have been the first documented case of inter-American literary scholarship), a brilliant Mexican poet and intellectual, Sor Juana Inés de la Cruz, incurred the wrath of her superiors for writing a critique of a sermon by the venerated Brazilian orator, Father Antônio Vieira. In the seventeenth century, Puritan leaders Samuel Sewall and Cotton Mather raised concerns about the growing influence of Catholic Spain in the New World; they suggested that a more aggressive Puritanism might counteract it, creating in the process a Puritan American continent.

The modern Pan American movement came into being two centuries later, but inter-American literary study as practiced today is largely a twentieth-century creation. Published in 1933, and reflecting the Pan Americanism of President Franklin D. Roosevelt's Good Neighbor policy, Herbert Bolton's seminal study, *The Epic of Greater America* can be taken as a conceptual basis for inter-American commentary and analysis. Bolton argued that, very real differences notwithstanding, the Americas could claim a common history: A frontier experience provided the various American republics with their common denominator. As the embodiment of the cultural rapprochement that characterized the more public components of Pan American relations in the pre–World War II era, Bolton's historically oriented argument is easily transferred to the literary sphere.

Literary history marked a first approach to inter-American literary study. Written during World War II, George W. Umphrey's "Spanish American Literature Compared with That of the United States" (1943) represents the first systematic attempt to read the literature of the United States against that of one of its American neighbors. Noting, as Bolton does for the historical record, what he takes to be commonalities in main trends and developments of New World literature, Umphrey discusses Inca Garcilaso de la Vega, Sor Juana Inés de la Cruz, and Anne Bradstreet in an early study comparing these latter two writers across national boundaries[1] as well as Fernández de Lizardi's *El Periquillo Sarniento* (1816), a text often said to be Spanish America's first novel. Umphrey establishes as vital points of comparison the literatures of our colonial eras, our revolutionary periods, Romanticism, and "contemporary" literature. He comments also on the positive influence of Edgar Allan Poe on Spanish American aesthetic sensibilities and concludes his groundbreaking study with a discussion of Spanish American Modernismo, a movement of the late nineteenth and early twentieth centuries that definitively established Spanish America's linguistic and literary independence from Spain.

Another text that reflects the proliferation of studies combining the literatures of the United States and Spanish America is Fernando Alegría's *Walt Whitman en Hispanoamérica*. Alegría discusses the liberating influence Whitman had on Latin America. Whitman's poetry had a deep impact on the evolution of modern Spanish American poetry,[2] especially that of the Modernistas and such later masters as Pablo Neruda. Alegría underscores the importance translation has played in the dissemination of inter-American literature.

Although contemporary inter-American scholarship has tended to focus on relations between Spanish America (neglecting Brazil) and the United States, Canada too has been historically well represented in the Pan American thinking of U.S. scholars. Appearing, for example, during the heyday of the Spanish American *nueva novela* (new novel) of the 1960s, Edmund Wilson's *O Canada: An American's Notes on Canadian Culture* did not receive the attention its appearance would now generate. As an early example of cultural criticism applied to the writing and reading of literature, Wilson's study ranges from the general (Canada's divided sense of national identity and its relationship to the United States) to the specific (the two sections he devotes to author Morley

Callaghan). Wilson also reminds us of Francis Parkman's enduring historical studies of Canada (*France and England in North America*), the novels of Hugh MacLennan (especially *The Two Solitudes*), and the poetry of Québec's Émile Nelligan, whose best sonnets merit comparison with those of Nicaragua's Rubén Darío and Brazil's Joao da Cruz e Sousa. Moving from Nelligan to the then contemporary scene—the mid-1960s "Quiet Revolution" in Québec—Wilson also discusses the literary, cultural, and political significance of Québecois nationalism. At the time, Québecois literature was experiencing a period of experimentation rivaling in scope the "new novel" of Spanish America and Brazil, but few Pan American connections had yet been made between Canada and Latin America.[3]

The literatures of Native peoples pose methodologically and conceptually vexing problems in contemporary inter-American literary scholarship. Although the final decades of the twentieth century are showing a remarkable surge in Native authors and texts, what is less clear is how these works should be considered in the inter-American context. In many ways, the issue of Native literature epitomizes the entire inter-American project, amply demonstrating its tremendous potential but also illustrating the profound methodological problems that accompany it. Should, as Robert Martin asks, Native literature be considered "American" literature at all?[4] If we decide that it should not, then we are faced with the problem of disregard: How can small literatures, whether written (typically in one of the European languages) or oral, survive on their own? On the other hand, if we do include Native literatures as part of the Pan American purview, then how do we avoid "Americanizing" them, generalizing about them so much that their unique characteristics are lost? Because there is probably no perfect solution, it seems prudent to consider something of a methodological compromise: including Native literatures in an inter-American perspective, but treating them as other national literatures—read, listened to, and interpreted in their unique cultural and historical contexts.

A number of literary scholars have moved in this direction. Karl Kroeber's 1979 study, "Deconstructionist Criticism and American Indian Literatures," is a case in point, as is Brian Swann's *Smoothing the Ground*, an excellent collection of essays that, touching on a range of topics and cultures from indigenous America, highlights unique features of Native oral literatures while also connecting them to trends and developments in the better known literatures of our time.[5] Whereas Kroeber places Native poetry in the context of major twentieth-century critical theory and thus tries to bring the Native tradition to the attention of readers who otherwise might not be cognizant of it at all, Swann's book cuts a much wider swath, addressing issues of translation, the aesthetics of the oral tradition, and the relationship of Native American literature to the dominant, Anglo culture. Comparing the larger, more hegemonic culture of the United States with the cultures of Mexicans and Natives, Swann, citing Octavio Paz, writes that while Mexico is the most Spanish country in Latin America, it is also the most Indian. On the other hand, the Indian element in the United States is invisible, the reason being that "the Christian horror of 'fallen nature' extends to the natives of America: The United States was founded on a land without a past. The historical memory of Americans is European, not American."[6]

Emphasizing spiritual, mechanical, and linguistic divides within inter-American literatures, Kroeber picks up on a related theme. He argues that "all Native American poetry is radically different from Western European poetry." Citing the importance of repetition to Native American poetry, in contrast to the relatively minor role it plays in Western poetics, Kroeber proceeds to assert two fascinating points. First, in contrast to the literature of the Western tradition, Native literature understands language as possessing a sacred function. It does not make a sharp distinction between poetry and prose. Second, "most Indian poetry appears to be built more upon a form of metonymy, synecdoche, than upon metaphor," the fundamental building block of Western poetry.[7]

Such stark divisions continue to engage those trying to craft an understanding of a Pan American literature. As a standard feature of such prestigious professional organizations as the Modern Language Association and the International Comparative Literature Association, inter-American literature is a discipline that has grown far faster in numbers of participants than in sense of professional identity and praxis of its exponents. Moreover, while literary scholars owe much to Herbert E. Bolton and other historians for helping to outline the very concept of inter-American study itself, contemporary historians like Arthur Quinn and Lester D. Langley[8] are continuing to define the literary undertaking, to legitimize its methodologies, and to establish its intellectual parameters. Methodological problems persist, however. Allowing for the many Native literatures, there are far more literatures to be studied than any scholar or team of scholars could ever hope to speak of authoritatively. In addition, can we ever completely justify discussing, for example, Brazilian, Mexican, or Canadian literatures as both national and "American" literatures? Or is this precisely the multiple, interrelated perspective that *should* be employed in examining these literatures? If we adhere to the old sense of literary study as an exercise in nationalism, do we not risk perpetuating the fragmentation and hegemony that have marked literary study in the Americas for so long? At the same time, if we accept too uncritically the premise of an inter-American relationship between the literatures of the Western Hemisphere, do we not risk homogenizing the texts?

In the evolution of inter-American literature, methodology and perspective have emerged as paramount. There is a controversy between scholars who believe in a comprehensive approach to the literature of the Americas (where authors and texts from all the cultures of the Americas should be included in any single study) and those who believe that this approach is necessarily too broad, that a narrower approach is more appropriate. Until now, the more limited focus has had the upper hand. The great danger of this approach, however, according to those who espouse a more broad-based approach, is that it is too narrow, that it undermines the very concept of Pan Americanism, and, most damaging, that through omission it relegates some New World literatures and cultures (all too often those of Brazil and Canada) to what amounts to a second-class or marginalized status. That this methodological controversy tends to have been settled in favor of the more narrow focus is not surprising; most literary scholars are trained as specialists in a single national literature. This problem has been exacerbated in the United States, where the majority of American Studies or English Department university graduates are monolingual. In fact, the inter-American perspective has been recognized and addressed for a much longer time in other countries than in the United States.

Two key essays take up this entwined question of nomenclature and identity: Larry Shouldice's "Wide Latitudes: Comparing New World Literature" and Robert K. Martin's "North of the Border: Whose Postnationalism?"[9] Shouldice begins with what it means to call oneself "American" or to deal with "American" literature, then questions whether works written by "New World" authors that reflect little of "New World" reality (Henry James and Brazil's Machado de Assis, for example) should really be termed "New World" literature at all. He goes on to discuss the problem of authorship and identity, especially in the context of works written during the various colonial eras of the Americas, when the heavy influence of the European mother country was itself gradually being influenced by nascent American nationalisms. Larger patterns of influence and reception are also discussed, as are the problems of linguistic diversity. Shouldice argues that although the act of juxtaposing "New World" literatures and texts has flaws and limitations, it allows a scholar to highlight similarities while permitting us to compare and contrast important differences—special characteristics of texts, authors, and literary traditions that render works uniquely Brazilian, Québecois, Mexican, or English Canadian.

More well known, Martin's study is also important for the methodological and conceptual questions that it raises. Concerned that inter-American studies will proceed by making the literature of the United States the model or prototype, the "hegemonic center" of analysis, and that U.S. scholars will then merely "add on" other American literatures as marginalized "others," Martin points out the urgent need for the United States to work on the histories and cultures of neighboring nations. Referring specifically to the superficiality of blithely sticking Canadian titles, for example, on reading lists, Martin cites four problems: the tendency for U.S. literary study to focus "on an ethnic model," one in which "ethnics are simply Americans with a difference, somewhere along the path of full participation in the American nation"; the inadequacy of language training for American academics; the tendency of American studies scholars to absorb Canada and Québec into their field as if they were not sovereign nations but regions or states; and the difficulty in applying "the multicultural approach of the United States" to Canada.[10] Martin also questions whether the "appeal of a deconstructed nationality cannot be as strong in a nation that has yet to achieve its selfhood as in one that sees the need to put itself into doubt." Applicable to the relationship between the literature of the United States and Canada as well as between the United States and Latin America, this concern speaks directly to the issue of balance in comparative studies and to a number of contemporary literary concerns, including the volatile problems of nationhood, racial identity, gender, and sexuality.[11]

Similar themes are addressed by José David Saldívar, who notes that "American literary history can no longer be written by separating the ethnic groups . . . that produced the literatures." The question of Native authors and their relationship to American literature continues to be a thorny one. Arguing for a broader and "more oppositional American literary history,"[12] Saldívar concurs with Werner Sollors, who contends that the old, ethnic-based model of literary history "obfuscated important literary and cultural connections" between the Americas. A new and more deliberately inter-American literary history

ought to increase our understanding of the cultural interplays and contacts among writers of different [national] backgrounds, the cultural mergers and secessions that took place in [the] America[s], all of which can be accomplished only if the categorization of writers as members of [national] ethnic groups is understood to be a very partial, temporal, and insufficient characterization at best.[13]

"Recast in this light," Saldívar asserts, invoking the legacy of Cuban essayist and political leader José Martí, "American literatures can only be understood as part of the larger debates and confrontations between 'our America' and the 'other America,' which is not ours." Saldívar then goes on to credit the Cuban publishing house, Casa de las Américas, and Cuban poet and essayist Roberto Fernández Retamar for their leadership in formulating this new and more "oppositional" inter-American literary history:

Fernández Retamar, in particular, has attempted to develop a new terminology that goes beyond a North American and Latin American 'idealist' criticism, for Casa de las Américas was born in the very struggle between American imperialism, on one hand, and Latin American Marxism, on the other.[14]

Most inter-American literary studies continue to offer a binary (English-Spanish) analysis of the literatures of the United States, Spanish America, and the Caribbean, with Canada, Native societies, Brazil, Suriname, and other nations left aside. Two texts that reflect this tendency are Bell Gale Chevigny and Gary Laguardia's *Reinventing the Americas: Comparative Studies of Literature of the United States and Spanish America* and Gustavo Pérez Firmat's *Do the Americas Have a Common Literature?* Each calls attention to the methodological pitfalls in inter-American literary study which, observes Firmat, is still something of a terra incognita in its organization and praxis. Holding to a narrower focus, Chevigny and Laguardia lay out what they take to be shared points of experience between the United States and Spanish America. Perhaps unintentionally echoing Herbert Bolton's original thesis, Chevigny and Laguardia begin by asking whether we can speak of the literatures of the Americas in the same way that we speak of European literature, a similarly diverse entity: "Although we are accustomed to stressing the differences between the Americas, it is possible to argue that they share fundamental historical experiences, experiences articulated and imaginatively transformed in their literatures, that underwrite the integrity of a comparative exploration."[15] The authors then go on to cite several examples of these historical commonalities: All present-day nations of the Americas arose from European conquest and settlement; this process involved, in all cases, the defeat and displacement of indigenous populations. European colonizers appropriated large expanses of territory (giving rise to the concept of "frontier"). Development throughout the region is tied to slavery. Present-day hybrid cultures are the result of a mixing of races. At some point, all of the Americas experienced a "revolutionary rupture with the colonizing power." New nations were formed that found themselves forced "to reconstitute themselves self-consciously as something new." Finally, Chevigny and Laguardia point out a crucial difference between the ways the United States was formed and the ways Spanish America evolved:

The United States was first settled by individuals . . . who were escaping from religious or political conditions they found unacceptable. The colonization of Spanish America, in contrast, was carried out by people who, on the whole, had no fundamental quarrel with their society and sought to extend it while enriching themselves.[16]

Inspired by another historian's work (Lewis Hanke's 1964 study, *Do the Americas Have a Common History?*), Firmat's *Do the Americas Have a Common Literature?* also concentrates on connections between Spanish-speaking America, the Caribbean, and the United States. Firmat adopts four distinct approaches in his search for a Pan American literature: the generic, which "attempts to establish a hemispheric context by using as a point of departure a broad, abstract notion of wide applicability"; the genetic, which emphasizes the "causal links among authors and texts," including "the uses to which a given author or text have been put by his or her successors"; the oppositional, or the placement of works "side by side without postulating causal connections"; and the mediative, which "concentrates on texts that already embed an inter-American or comparative dimension." In discussing his own "exposition of the Pan American poetics of José Lezama Lima," Firmat's terminology affirms the debt his methodology owes to the spirit of Pan Americanism, a movement that can be taken as the conceptual progenitor of inter-American literary study.[17]

Unlike some other works, *Do the Americas Have a Common Literature?* includes essays that deal with Brazil and Québec. David T. Haberly argues in "Form and Function in the New World Legend," that the legend "was of fundamental importance in explorations of the past throughout the Americas . . .

and that the nature and requirements of that form . . . imposed a remarkable degree of uniformity upon those explorations."[18] Examining works by Washington Irving, José de Alencar of Brazil, and Mexico's Justo Sierra, Haberly shows how central the role of history is to the development of literature in the Americas, how "the creation of historical or pseudohistorical frames, the seamless mixing of history and parahistory, the disconcerting juxtaposition of reality and fantasy" have all played fundamental roles in fomenting a particular "New World" consciousness about the relation of the past to the present.[19]

In another essay in the same volume, René Prieto compares and contrasts the poetics of a Cuban avant-garde narrativist and a Québecois feminist poet: "[Severo] Sarduy and [Nicole] Brossard set out to transgress the canonical formulas of the art they practice." Focusing on the malaise of the postcolonial condition that he believes permeates their work, and asking whether their "unswerving iconoclasm" evolves "in a direction that is distinctively American," Prieto finds that what Sarduy and Brossard have in common as American authors "is that their own version of the tale of rejection is dramatized as an erotic metaphor which brings together body and language," an argument that might also be extended to the work of the Brazilian narrativist Clarice Lispector.[20]

Because Québec's situation is comparable in many ways to that of Latin America, particularly with respect to the impacts felt from the regional predominance of English-language culture, more Pan American studies integrating Québecois literature with both Brazilian and Spanish American literature are likely. Indeed, both *Confluences littéraires: Brésil, Québec, les bases d'une comparaison*, edited by Michel Peterson and Zila Bernd (1992), and the Fall 1994 issue of the periodical *Canadian Literature* take this approach. In one important respect, an earlier work—Ronald Sutherland's *Second Image: Comparative Studies in Québec/Canadian Literature* (1971)—established a basis for comparative Pan American study, including and excluding Québec. For Sutherland, Canadian comparative literary study represents part of a larger process by which the nation must come to grips with the multiplicity of its own identity. There is a parallel for Latin America, whose national components have been the infrequent subject of comparative analysis, particularly with reference to Brazil. Emir Rodríguez Monegal is one of the few[21] who have attempted to integrate Brazil into a larger inter-American approach to literature:

It cannot yet be said that there is a cohesive Latin American literature, at least in the continental sense. There is, rather, a continental literature in process, an ongoing development. . . . Despite their common peninsular origin, Spanish America and Brazil have always been separate and apart, since the first days of the discovery and conquest of the New World.[22]

Rodríguez Monegal's Borzoi Anthology, a seminal two-volume work, has been instrumental in helping to bridge the gap between Spanish Americanists and Brazilianists. Of his methodology in selecting the Brazilian and Spanish

American texts to be included in the collection, Rodríguez Monegal declares that for "the normal diachronic perspective used in literary history I have substituted a synchronic model in which texts produced in different times and circumstances are brought together to form a coherent and unified whole," one in which "an integrated image of a whole continent will at long last be possible."[23] Two books in particular build on the *Borzoi Anthology*, Lois Parkinson Zamora's *Writing the Apocalypse: Historical Vision in Contemporary U.S. and Latin American Fiction* and Renata R. Mautner Wasserman's *Exotic Nations: Literature and Cultural Identity in the United States and Brazil, 1830–1930*. The former, which explains the significance that the apocalypse[24] has for certain postmodern writers in North and South America, undertakes a comparative analysis of themes and narrative techniques in works by Gabriel García Márquez, Thomas Pynchon, Julio Cortázar, John Barth, Walker Percy, and Carlos Fuentes. Merging the artistic and the political, Zamora contends that

the pressures of national identity and political self-definition in Latin America differ greatly from those in the United States, and, with the exception of the U.S. South, those pressures have recently served as subject for literature in Latin America for a far greater extent that in the United States.

It is in this sociopolitical context that Zamora finds "the basic difference in the use of the myth of apocalypse in contemporary Latin American and U.S. literature":

Whereas visions of apocalypse in U.S. fiction focus primarily on *individual* identity or narrative strategy, they are more often used in Latin American fiction as a means of expressing the *communal* realities of historical identity.... There is an essentially different proportion of the personal to the political, of the subjective to the political, in contemporary U.S. and Latin American fiction.[25]

Wasserman's study concentrates on relations between the United States and Brazil, a pairing not seen since the appearance, in the heyday of Pan Americanism, of Samuel Putnam's *Marvelous Journey*. It is Wasserman's thesis that in the decades following political independence, both Brazil and the United States sought through their novels to establish a national identity, both adopting but at the same time departing from the ways they were viewed by their European forebears. Devoting much of her attention to novels by James Fenimore Cooper and José de Alencar, and taking into account the pervasive influence of French masters Jean-Jacques Rousseau, Bernardin de Saint-Pierre, René de Chateaubriand, and others, Wasserman argues that while such issues as "wilderness" play similar roles in the formative years of Brazil and the United States, another issue, miscegenation, dramatically marks their differences. Like Zamora's study, Wasserman's book clearly demonstrates the value of closely argued comparisons (including the crucial contrasts) between a limited number of "New World" literatures.[26]

By focusing only on the United States and Brazil, Wasserman pursues her argument with greater depth, analysis, and textual evidence than she might otherwise have done had she broadened her coverage to other national literatures. Nevertheless, it is imperative that scholars reach beyond two-nation studies in inter-American literature. To do otherwise distorts the field's enormous potential for meaningful study and sets up the kind of cultural hegemony that has made the investigation of "different" literatures so difficult in other parts of the world. Although it is true that scholarship involving the literatures of the United States and Spanish America is the most prevalent variety of inter-American research,[27] with Canadian and Latin American being the least cultivated, we should not allow ourselves to believe that this is the only, or most efficacious, way to examine literary relations between the Americas.

A broad range of topics might inform the ongoing expansion of inter-American literary study toward a systematic, comprehensive and methodologically profound field.[28] These include Native literatures; the novel of the land; the immigrant novel; the concept of the West and westward movement in the Americas; the "new novel" of the 1960s; translation; nineteenth-century poetry in the Americas; a comparative assessment of Whitman's influence in the Americas; fin-de-siècle poetry in the Americas; a history of drama as it has evolved in the "New World," a comparative study of colonial literature in the Americas; a summary of inter-American literary relations, from the earliest times to the present day; a reassessment of American literary history (from an inter-American point of view); the concept of "mirage" as it pertains to inter-American literature and culture; the use of drama during and after the era of conquest; and, finally, the differing attitudes of Catholics and Protestants toward Natives.

These topics range considerably in theme, genre, and period, but what they share is a common applicability to the American experience. The concept of the "new novel," for example, is well-known in the context of Spanish America and increasingly in Brazilian literature. Less well known outside the field of Spanish American literature, however, is the debt it owes to the modern narrative tradition of the United States, especially William Faulkner. Chilean novelist José Donoso wrote, in *Una historia personal del boom*, that several writers from the United States and elsewhere had served as models for aspiring Spanish American novelists who wished to liberate their narratives from the confines of rote realism. Other writers and critics, including Argentina's Jorge Luis Borges (who translated Faulkner's *The Wild Palms* in 1940), Peru's Mario Vargas Llosa, and Colombia's Gabriel García Márquez, have often reiterated how much Faulkner in particular meant to them. More recently, the impact of the "new novel" on Margaret Atwood and other U.S. and Canadian authors has been far-reaching. The *nueva novela* helped to establish Spanish America as a major international literary player. Beginning in the 1960s, writers and critics in the United States and Canada began to take notice of the new Spanish American narrative.[29] In a pair of now-famous essays—"The Literature of Exhaustion" and "The Literature of Replenishment"—John Barth discusses the influence of Borges and other Spanish American authors on his own development as a writer. Another eminent critic, Canada's Linda Hutcheon, has examined the impact that Spanish American "magical realism" has had on the evolution of the modern English Canadian novel. What is there about magical realism that has made it so attractive to an entire generation of English Canadian narrativists?

Like its Latin American counterpart, the novel of Québec during the 1960s was characterized by a determination to free itself, formally and thematically, from the traditions represented by its predecessors and from conventional novelistic techniques. The Québecois novel, a vital part of the "Quiet Revolution," became an instrument of protest and cultural liberation. Using self-conscious first-person narrators and often focusing on the political and ontological implications of the act of writing, authors like Anne Hébert, Gérard Bessette, and Réjean Ducharme dispensed with traditional concepts of plot, character, style, and structure. Although the history of the Latin American "new novel" is well known, there is still a need for a comparative study of the political and other implications of this iconoclastic form as practiced in Canada, particularly in Québec—a culture that has much in common with the nations of Spanish America and with Brazil.

The current field of inter-American literature owes much of its conceptual foundation to the Pan Americanism of the 1930s and 1940s, a movement that can be regarded as its intellectual progenitor. Even so, as inter-American literary studies are proliferating, many of the objections to Bolton's 1933 thesis are being repeated today by critics of the more ample approach to American literature. Just as the Mexican philosopher Edmundo O'Gorman regarded Bolton's view of an intercontinental America unified by a common historical experience as illusory, so too does the contemporary Cuban poet Roberto Fernández Retamar argue that U.S. and Latin American literatures are incongruous. While the historical and political realities of the United States and its American neighbors differ tremendously, it is also true that in spite of these differences they share many things. Moreover, the objections raised by scholars like O'Gorman and Fernández Retamar seem to stem from a common misconception about the comparative method—namely, that a comparison can be successfully carried out only if there are sufficient similarities between the objects studied. In fact, the most useful and revealing comparative studies tend to be those that—after establishing the common ground that connects two or more objects (in this case, literary texts, authors, or literary traditions)—take pains to explicate the differences between them, these differences being the qualities that make each work of art (or culture) unique. We do not need to insist that things be identical, or even mostly similar, in order to study them together. At stake is not whether we can legitimately attempt broadly comparative studies, but how well we design and execute such analyses, and how conscious we are of the complexities involved. If we exact rigorous methodologies (perhaps alternating binary studies with those that are more comprehensive), if we do our historical and cultural homework (including that relating to the various literary histories of the Americas), and if we pay proper attention to the differences that inform this area of study, then the future of inter-American comparatism, the literary analogue of Pan Americanism, is very bright indeed.

NOTES

1. George W. Umphrey, "Spanish American Literature Compared with That of the United States," *Hispania* 26 (February 1943): 21–34. See also Owen Aldridge, *Early American Literature: A Comparatist Approach* (Princeton, 1982).

2. Fernando Alegría, *Walt Whitman en Hispanoamérica* (Mexico City, 1954). Whitman's influence in the Americas deserves more comprehensive study. Although his impact on Brazil and Spanish America is well-known—see Gay Allen and Ed Folson, eds., *Walt Whitman and the World* (Iowa City, 1995), and Sylvia Molloy, "His America, Our America: José Martí Reads Whitman," *Modern Language Quarterly* 57 (1996): 369–79)—Whitman's presence in Canadian literature is not nearly as well understood.

3. See also Eva-Marie Kröller, "Comparative Canadian Literature: Notes on its Definition and Method," *Canadian Review of Comparative Literature* 6 (Spring 1979): 139–50.

4. Robert K. Martin, "North of the Border: Whose Postnationalism?", *American Literature* 65, no. 2 (June 1993): 361.

5. Karl Kroeber, "Deconstructionist Criticism and American Indian Literature," *Boundary* 27, no. 3 (Spring 1979): 73–92; Brian Swann, ed., *Smoothing the Ground: Essays on Native American Oral Literature* (Berkeley, 1983).

6. Octavio Paz, "Reflections: Mexico and the United States," *New Yorker*, 17 September 1979, p. 40.

7. Karl Kroeber, "The Wolf Comes: Indian Poetry and Linguistic Criticism," in Swann, 98, 104.

8. See Arthur Quinn, *A New World: An Epic of Colonial America from the Founding of Jamestown to the Fall of Quebec* (Boston, 1994); Lester D. Langley, *The Americas in the Age of Revolution, 1750–1850* (New Haven, 1997).

9. Larry Shouldice, "Wide Latitudes: Comparing New World Literature," *Canadian Review of Comparative Literature* 17 (March 1982): 46–55; Martin, 358–61.

10. Martin, 359.

11. Emphasizing the need to "highlight differences," Martin notes the need for "a joint study of the colonial period," the interconnections that exist between Canadian literature and that of the United States, the identities of Native American authors and studies that investigate "Margaret Atwood's indebtedness to Perry Miller," the "claustrophobic world of Faulkner's South and that of Marie-Claire Blais's Québec." See Martin, 360–61.

12. José David Saldívar, "The Dialectics of Our America," in *Do the Americas Have a Common Literature?*, edited by Gustavo Pérez Firmat (Durham, 1990), 77.

13. Werner Sollors, *Beyond Ethnicity: Consent and Descent in American Culture* (New York, 1986), 15.

14. Saldívar, 78.

15. Bell Gale Chevigny and Gary Laguardia, *Reinventing the American: Comparative Studies of Literature of the United States and Spanish America* (New York, 1986), 3.

16. Ibid., 3–4.

17. Gustavo Pérez Firmat, *Do the Americas Have a Common Literature?* (Durham, 1990), 3–4.

18. David T. Haberly, "Form and Function in the New World Legend," in Firmat, 42.

19. Ibid. In another essay from the same volume, "The Usable Past: The Idea of History in Modern U.S. and Latin American Fiction," Lois Parkinson Zamora argues that the New World possesses a unique historical consciousness, one that manifests itself in several of the American national literatures. Another singular work in this regard is Eduardo Galeano's three-volume masterpiece, *Memoria del fuego* (Montevideo, 1986), a narrative that merges history with literature and that, in the process, systematically integrates the stories of North, Central, and South America. Finally, V. S. Naipaul's *A Way in the World* (New York, 1994) also entwines history and fiction in telling a story that involves New World nations.

20. René Prieto, "In-Fringe: The Role of French Criticism in the Fiction of Nicole Brossard and Severo Sarduy," in Firmat, 267, 280.

21. See also Renata Mautner Wasserman, "Mario Vargas Llosa, Euclides da Cunha, and the Strategy of Intertextuality" *Proceedings of the Modern Language Association* 108, no. 3 (May 1993): 460–73.

22. Emir Rodríguez Monegal, *The Borzoi Anthology of Latin American Literature* (New York, 1984), xii.

23. Ibid., xv.

24. See also Sherrill E. Grace, *Regression and Apocalypse: Studies in North American Literary Expressionism* (Toronto, 1989).

25. Lois Parkinson Zamora, *Writing the Apocalypse: Historical Vision in Contemporary U.S. and Latin American Fiction* (Cambridge, England, 1989), 179.

26. Renata R. Moutner Wasserman, *Exotic Nations: Literature and Cultural Identity in the United States and Brazil, 1830–1930* (Ithaca, 1994).

27. See, for example, Deborah Cohn, "To See or Not to See: Invisibility, Clairvoyance, and Re-Visions of History in *Invisible Man* and *La casa de los espíritus*," *Comparative Literature Studies* 33, no. 4 (1996): 372–95.

28. See also Earl E. Fitz, *Rediscovering the New World: Inter-American Literature in a Comparative Context* (Iowa City, 1991).

29. See Emir Rodríguez Monegal, *El boom de la novela latinoamericana* (Caracas, 1972); Paul Dixon, *Reversible Readings* (Tuscaloosa, 1985).

13

The Myth of Pan Americanism: U.S. Policy toward Latin America during the Cold War, 1954–1963

Stephen M. Streeter

After World War II, Pan Americanism became virtually synonymous with the Organization of American States (OAS), a multilateral institution established in 1948 to govern the inter-American system under a series of treaties. In the 1950s and 1960s, the OAS became embroiled in controversies over Washington's attempts to roll back leftist revolutions in Latin America, especially in Guatemala and Cuba.[1] As Latin American nationalism surged in these turbulent decades, the credibility of Pan Americanism suffered greatly. The scholar Gordon Connell-Smith, for example, described Pan Americanism as "no more than a cloak for . . . 'Yankee imperialism.' "[2] Another commentator concluded that "the primary purpose of the OAS has been to cloak and thereby legitimize the predominant role of the United States in the settlement of most hemispheric conflicts."[3] Chilean socialists denounced the OAS as a "tool and agent of North American imperialism."[4]

Defenders of Pan Americanism responded by denying that the United States dominated the inter-American system during the Cold War. These commentators generally blamed Latin American members of the OAS for failing to rally against the communist threat, especially in Cuba.[5] A few studies also contended that for many Latin Americans, Pan Americanism actually served as a rhetorical device to challenge U.S. imperialism. The scholar Tom Farer, for example, has maintained that Latin American leaders "devised the institutions of the Inter-American System not to legitimate but rather to contain American power."[6]

The recent declassification of records of the Eisenhower and Kennedy administrations permits scholars to reassess Pan Americanism from a new angle. This essay will contrast the public and private statements of U.S. policy makers from 1954 to 1963, a crucial period that spans the U.S. intervention in Guatemala and the formation of the Alliance for Progress (AFP), a $20-billion development assistance program for Latin America. The evidence sampled here suggests that during the Cold War U.S. officials used Pan Americanism to dampen Latin American criticisms of the United States and to convince the U.S. public to support Washington's economic and military aid programs in Latin America. In short, Pan Americanism served as a hegemonic myth that justified U.S. imperialism.[7]

Imperialism has been defined as "the imposition of control by a powerful nation over other peoples and regions to the point that they lose their freedom to determine their own lives."[8] Such control can be achieved by "force, by political collaboration, by economic, social, or cultural dependence."[9] Hegemony, a Gramscian concept that emphasizes cultural and ideological forms of domination, helps to explain how Pan Americanism functioned to perpetuate U.S. imperialism: Pan Americanism "is expressed in universal norms, institutions and mechanisms which lay down general rules of behaviour for states and those forces of civil society that act across national boundaries—rules which support the dominant mode of production."[10] Through Pan Americanism

the fiction of hemispheric solidarity is shored up by constant and powerful rhetoric about partnership against external, un-American threats and about shared goals of freedom and democracy. Continued U.S. dominance is bolstered by Pan Americanism and a vision of a unitary America.[11]

Declassified policy guidelines reveal that Washington sought in Latin America, as it did in the Third World generally, Cold War allies, military bases, raw materials, open markets, free trade, foreign investment, and political stability. Such hegemonic goals obviously could not be announced publicly, but Pan Americanism provided the perfect guise for attacking real and perceived communist and nationalist threats to U.S. interests.[12] Eisenhower and Kennedy administration officials could equate U.S. and Latin American interests because they believed that all Americans shared common economic, political, social, and religious ideals, including a strong belief in democracy, justice, freedom, human rights, progress, and free-market capitalism. U.S. Ambassador to the OAS John C. Dreier, for example, celebrated Columbus Day 1954 by asserting that Columbus's "discovery" represented "the first great historical fact which all the peoples of North and South America share in common."[13] A few months later Secretary of State John Foster Dulles announced that the inter-American system envisioned by Simon Bolívar had finally been realized in the "family tree of America—its multiple roots deep in our common New World history—its 21 branches each a proud, independent nation, its rich fruits beneficial to all mankind."[14] To persuade members of the U.S. Congress and Latin American diplomats to support the AFP, President Kennedy declared that our continents are bound together by a common history, the endless exploration of new frontiers. Our nations are the product of a common struggle, the revolt from colonial rule. And our people share a common heritage, the quest for the dignity and the freedom of man.[15]

Secretary of State Dean Rusk assured Americans that the Alliance rested on "those indissoluble ties of geography and history, of common culture and common interest, which have always bound our nations together."[16]

Nearly all of these history lessons rested on some version of the Monroe Doctrine. In 1823 President James Monroe unilaterally appointed the United States the watchdog of the hemisphere and warned European powers to stay out. The Monroe Doctrine, which served thereafter to justify numerous U.S. military interventions in Central America and the Caribbean, fostered bitter resentment in Latin America. Although the Good Neighbor policy of Franklin D. Roosevelt briefly eased inter-American tensions, many Latin Americans did not forgive the U.S. for big stick diplomacy. One Mexican writer described the Monroe Doctrine as a "wrapper concealing . . . the ambitions of a strong people who claim to exercise hegemony over a group of weak peoples, giving to their domination over them the hypocritical appearances of disinterest and benevolence." According to the Bolivian diplomat Raúl Diez de Medina, "The Monroe Doctrine did not create Pan-Americanism, but, on the contrary, it arrested the Bolivarian Pan-Americanism of equal rights and mutual obligations."[17]

During the Cold War, U.S. officials frequently turned to Pan Americanism to counter charges of "Yankee imperialism." Assistant Secretary of State for Inter-American Affairs Roy R. Rubottom, Jr., for example, compared previous U.S. interventions in Latin America to the blundering of a "well-intentioned neighbor" who tries to settle a domestic dispute between a wife and husband but ends up alienating both of them.[18] The shifting of responsibility for collective hemispheric defense from the United States to the OAS, through the Treaty of Rio de Janeiro (1947) and the Caracas Declaration (1954), emerged as a common theme in speeches on Pan Americanism. These treaties endorsed the principle of hemispheric unity against "external aggression" in countries like Guatemala, which, according to Washington, had barely escaped a Soviet-backed communist takeover in 1954.[19]

The idea that the Americas shared common ideals based on Enlightenment values of democracy, justice, and human rights flowed from the belief that most nations in the hemisphere had liberated themselves from European colonialism in order to establish less tyrannical forms of government. The "inter-American way of life," explained Assistant Secretary Rubottom to the Milwaukee Foreign Policy Institute, remains strong because "we believe in representative democracy based on free elections, not in government imposed by threat or intimidation."[20] President Kennedy pledged allegiance to the OAS charter, which demanded "social justice based on respect for the essential rights of man."[21] He proclaimed before the OAS council that "in the end our moral unity as a family of nations rests on the ultimate faith that only governments which guarantee human freedoms, respect human rights, and vindicate human liberties can advance human progress."[22]

The economic component of Pan Americanism represents an ideology described by the historian Emily Rosenberg as "liberal developmentalism." After World War II, inter-governmental agencies such as the International Cooperation Administration, the World Bank, and the U.S. Information Agency began promoting the idea that "other nations could and should replicate America's own developmental experience." Liberal developmentalism, in essence, replaced the "Open Door," Washington's earlier metaphor for free trade and investment opportunities.[23] Once again, U.S. officials drew upon a mythical past to convince their audiences that Latin America should welcome foreign investment and free trade. Assistant Secretary Rubottom, addressing a banquet of the International Institute for Education in Houston, Texas, recalled that the United States had industrialized by encouraging foreign investment: "The money poured in—pounds, francs, guilders, marks, lire, and pesos, too—hundreds of millions. We developed, and they made profit." Surprisingly, "we never found the foreign investors to be an impediment to the full exercise of our freedom or our sovereignty."[24] President Kennedy informed a group of Brazilian students in 1963, "I don't think that the United States would ever have been developed without foreign capital."[25]

However, a comparison of U.S. policy makers' rhetoric with historical reality exposes numerous fallacies in Pan Americanism. The notion that the Americas had a common history, though popular briefly before World War II, had few scholarly adherents by the 1950s. Critics pointed out that this hypothesis erased vast linguistic, religious, and cultural differences. It also ignored widely divergent developmental paths. One historian demolished the geographical basis for Pan Americanism by the simple observation that Madison, Wisconsin lay closer to most European capitals than to Buenos Aires.[26] U.S. officials also drew selectively on Latin American history to support their version of Pan Americanism. When invoking Simon Bolívar as a founder of Pan Americanism, they conveniently omitted his prophetic warning that the United States "seemed destined by Providence to invest America with wretchedness in the name of Liberty."[27] Nor did they recall that the Cuban patriot José Martí, whom they cited as a great defender of liberty and freedom, also assailed the "menace of United States imperialism" and rejected Pan Americanism in favor of Pan Hispanism.[28]

The central assumption of liberal developmentalism—that the United States developed through open markets and free trade policies—is not sustained by the historical record. After reviewing the impact of nineteenth-century commercial policies in various developed and underdeveloped countries, economic historian Paul Bairoch concluded that the United States represented "the mother country and bastion of modern protectionism."[29] Many U.S. leaders ascertained correctly that high tariffs would promote industrialization. One scholarly study estimates that the removal of the tariff from the cotton textile industry "would have reduced value added in textiles by, at a minimum, three-quarters," thereby bankrupting "about half of the industrial sector of New England."[30] In the late nineteenth century, the United States skillfully employed tariffs and reciprocity treaties to wrest control of Latin American markets from Great Britain. During the first half of the twentieth century, Washington made no principled commitment to the so-called Open Door policy. The United States shut the door to European competition in the Caribbean and the Middle East and never acted as if it were "motivated by some general belief in the magic of the market place." U.S. citizens "tolerated and even encouraged . . . government intervention in economic affairs."[31]

Foreign investment played a relatively minor role in U.S. industrialization, accounting for less than five percent of capital formation during the nineteenth century. Only after establishing itself as the supreme leader in the world market did the United States begin to lift some of its protectionist measures. Dependency and world systems analysts have maintained that strict adherence to the free trade doctrine after World War II doomed Third World countries to exchanging strategic raw materials and agricultural commodities for U.S. manufactured goods. The Economic Commission on Latin America (ECLA), for example, insisted that without a system of industrial protection similar to that enjoyed by the United States during its own period of industrialization, domestic industries in Latin America could not survive foreign competition in the postwar period. Yet State Department officials scorned ECLA and subverted its proposal for protecting infant industries under the Central American economic integration treaties. U.S. delegates to the 1963 meeting of the Inter-American Economic and Social Council also blocked Brazil's proposal to create a permanent Latin American coordinating committee to the UN Conference on Trade and Development. Brazil's "extreme positions" on trade and its bid for leadership in Latin America, Governor W. Averell Harriman alerted Washington, would threaten U.S. hegemony in the hemisphere.[32]

Contradictions and inconsistencies also plague the political component of Pan Americanism. The State Department's assertion that the United States finally began to honor the Good Neighbor policy after World War II, for example, is well described by what one social critic calls "the change of course." Whatever unintentional errors or sins the United States committed against Latin America in the past were explained away because the so-called great benefactor had seen the light and mended its ways.[33] Officials such as George F. Kennan, head of the State Department's policy planning staff, spoke more honestly in private. In 1950, Kennan advocated "harsh governmental measures of resistance" in Latin American countries where communism seemed to threaten. "It is better to have a strong regime in power," he explained, "than a liberal government if it is indulgent and relaxed and penetrated by Communists." By "communists," Kennan meant labor leaders, peasant organizers, priests, self-help groups, and virtually anyone in Latin America who opposed the status quo.[34] Kennan's willingness to abandon democracy comes as no surprise, given his realist approach to foreign policy. Because "we have about 50 percent of the world's wealth, but only 6.3 percent of its population," he warned, the United States will naturally become "the object of envy and resentment." To keep the wealth, we cannot "afford today the luxury of altruism and world-benefaction" or the pursuit of "vague and unreal objectives such as human rights, the raising of living standards, and democratization." The State Department should deal in "straight power concepts," Kennan recommended, because "the less we are then hampered by idealistic slogans, the better."[35]

Such Machiavellian confessions of raw power often coincided with admonitions about the need to promote democracy and human rights. Nonetheless, most U.S. officials distinguished clearly between propaganda and hard-headed policy. U.S. Secretary of the Treasury George Humphrey hammered the question at a high-level National Security Council meeting in December 1954: "We should . . . stop talking so much about democracy, and make it clear that we are quite willing to support dictatorships of the right if their policies are pro-American." When President Eisenhower interrupted the secretary to ask, "You mean they're OK if they're our s.o.b.'s[?]" Humphrey agreed, and then added that the United States "was being much too idealistic in its relations with other nations. Whatever we may choose to say in public about ideas and idealism, among ourselves we've got to be a great deal more practical and materialistic."[36] President Kennedy's policy guideline for Latin America is strikingly similar to Kennan's:

There are three possibilities in descending order of preference: a decent democratic regime, a continuation of the [Dominican Republic's] Trujillo regime, or a Castro regime. We ought to aim at the first, but we really can't renounce the second until we are sure we can avoid the third.[37]

The consequences of these policy prescriptions surely undermined the ideals of Pan Americanism. President Eisenhower, as many studies have shown, used U.S. government agencies to plot assassinations of foreign leaders, encourage military coups, and reward dictatorships with economic and military aid. His administration also blocked OAS initiatives that would have authorized the Inter-American Commission on Human Rights to review individual cases of alleged human rights violations. President Kennedy, who spoke eloquently on democracy and human rights, continued the trend begun by his predecessor of shifting the mission of the Latin American military from hemispheric defense to internal security. The innocuous-sounding "Public Safety Program," for example, trained counterinsurgency forces in Central America that committed some of the worst human rights violations in the hemisphere. In Guatemala alone, more than 100,000 civilians perished at the hands of U.S.-trained and -equipped death squads. The Kennedy administration launched covert operations, plotted assassinations, and encouraged military coups in at least half a dozen Latin American countries.[38]

The sharp contrast between the rhetoric of Pan Americanism and the historical reality raises the question of whether U.S. officials truly believed the myth they were propagating. Doubts about Pan Americanism did surface occasionally. An intelligence report, for example, warned of "the increasing tendency of Latin Americans to look towards Pan Latin Americanism instead of toward Pan Americanism."[39] By the late 1950s, U.S. officials had learned that the Monroe Doctrine could not be mentioned casually in front of Latin American audiences. When U.S. congressional leaders suggested invoking the Monroe Doctrine to justify ending aid to Cuba in 1958, President Eisenhower demurred, pointing out that "our neighbors . . . resist the unilateral nature of the Monroe Doctrine."[40] President Kennedy, despite unrelenting pressure from his hawkish critics, declined to publicize the Monroe Doctrine as the basis for intervening in Cuba, probably because he feared offending members of the OAS.

Latin American resistance to Washington's policies exposed many of the fallacies of Pan Americanism, but U.S. diplomats proved to be remarkably insular. Washington seemed entirely unprepared for the vitriolic reception that Vice President Richard M. Nixon received during his 1958 tour through South America. Unruly demonstrators, angered by Washington's coddling of dictators such as Venezuelan dictator Marcos Perez Jimenez, spat at Nixon and threw stones at his motorcade, nearly killing him in Caracas.[41] Although the backlash against Nixon sparked a debate within the Eisenhower administration about its Latin American policy, officials continued to blame social unrest on communist agitators. They did not consider the danger grave enough to reexamine the premises of Pan Americanism. Certain officials in the Kennedy administration appeared equally obtuse about the depth of discontent in Latin America. In 1962, for example, Undersecretary of State for Economic Affairs George Ball dedicated a new bridge in the Panama Canal Zone with flattering prose about the "creative spirit of common endeavor" and the "enduring partnership between our sister Republics." Carried away by his own rapturous exposition of Pan Americanism, he seemed unaware that someone in the crowd just might remember that three years earlier U.S. troops had wounded or killed more than 120 Panamanian students for trying to plant their national flag in the Canal Zone.[42]

Many U.S. officials failed to grasp the depth of anti-Americanism in Latin America because their own propaganda efforts insulated them from the unpleasant reality. The Eisenhower administration's attempt to rally the hemisphere against the leftist government of Guatemala in 1954, for example, illustrates that the OAS voting record could be misleading. At the Tenth Conference of America States in Caracas, Secretary Dulles wrangled with Guatemalan Foreign Minister Guillermo Toriello Garrido over the passage of an anticommunist resolution that never mentioned Guatemala by name but which obviously targeted the Jacobo Arbenz administration. The key sentence in the resolution read: "The domination or control of the political institutions of any American state by the international communist movement . . . would constitute a threat to the sovereignty and political independence of the American States."[43] The Eisenhower administration hoped to use the Caracas resolution to invoke Article 6 of the Rio Treaty of

1947, which sanctioned punishment of any American state after two-thirds of the OAS members voted that the accused had committed "aggression which is not an armed attack."[44]

After days of acrimonious debate and "arm twisting" by the United States, the Caracas resolution passed 17 to 1, with 2 abstentions. Guatemala stood alone in opposition; Argentina and Mexico abstained. Yet Dulles had not won the hearts, or even the minds, of most Latin Americans. The delegates cheered the speeches of Toriello, who castigated the United States for trying to undermine Guatemalan sovereignty. To Mexican jurist Isidro Fabela, the Caracas resolution represented an "assault on the principle of nonintervention which is the keystone of Pan Americanism." Most Latin American nations supported the Caracas resolution only because they feared economic reprisals.[45] The State Department reacted to these criticisms by organizing a public relations campaign to cover up the CIA's role in removing Arbenz. President Eisenhower announced at the Illinois State Fair that Guatemalans "rose up and rejected the Communist doctrine, and said in the terms of the spirit of the agreement at Caracas, 'You shall not come here and establish yourselves.' "[46] Secretary Dulles ordered U.S. embassies throughout the world to deny all allegations that the United States had supplied arms to the Guatemalan rebels. The U.S. Information Agency devoted itself to promoting the view that under Arbenz, Guatemala had become a "metastasizing cancer."[47]

When the cover-up failed, angry demonstrations and protests erupted throughout Latin America against the U.S. intervention in Guatemala. U.S. officials blamed communist agitators who had allegedly duped Latin American nationalists into attacking the United States and Pan Americanism.[48] Ambassador Dreier warned:

If either communism on the one hand or fanatic nationalism on the other—or the two working together—should ever capture any considerable portion of the population of this continent, the possibility of our achieving the high purposes of inter-American cooperation would indeed be dim.[49]

After touring South America, President Eisenhower reported:

On occasion I heard it said that economic advance in some American Republics only makes the rich richer and the poor poorer, and the United States should take the initiative in correcting this evil. This is a view fomented by communists, but often repeated by well meaning people.[50]

President Kennedy, shaken by the Cuban missile crisis and the popularity of Marxist leader Cheddi Jagan of British Guyana, came to regard Latin America as "the most dangerous area in the world."[51] In 1962 Washington prodded the OAS into creating the Special Consultative Committee on Security Against the Subversive Action of International Communism.[52]

Although U.S. officials exaggerated the communist threat, they did not lose track of reality. In 1958, the CIA estimated that there were only 200,000 communists in all of Latin America.[53] Throughout the 1950s and 1960s U.S. intelligence reports judged the Communist Party to be incapable of seizing power anywhere in the hemisphere outside Cuba. Political instability throughout Latin America, one study commented, "is the product of fundamental inequities and historic circumstances; it is not the creation of Castro and the Soviets." A much more serious problem was "the attractiveness of the Cuban example." If the "growth of indigenous, noncommunist, radical nationalism" continued unchecked, CIA intelligence analysts predicted in early 1962, "the U.S. freedom of action will probably become increasingly restricted."[54]

Unable to face reasons for anti-Americanism, some U.S. officials tried to deny the problem. Kennedy administration aide Arthur Schlesinger regarded the Punta del Este conference in 1962 as a "substantial success" because the United States had managed to obtain several resolutions against Cuba.[55] "Everyone went home reasonably well satisfied," recalled U.S. participant Walt W. Rostow. OAS members, in his opinion, had demonstrated their "ultimate loyalty to the Inter-American system."[56] Opposition to the U.S. stand was attributed to the evil forces of communism. U.S. Representative to the OAS DeLesseps S. Morrison declared: "Most Latin American countries would have liked to move against the Cuban regime, but [they] feared to do so, some because Fidelismo elements at home might be stirred up, others because they might be denounced as lackeys of the United States."[57]

Most studies of the Punta del Este conference suggest that dissension rather than unity on the Cuban issue prevailed. U.S. representatives had to twist the arms of reluctant OAS members who upheld the principle of nonintervention, raised legal technicalities, and questioned the seriousness of the Cuban threat. "We achieved our aims," one U.S. participant confessed, "by the toughest cracking of skulls reminiscent of the days of the big stick." Several Latin American foreign ministers complained that the United States had threatened to cut off foreign aid to their countries if they did not oppose Cuba.[58] A similar pattern of self-interested deception can be found in the Kennedy administration conviction that Pan Americanism had triumphed when the OAS voted unanimously to support President Kennedy's request for a quarantine of Cuba during the Cuban missile crisis. "I didn't have to twist arms or bludgeon anyone," Secretary of State Dean Rusk remembered.[59] A State Department legal expert concluded that "all in all, the record shows that, although the Organ of Consultation, like every parliamentary assembly, was not an assemblage of equals, it was neither supine nor a rubber stamp for a United States initiative."[60]

Many Latin American leaders grew alarmed that the confrontation between Castro and Kennedy threatened to drag the hemisphere into a nuclear holocaust. When the crisis struck, most members of the OAS were already turning against Castro, in part because his adherence to Marxist doctrine, which he had announced in December 1961, disturbed Latin America's socially conservative diplomatic corps. Nevertheless, Latin America hardly rallied behind the United States during the Cuban missile crisis. The Kennedy administration interpretation of the Cuban missile crisis glosses over the hostile reaction in Latin America to the Bay of Pigs invasion in April 1961. In several Latin American capitals, pro-Cuba rallies defended Castro and denounced the United States for violating Cuban sovereignty. The historian Thomas G. Paterson points out that had the United States not sought to destroy the Cuban revolution by military invasion and sabotage, the Cuban missile crisis probably could have been avoided.[61] In addition, at the time of the crisis, most Latin American diplomats preferred that Kennedy negotiate a trade with the Jupiter missiles in Turkey rather than raise the level of the confrontation by imposing a quarantine.[62]

Illusions about Pan Americanism also persisted because officials tended to exaggerate the advances being made in economic development and human rights in Latin America. Assistant Secretary of State for Inter-American Affairs Henry Holland, for example, declared in 1955 that "some of us are passing through temporary periods of adversity, but there are no cripples among us. There is not a stagnant economy in the hemisphere. On all sides there is activity and progress."[63] Secretary Dulles lectured skeptics at the Pan American Union:

If there be any who believe that inter-American solidarity is something at which we toss bouquets of words every April 14 and forget for the rest of the year, it would be well for them to look at the record. It is a continuous advancing record of positive accomplishment resulting from day-by-day efforts. It shows our united determination to make America a happier, better home for Americans.[64]

In 1963, President Kennedy informed the Central American ministers (nearly all of them representing dictatorships): "Democracy rules in most of our lands. It will prevail over the last vestiges of tyranny in every land in this hemisphere."[65] A year later, U.S. Representative to the United Nations Adlai E. Stevenson alleged that in several Latin American countries "the army is proving [to be] democracy's strongest bulwark and most constructive promoter."[66] That U.S. officials could so easily ignore the tragic consequences of equipping and training the Latin American military should not be surprising. As the anthropologist Leigh Binford has observed, "Capacity for cynicism . . . varies directly with rank within a hierarchy of power; those least likely to be touched by suffering are also those most insulated (by social and economic distance) from it."[67]

Shunning responsibility for the failures of Pan Americanism, many U.S. officials practiced "blame the victim." John Moors Cabot, a foreign service officer with lifelong experience in Latin America, once explained that when Latin Americans criticized the United States, "this is the hurt of the pupil whose mentor falls below preconceived ideals. He knows that in his own country he is not likely to see so genuine a democracy." The economically frustrated Latin American "does not realize that he himself is to blame for most of his economic limitations and difficulties and he therefore turns his attack on the United States and American interests."[68] Secretary Dulles shared Cabot's paternalism. He regarded Latin Americans as "people who have practically no capacity for self-government and indeed are like children."[69]

Through all of these devices—anticommunism, denial, optimism, and paternalism—Eisenhower and Kennedy administration officials sought to rationalize the contradictions of Pan Americanism. The occasional appearance of Pan American ideals in top-secret documents suggests that at least some U.S. officials took the myth to heart, but if we adopt one prominent historian's suggestion to "judge a country's actions as much by what the *outcomes* are, as what the intentionality and the procedures for arriving at an intention (that is a decision) might have been," then it is clear that traditional U.S. hegemonic objectives overrode any consideration for humanitarian ideals.[70] This contradiction between myth and reality becomes more understandable if we recognize that the leaders of Great Powers generally believe their own propaganda. Pan Americanism, in this respect, differs little from other imperial ideologies such as social Darwinism or Orientalism.[71]

NOTES

1. Larman C. Wilson and David W. Dent, "The United States and the OAS," in *U.S.–Latin American Policymaking: A Reference Handbook*, edited by David W. Dent (Westport, 1995), 30–31.

2. Gordon Connell-Smith, *The Inter-American System* (New York, 1966), 54, 318–19.

3. Jerome Slater, *The OAS and United States Foreign Policy* (Columbus, 1967), 25–26.

4. Quoted in Heraldo Muñoz, "The International Policy of the Socialist Party and Foreign Relations of Chile," in *Latin American Nations in World Politics*, edited by Heraldo Munoz and Joseph S. Tulchin (Boulder, 1984), 159–60. Latin American works highly critical of Pan Americanism include Ezequiel Ramirez Novoa, *La farsa del pan-americanismo y la unidad indoamericana* (Buenos Aires, 1955), and Ricardo Martinez, *De Bolívar a Dulles: El Panamericanismo doctrina y práctica imperialista* (Mexico City, 1959).

5. Jesús de Galindez, *Iberoamérica: su evolución política, socio-económica cultural e internacional* (New York, 1954); Ann Van Wynen Thomas and A. J. Thomas, Jr., *The Organization of American States* (Dallas, 1963); George Meek, "U.S. Influence in the Organization of American States," *Journal of Interamerican Studies and World Affairs* 17, no. 3 (August 1975): 311–25.

6. Tom Farer, *The Grand Strategy of the United States in Latin America* (New Brunswick, 1988), 25. On the U.S. left's attempt to define Pan Americanism in a counterhegemonic fashion, see Van Gosse, *Where the Boys Are: Cuba, Cold War America and the Making of a New Left* (New York, 1993).

7. On myth in inter-American relations, see Eldon Kenworthy, *America/Americas: Myth in the Making of U.S. Policy toward Latin America* (University Park, PA, 1995);

and Mark T. Berger, *Under Northern Eyes: Latin American Studies and U.S. Hegemony in the Americas 1898–1990* (Bloomington, 1995).

8. Thomas G. Paterson and Stephen G. Rabe, *Imperial Surge: The United States Abroad the 1890s—Early 1900s* (Lexington, KY, 1992), xvi.

9. Michael W. Doyle, *Empires* (Ithaca, 1986), 45.

10. Robert W. Cox, "Gramsci, Hegemony and International Relations: An Essay in Method," *Millenium: Journal of International Studies* 12, no. 1 (Spring 1983): 172–73. See also Guy Poitras, *The Ordeal of Heremony: The United States and Latin America* (Boulder, CO, 1990); Jorge I. Domínguez, *To Make a World Safe for Revolution* (Cambridge, MA, 1989); Louis A. Pérez Jr., "Intervention, Hegemony, and Dependency: The United States in the Circum-Caribbean, 1898–1980," *Pacific Historical Review* 51 (May 1982): 165–94.

11. Berger, *Under Northern Eyes*, 18.

12. See Stephen G. Rabe, *Eisenhower and Latin America: The Foreign Policy of Anticommunism* (Chapel Hill, 1988); *Foreign Relations of the United States, 1961–1963* (Washington, 1996) (FRUS). For definitions of Pan Americanism, see J. Lloyd Mecham, *The United States and Inter-American Security, 1899–1960* (Austin, 1961), 475; Thomas L. Karnes, "Pan-Americanism," in *Encyclopedia of American Foreign Policy: Studies of the Principal Movements and Ideas*, edited by Alexander DeConde (New York, 1978), 730; David Sheinin, "Pan Americanism," in *Encyclopedia of U.S. Foreign Relations*, edited by Bruce W. Jentleson and Thomas G. Paterson (New York, 1997).

13. *Department of State Bulletin* [hereafter DSB], vol. 31 (25 October 1954), 596.

14. DSB, vol. 32 (2 May 1955), 729.

15. *Public Papers of President John F. Kennedy* (Washington, 1961), 171 [hereafter PPPJFK].

16. DSB, vol. 46 (14 May 1962), 787.

17. Quoted in Donald Marquand Dozer, ed., *The Monroe Doctrine: Its Modern Significance*, rev. ed. (Tempe, 1976), 25, 106.

18. DSB, vol. 36 (27 May 1957), 856.

19. DSB, vol. 38 (5 May 1958), 716–17; Adolf A. Berle, *Latin America: Diplomacy and Reality* (New York, 1962), 77–78; DSB, vol. 31 (25 October 1954), 597.

20. DSB, vol. 42 (4 April 1960), 520.

21. PPPJFK (1963), 873.

22. DSB, vol. 44 (1 May 1961), 616–17.

23. Emily S. Rosenberg, *Spreading the American Dream: American Economic and Cultural Expansion* (New York, 1982), 7.

24. Roy R. Rubottom, Jr., "Progress through Cooperation in Latin America," DSB, vol. 42 (22 February 1960), 286.

25. PPPJFK (1963), 608.

26. Arthur P. Whitaker, *The Western Hemisphere Idea: Its Rise and Decline* (Ithaca, 1954), 163.

27. Quoted in Lewis Hanke, ed., *Do the Americas Have a Common History? A Critique of the Bolton Theory* (New York, 1964), 26.

28. DSB, vol. 46 (2 April 1962), 539; DSB, vol. 46 (30 April 1962), 705; James Kirk, *José Martí: Mentor of the Cuban Nation* (Gainesville, 1969), 9; José Martí, *Inside the Monster: Writings on United States Imperialism* (New York, 1975).

29. Paul Bairoch, *Economics and World History: Myths and Paradoxes* (New York, 1993), 32, 54.

30. Mark Bils, "Tariff Protection and Production in the Early US Cotton Textile Industry," *Journal of Economic History* 44 (December 1984): 1033–45; D. G. Harriman, *American Tariffs from Plymouth Rock to McKinley: A Complete and Impartial History* (New York, 1892), 23–27; Susan Previant Lee and Peter Passell, *A New Economic View of American History* (New York, 1979), 88–89; Robert A. Lively, "The American System: A Review Article," *Business History Review* 34 (March 1955), 81–96.

31. Jeffrey A. Frieden, "The Economics of Intervention: American Overseas Investments and Relations with Underdeveloped Areas, 1890–1950," *Comparative Studies in Society and History* 31 (January 1989): 75; Edward P. Crapol and Howard Schonberger, "The Shift to Global Expansion 1865–1900," in *From Colony to Empire: Essays in the History of American Foreign Relations*, edited by William Appleman Williams (New York, 1972), 172–77.

32. Lance C. Davis and Robert J. Cull, *International Capital Markets and American Economic Growth 1820–1914* (Cambridge, 1994), 1; Susan Ariel Aaronson, *Trade and the American Dream: A Social History of Postwar Trade Policy* (Lexington, KY, 1996), 14–17; Thomas J. McCormick, "World Systems," in *Explaining the History of American Foreign Relations*, edited by Michael J. Hogan and Thomas G. Paterson, (Cambridge, England, 1991), 94; United Nations, *The Economic Development of Latin America in the Post-War Period* (New York, 1964), 9; United Nations, *Towards a Dynamic Development Policy for Latin America* (New York, 1963), 74; Stephen M. Streeter, "Managing the Counterrevolution: The United States and Guatemala" (Ph.D. diss., University of Connecticut, 1994), 444–49; FRUS, 1955–1957, vol. 6, 316; FRUS, 1958–1960, vol. 5, 385; FRUS, 1961–1963, vol. 12, 161–62; W. Michael Weis, *Cold Warriors & Coups D'etat: Brazilian-American Relations, 1945–1964* (Albuquerque, 1993), 164–65. For a discussion of ECLA's strategies and the failure of Latin America's "inward-looking development model" in the postwar period, see Victor Bulmer-Thomas, *The Economic History of Latin America since Independence* (Cambridge, England, 1994), 276–322.

33. Noam Chomsky, *Powers and Prospects: Reflections on Human Nature and the Social Order* (Boston, 1996), 99.

34. FRUS, 1950, vol. 2, 607; Noam Chomsky, *Deterring Democracy* (London, 1991), 49.

35. FRUS, 1948, vol. 1, 524.

36. FRUS, 1952–1954, vol. 2, 838.

37. Arthur M. Schlesinger, Jr. *A Thousand Days: John F. Kennedy in the White House* (Boston, 1965), 769.

38. Rabe, 175; Lars Schoultz, *Human Rights and United States Policy toward Latin America* (Princeton, 1981), 250; FRUS, 1958–1960, vol. 5, 348–56; Michael McClintock, *The American Connection: State Terror and Popular Resistance in Guatemala*, vol. 2 (London, 1985); Stephen G. Rabe, *The Most Dangerous Area in the World: John F. Kennedy Confronts Communist Revolution in Latin America* (Chapel Hill, 1999); William O. Walker, "Mixing the Sweet with the Sour: Kennedy, Johnson, and Latin America," in *The Diplomacy of the Crucial Decade: American Foreign Relations during the 1960s*, edited by Diane B. Kunz (New York, 1994), 42–79; Octavio Ianni, "Imperialism and Diplomacy in Inter-American Relations," in *Latin America and the United States: The Changing Political Realities*, edited by Julio Cotler and Richard R. Fagen (Stanford, 1974), 23–51; Federico G. Gil, "The Kennedy-Johnson Years," in *United States Policy in Latin America: A Quarter Century of Crisis and Challenge*, edited by John D. Martz (Lincoln, NE, 1988), 3–27.

39. FRUS, 1958–1960, vol. 114, 5.

40. FRUS, 1958–1960, vol. 114, 516–17.

41. Richard Nixon, *Six Crises* (New York, 1962), 215–77; FRUS, 1958–1960, vol. 5, 918; Marvin R. Zahinser and W. Michael Weis, "A Diplomatic Pearl Harbor? Richard Nixon's Goodwill Mission to Latin America in 1958," *Diplomatic History* 13 (Spring 1989): 163–90.

42. DSB, vol. 47 (29 October 1962), 647; Walter LaFeber, *The Panama Canal: The Crisis in Historical Perspective* (New York, 1989).

43. Department of State, *Tenth Interamerican Conference* (Washington, 1955), 157.

44. Arthur Schlesinger and Stephen Kinzer, *Bitter Fruit: The Untold Story of the American Coup in Guatemala* (New York, 1982), 142–43.

45. Quoted in Piero Gleijeses, *Shattered Hope: The Guatemalan Revolution and the United States, 1944–1954* (Princeton, 1991), 275–76.

46. Quoted in Richard H. Immerman, *The CIA in Guatemala* (Austin, 1982), 178.

47. Opal to Clark, 19 July 1954, Lots 58 D 18 and 58 D 78, box 3, folder "Guatemala 1954, USIA," Lot Files, Record Group (RG) 59, National Archives of the United States, Washington, DC (NA).

48. FRUS, 1952–1954, vol. 6, 388–389.

49. DSB, vol. 31 (25 October 1954), 599.

50. DSB, vol. 42 (28 March 1960), 471–86.

51. FRUS, 1961–1963, vol. 12, 608.

52. Lars Schoultz, *National Security and United States Policy toward Latin America* (Princeton, 1987), 134–35.

53. "OCB Report on NSC 5613/1, CIA Intelligence Annex B, Sino-Soviet Bloc Activities in Latin America," 15 April 1958, White House Office of the Special Assistant for National Security Affairs Records, NSC Series, Policy Papers Subseries, box 18, folder "NSC 5613/1 (1)," Dwight D. Eisenhower Library, Abilene, KS.

54. FRUS, 1961–1963, vol. 12, 211–212, 234. On the weakness of the Soviet threat in Latin America, see Nicola Miller, *Soviet Relations with Latin America 1959–1987* (Cambridge, MA, 1989), 220; Thomas G. Paterson, *Contesting Castro: The United States and the Triumph of the Cuban Revolution* (New York, 1994), 28.

55. Schlesinger, 783.

56. W. W. Rostow, *The Diffusion of Power: An Essay in Recent History* (New York, 1972), 221.

57. DeLesseps S. Morrison, *Latin American Mission: An Adventure in Hemisphere Diplomacy* (New York, 1965), 96.

58. John Gerassi, *The Great Fear: The Reconquest of Latin America by Latin Americans* (New York, 1963), 321–25; Morris H. Morley, *Imperial State and Revolution: The United States and Cuba, 1952–1986* (New York, 1987), 157.

59. Dean Rusk, *As I Saw It* (New York, 1990), 237.

60. Abram Chayes, *The Cuban Missile Crisis* (New York, 1974), 53.

61. Thomas G. Paterson, "Fixation with Cuba: The Bay of Pigs, Missile Crisis, and Covert War against Castro," in *Kennedy's Quest for Victory: American Foreign Policy 1961–1963* (New York, 1989), 140.

62. Barton J. Bernstein, "Reconsidering the Missile Crisis: Dealing with the Problem of the American Jupiters in Turkey," in *The Cuban Missile Crisis Revisited*, edited by James Nathan (Lexington, KY, 1992), 82.

63. DSB, vol. 33 (25 July 1955), 137–38.

64. DSB, vol. 38 (5 May 1958), 718.

65. DSB, vol. 48 (8 April 1963), 513.

66. DSB, vol. 45 (21 August 1961), 315.

67. Leigh, Binford, *The El Mozote Massacre: Anthropology and Human Rights* (Tucson, 1996), 66.

68. John Moors Cabot, *Toward Our Common Destiny: Speeches and Interviews on Latin American Problems* (Medford, 1955), 115, 120. On Cabot's paternalism, see Stephen M. Streeter, "Campaigning Against Latin American Nationalism: John Moors Cabot in Brazil, 1959–1961," *The Americas* 51 (October 1994): 193–218.

69. FRUS, 1958–1960, vol. 5, 29.

70. Bruce Cumings, " 'Revising Postrevisionism' Revisited," in *America in the World: The Historiography of American Foreign Relations since 1941*, edited by Michael J. Hogan (New York, 1995), 135–36.

71. Berger, 16; Tony Smith, *The Pattern of Imperialism: The United States, Great Britain and the Late-Industrializing World since 1815* (Cambridge, 1981), 193; Terry Eagleton, *Ideology: An Introduction* (London, England, 1991), 96–97; Edward W. Said, *Culture and Imperialism* (New York, 1993), 8–9; Noam Chomsky, "What Directions for the Disarmament Movement? Interventionism and Nuclear War," in *Beyond Survival: New Directions for the Disarmament Movement*, edited by Michael Albert and David Dellinger (Boston, 1983), 292–93.

14

Ecuador and the Organization of American States: A Less Than Perfect Union

Jeanne A. K. Hey

INTRODUCTION

An intuitive judgment of the relationship between Ecuador and the Organization of American States (OAS) would most likely conclude that the two were made for each other. The OAS is a prominent organization but unquestionably one that takes a back seat in global regional alliances, owing to its representation of mostly underdeveloped countries. The imbalance of power within the organization—namely, that the United States overwhelms other members in military and economic capabilities—further weakens the OAS's promise as an effective international organization. That said, the OAS has been the author of important agreements and treaties, not the least its recent intervention in the Peru–Ecuador border dispute.

Ecuador's position within the Western Hemisphere mirrors that of the OAS within the global community. Ecuador is an accepted and respected member of the Pan American system but is nonetheless acknowledged to be a minor player. Ecuador's relatively small size, weak economy and power base, and unexceptional diplomatic history contribute to its reputation as a country whose interests are as likely to be ignored as respected in international negotiations. These parallels between the OAS and Ecuador might invite the conclusion that Ecuador would see the OAS as an ideal vehicle for its foreign policy goals. Because Ecuador's own diplomatic, military, and economic means are limited, it would appear sensible that Quito use the regional organization to enhance the weight of its foreign policies. Within the OAS, Ecuador is technically an equal player, on par with and sharing the same voting power as Brazil, Argentina, Mexico, and the United States. Certainly Ecuadorans cannot enjoy that same sense of equality in other areas of hemispheric affairs, where they almost always come up short in comparison to their neighbors. Similarly, Ecuador's own subordinate position within the inter-American system might suggest that Quito would support the OAS, which plays a subordinate role among global regional organizations. Indeed, Ecuadoran ex-President Galo Plaza Lasso's assumption of the post of secretary general of the OAS early in the organization's history suggested that Ecuador might become a major player within the organization.

Alas, this was not to be the case. Although Ecuador has certainly taken its role as an OAS member seriously, it has not made the multilateral organization its principal or even frequently used foreign policy vehicle. Before one blames Ecuadorans for their failure to take advantage of the OAS, it must be remembered that the structure and operation of the OAS reflects the wealth and power distribution in the global political economy. The OAS is alternately dominated and ignored by the United States as the regional hegemon sees fit to meet its foreign policy goals. Even within this constraint, however, there is a sense in the literature on Ecuador's foreign policy that the OAS is underutilized. Francisco Carrión Mena, a foreign policy scholar and adviser to a former Ecuadoran president, barely mentions the OAS in his volume on Ecuador's foreign policy.[1] Most glaring, he fails to identify the OAS as a potential mediator in his discussion of third party arbiters for the Peru-Ecuador border dispute. The pertinent literature reveals a theme in which Ecuador participates fully in the OAS and ascribes to all of its lofty principles of Pan Americanism, mutual recognition of sovereignty, peaceful resolution of disputes, and economic development. Yet there is little evidence of, or even hope for, an Ecuadoran foreign policy that would take advantage of the OAS as a unique institutional vehicle for a relatively weak Ecuador to maximize its foreign policy interests.[2] One is left wondering, why not? If the OAS appears to be a weak country's brightest hope of increasing its level of power and foreign policy effectiveness, why is this opportunity not seized? This chapter addresses this question.

TWO EMPIRICAL QUESTIONS

Two empirical questions help to operationalize this study. First, is there evidence that Ecuador actively employs the OAS as a foreign policy instrument? Examination of this question will reveal whether Ecuador has used the OAS to its fullest potential. A second question is whether Ecuador has opposed the United States within the OAS. This empirical question concerns Ecuador's level of autonomy within the organization.

Has Ecuador Used the OAS as a Foreign Policy Instrument?

Is the OAS a first or second option when Ecuadoran foreign policy makers seek to address a problem or an opportunity? Does Ecuador take advantage of the OAS's diplomatic offices and bureaucracy to meet its foreign policy goals? The preponderance of the evidence suggests that although Ecuador does participate in the OAS regularly, it does not see the organization as its most important, or even as a ranking, foreign policy instrument. Certainly Quito has consistently maintained high official regard for the institution. Ecuadoran leaders have often repeated their adherence to the lofty principles on which the OAS is founded and their commitment to Pan Americanism. The Ministry of Foreign Affairs' annual reports show that Ecuador always participates in regional meetings, electoral observations, special missions, and other activities sponsored by the OAS. Indeed, Ecuador is a good citizen within the regional body. In 1989–1990, Ecuadoran Foreign Minister Diego Cordovez noted in the Ministry's annual report that Ecuador was the first state to propose a plan for the strengthening of the OAS, including new rules that would assure that members would pay their OAS dues.[3]

One example where Ecuador successfully appealed to the OAS is the 1995 flare-up of the Ecuador-Peru border dispute. The administration of President Sixto Durán Ballén (known in Ecuador as Sixto) used the OAS offices to mediate the negotiations and ameliorate the conflict situation. In contrast to Peruvian President Alberto Fujimori, Sixto was praised for welcoming the OAS into the negotiations and approaching the conflict in a diplomatic, multilateral way.[4] OAS Secretary General Cesar Gaviria travelled to Quito and Lima early in the militarized conflict. In a rather undiplomatic move, Fujimori argued publicly that the OAS had no role in mediating the conflict, preferring the four guarantor countries of the Rio Protocol (Argentina, Brazil, Chile, and the United States) as negotiators. In contrast, Sixto welcomed the secretary general and succeeded in putting the war on the OAS Permanent Council's agenda. While Sixto acted as a perfect diplomat in regional meetings, he fomented nationalism and anti-Peruvianism at home, thereby maximizing political points with both hemispheric and national audiences.

This important exception noted, Ecuador's OAS participation is more ordinary than outstanding. Rather than using the OAS as a foreign policy instrument of first, or even usual, resort, Ecuador has taken what might be seen as a more practical approach. Quito seeks out OAS offices when it clearly maximizes Ecuador's advantage. Although this certainly makes sense from a national interest point of view, it does not exploit the OAS's Pan Americanist theme, nor does it exhibit any particular creativity on the part of Ecuadoran foreign-policy makers. Moreover, unlike the 1995 border dispute with Peru, there are several instances in which Ecuador did not make use of OAS offices in a creative and effective way. One such case is the 1984 Conferencia Económica Latinoamericana (CEL) sponsored by Ecuadoran President Osvaldo Hurtado. This was the first regional meeting that looked seriously at the emerging debt crisis in Latin America. Hurtado secured the participation of numerous heads of state and foreign ministers who signed the "Declaration of Quito" and "Plan of Action" documents that established creditors' responsibility in the debt crisis and called for debt relief.[5] The conference was a high point of Hurtado's policy making and in Ecuador's foreign policy history, but its principles and plans were soon forgotten or molded into future declarations made in other multilateral meetings, including the Cartagena Consensus and the Group of Eight. Just as significant for Ecuador, the OAS played almost no role in CEL. Hurtado included CEPAL, a UN body devoted to Latin American development, in the planning of CEL, but although the OAS had been an important forum for the preconference advertising and postconference "selling" of CEL policy recommendations, its role in the conference itself was limited. The OAS might have been an ideal forum for Latin American debtors to meet with representatives from their major creditor, the United States, to discuss emerging problems. Furthermore, the OAS might have served as a permanent home for future negotiations. Instead, Ecuador went it alone, with the result that later meetings on the debt question were dispersed throughout the region, diluting the strength of debtors' demands and their ability to attain them.

Ecuadoran policy makers have also taken important diplomatic initiatives on drug trafficking, natural resources policy, and attraction of foreign investment that also sidestepped the OAS as a potential Pan American forum. These areas are instead managed bilaterally (e.g., drug trafficking operations with the United States) or though multilateral offices other than the OAS (e.g., OPEC and the Rio Conference on the environment).

Does Ecuador Oppose the United States in the OAS?

A second manner by which to examine Ecuador's activity in the OAS is to ask whether Quito has used the organization to oppose the United States and its hemispheric hegemony. The question presumes that an active Ecuador within the OAS would, by definition, be a contrary influence to the United States. The presumption is problematic; foreign policy makers in Ecuador do not always perceive their interests as inimical to those of Washington. This is especially true under more right-wing administrations, such as those of León Febres Cordero (1984–1988) or Sixto Durán Ballén (1992–1996).[6] Even so, it is generally safe to argue that during the 1970s and into the 1980s, much of Latin America resisted U.S. influence in the region. While Latin American regimes courted U.S. development aid, they rejected U.S. hegemony over political, military, and economic decisions made within the hemisphere. Dependency theory and Latin nationalism remained popular ideologies as well as rallying points for politicians. For example, the region was united in its opposition to U.S. involvement in Central America in the 1980s. Anti-U.S. sentiment in the region has dissipated in the 1990s owing to the neoliberal "revolution" and the democratization of the hemisphere. It nonetheless remains useful, in addressing Ecuador's activity within the OAS, to ask whether Quito has demonstrated autonomy from Washington. One indicator of such autonomy is expressed opposition to the hegemon.

In examining Ecuador's autonomy from the United States, especially within the OAS, it is helpful to ask whether Osvaldo Hurtado is correct in his description of the evolving relationship between Ecuador and the OAS. Hurtado founded the Democracia Popular party and unexpectedly became a young president of Ecuador when the first democratically elected president in the postmilitary era, Jaime Roldós, died in an airplane crash in 1981. In his tome, *Political Power in Ecuador*, Hurtado presents a foreign-policy making establishment in Quito whose activity in the OAS and other bodies reveals increasing autonomy vis-à-vis the United States. He describes Ecuador's relationship with the United States and the OAS during the Cold War:

the United States put into effect a world system of alliances, which in Latin America was consolidated in the Inter-American Reciprocal Assistance Pact of 1947 and the Organization of American States of 1948, instruments employed by the United States Department of State to dictate Ecuador's foreign policy and manipulate its internal affairs in pursuit of a single goal: the "defense of democracy" against "international Communism." As a consequence, Ecuador was discouraged from maintaining diplomatic or commercial relations with Socialist countries, and in international meetings its vote was secured to oppose Soviet policy, to support North American initiatives, and to legitimize interventions carried out in Latin America by North American imperialism.[7]

For Hurtado, the OAS was little more than one weapon in the U.S. arsenal of methods to "dictate Ecuador's foreign policy," but by the 1970s that OAS role had begun to change. Assessing the Cuban revolution as "the beginning of the end for the ideological hegemony consecrated in the Inter-American Reciprocal Assistance Treaty," Hurtado argues that events throughout the 1960s and 1970s led to a breakdown of the "North American system" in the hemisphere. The assent of leftist governments to power in Chile, Peru, and elsewhere; the reacceptance of Cuba into the inter-American system by nearly all Latin states; and the 1973 OAS resolution admitting ideological pluralism in the hemisphere contributed to the weakening of U.S. hegemony. Hurtado argued that "it can no longer be sustained that the OAS is merely another instrument of North American hegemony in the Western Hemisphere" and that "the participation of Ecuador in the OAS and the United Nations is now independent of United States control."[8]

If Hurtado is correct that Ecuador can no longer be called a puppet of the United States and is now "independent of United States control" within the OAS, there should be indications that Ecuador has opposed U.S. positions within the organization. There is some evidence that Ecuador has been willing to do so, especially when joining with other OAS members on questions that afford Quito some diplomatic safety in numbers. In the 1970s, as part of an ostensibly "independent" foreign policy, Ecuador undertook several independent initiatives within the OAS, particularly with reference to Cuba. Ecuador opposed Cuba's expulsion from the OAS and hosted OAS meetings that called for lifting the sanctions against Cuba,[9] but these independent endeavors, especially those that are anti-United States, are more the exception than the rule. Quito appears unwilling to trust that a united Latin America front against the United States, operating within the OAS, is strong enough to shield Ecuador from the consequences of U.S. ire.

One example of this unwillingness to join in a strong effort against the United States—and one not limited to Ecuador—is the collective inaction by Latin American OAS members in the wake of Washington's support of Great Britain in the Malvinas War with Argentina. Although many Latin Americans considered the U.S. endorsement of Britain a direct violation of the inter-American military assistance treaty, they failed to punish the United States within the OAS. To critics of Ecuador's inaction in this matter, and to those who argued that the U.S. reaction to the Malvinas War indicated that Washington was uncommitted to the OAS, then–Foreign Minister Luis Valencia responded that even with all the "structural faults" within the OAS, it was important to maintain a "mechanism of understanding" with the United States, especially in light of Ecuador's economic crisis.[10] In other words, Ecuador had refused to alienate the United States in a time of economic hardship, even when the latter had violated the most important inter-American military treaty.

A more recent example of Ecuador's failure to oppose the United States within the OAS came during the 1994 election of OAS Secretary General César Gaviria. Gaviria was pitted against former Costa Rican Foreign Minister Bernd Niehaus. Months prior to the March election, Niehaus had announced that he had it wrapped up, citing public support and promised votes from all thirteen CARICOM (the Caribbean Community) states as well as many others, including Ecuador. However, at the last minute, Sixto changed his mind and directed his OAS ambassador to cast Ecuador's ballot for Gaviria.

Despite Gaviria's strong backing from not only the United States but also Canada, Brazil, Argentina, and Mexico, Sixto had at first maintained the commitment he made to Niehaus months before the vote. Sixto had personal ties with Niehaus, a member of whose family had worked with the Ecuadoran president in earlier years at the Inter-American Development Bank. A looming banana conflict also played a part in his original decision to support Niehaus. The European Union had recently announced plans to favor Caribbean banana producers over mainland growers, a policy that promised to cut Ecuador's exports dramatically. Niehaus had promised to aid Ecuador and other mainland banana growers in their dispute with the European Union, whereas Gaviria led a multilateral effort to cooperate with the Europeans. Finally, local politics played a role. Sixto's immediate predecessor in the presidential palace, Rodrigo Borja, had expressed interest in the OAS secretary general's job. Sixto did not relish the prospect of his political foe gaining regional renown, so he offered him only the most unenthusiastic support. When Borja withdrew, citing his own government's failure to support him, Sixto immediately endorsed Niehaus, apparently to lock the door on any chances Borja might have of resurrecting his candidacy.[11]

However, Gaviria was clearly Washington's top choice. The Colombian president had distinguished himself among advocates of neoliberal economic reforms and hard-line tactics against drug traffickers and leftist guerrillas. The Clinton administration's agenda in Latin America would be much better served by Gaviria than by Niehaus, a Third World–oriented nationalist of limited prestige and from a small country. Indeed, U.S. State Department diplomats uncharacteristically lobbied for their candidate for secretary general, going so far as to deliver warnings to Quito about the future of the OAS were Gaviria not elected.[12]

Despite these clear indications of Washington's preferences, Ecuador had joined with many Caribbean and Central American countries to rally behind Niehaus. It was a dramatic reversal, then, when only one day before the vote, Sixto decided to support Gaviria. This sudden change of opinion can be attributed to many potential factors: U.S. pressure, Ecuador's fear of reprisals from Washington, Sixto's realization that Gaviria was a preferable candidate to Niehaus, and Sixto's desire for an Andean, as opposed to a Central American, in the secretary general's office, among other possible factors.[13]

Whatever the case, it showed Ecuador's unwillingness to oppose the United States within the OAS, even when many other regional members did so. This case is most important because there is evidence that, at least in the beginning, Sixto truly wanted to oppose the United States and support Niehaus. Indeed, he suffered serious public humiliation in the wake of his waffling decision. As one former Foreign Ministry official noted, "Ecuador ended up looking like a dependent country, totally submissive to the United States." In this situation, Ecuador might have opposed the United States, won the appearance of independence, gained for its president much-needed political points at home, and counted on some diplomatic protection from potential U.S. retaliation from OAS members who did vote for Niehaus. Instead, and in keeping with other examples of Ecuador's hesitation to challenge the United States within the OAS, Quito changed its policy to a pro-Washington position.

ANALYSIS AND CONCLUSIONS

The OAS appears to provide small countries like Ecuador with a unique opportunity to pursue their foreign policy goals within a Pan American framework. As a multilateral institution, the OAS offers diplomatic offices, access to all regional actors, strength in numbers, and protection from foes. It appears ideally suited for Ecuador, whose own foreign policy resources are limited. Yet this study finds that Ecuador has failed to take advantage of the OAS, neither regularly appealing to it for foreign policy initiatives nor displaying much independence from the United States within it. What accounts for this failure?

Four factors—two rooted in the global political economy, one rooted in the OAS, and one rooted in Ecuador—help to explain why Quito has not better exploited its opportunities in the OAS. First, it must be noted that the OAS reflects, rather than challenges, the global distribution of power. In this sense,

Ecuador's failure to demonstrate a more impressive foreign policy profile within the OAS may be seen as a function of constraints within the OAS that mirror those placed on all small and poor countries around the world. It is not Ecuador per se that is culpable then, but the global political and economic system that constrains it. This view is expressed by Ecuadoran foreign policy scholar John Martz, who argues that "[t]o understand the role of Ecuador in foreign affairs, then, is first and foremost to recognize its status as a small state." This means that external factors, such as the regional distribution of power and wealth and the U.S. ability and willingness to act, are "decisive and are best explored through the traditional power-politics approach, which relies fundamentally upon the capabilities of the state."[14]

Under this model, Ecuador's relatively low power capabilities put the country at as much a disadvantage within the OAS as anywhere else and help to explain both Ecuador's failure to use the OAS creatively and to implement anti-U.S. policies. At the same time, powerful actors such as the United States, Argentina, Mexico, and Brazil dominate debates and policies within the OAS just as they do outside the organization. We can thus interpret Sixto's vote in the secretary general election as a ballot of acknowledgement that the region's "heavy hitters" would attain their desired outcome—the election of Gaviria over Niehaus—and that Ecuador would have much to lose by contesting U.S. plans.

A second explanation for Ecuador's actions within the OAS is the economic relationship between Ecuador and the United States. Especially during times of economic hardship and crisis, Ecuador must weigh carefully its foreign policy decisions' popularity with the United States. The United States is Ecuador's primary trading partner, creditor, and donor of foreign aid. Ecuador's economic vulnerability makes any anti-U.S. activity, within or without the OAS, a risky maneuver that might prompt U.S. economic retaliation. Indeed, Hurtado's CEL appears to confirm this point. The CEL appeared to the outside world as a confrontational policy, pitting Ecuador and neighboring debtors against the United States and other creditors. Important to understand, though, is that Hurtado implemented CEL at the beginning of the debt crisis and before Ecuador's most terrible economic hardships arose. Furthermore, Hurtado and his advisers met privately with creditors from the United States, assuring them that Ecuador would continue to work bilaterally to arrive at mutually agreeable debt negotiations. In effect, then, the Hurtado administration undermined any potential for success for its own multilateral efforts at solving the debt problem. It did so at least in part because it was already so economically exposed to the United States.

A third explanation for Ecuador's lackluster performance within the OAS concerns the organization itself. Considered from the point of view of a rational foreign policy actor, the OAS may well appear to offer few benefits and numerous risks. The difficult and contentious negotiations over the European union teach us that states are often reluctant to forfeit their control over policy making even if a united effort promises a better future for the whole. Policy makers and heads of government worry that they will become unable to protect that national interest when it deviates from regional interests. Playing the "good guy" willing to pursue regional interests at the expense of parochial concerns is no guarantee to a positive outcome. Indeed, the "bad guys" who approach regional cooperation reluctantly and with a keen eye on national interest often win concessions that the "good guys" do not. Washington's recent success in ousting UN Secretary General Boutros Boutros-Ghali despite his global popularity is indicative of this phenomenon. This basic "prisoners' dilemma," in which individuals fail to cooperate even though it is in their mutual interest to do so, plagues all multilateral efforts, and the OAS is no exception. Hence, were Ecuador to frequent the OAS as a multilateral route to its foreign policy goals, Ecuadorans could lose out to other actors who take a more self-interested position.

The breakdown of the Andean Pact in the 1970s illustrates this point. Although many Andean leaders, stinging after the demise of the Latin American Free Trade Agreement (LAFTA), fully understood the potential pitfalls of regional economic agreements, they nonetheless proceeded to make many of the same errors in the Andean Pact.[15] Despite careful planning, inserting into the treaty safeguards against disintegration and parochialism, and a strongly vocalized commitment to the Andean Pact, partisan interests and actions fatally wounded the organization. Problems plaguing the young Pact culminated in the 1973 withdrawal of Chile, whose leaders claimed that its economic growth needs were incompatible with Pact regulations on foreign investment.[16] The early years of the Andean Pact are a case study in national interests overcoming regional promise.

Ecuadorans have asked the same question of the OAS that Chileans asked of the Andean Pact: What does the OAS offer Ecuador that unilateral policy making does not? The OAS does provide Ecuador with institutional channels of communication, regional treaties and norms to regulate behavior, diplomatic offices, and safety in numbers, but rarely have these assets helped to advance a truly successful policy for Ecuador. With the exception of help in Ecuador's border dispite with Peru, the OAS has infrequently acted as a powerful presence in regional or global debates. At the time of the Central American civil wars of the 1980s, for example, the OAS played a bit part. Individual and extra-OAS collective efforts, such as the Arias Peace Plan and Contadora, were much more visible and effective in shaping events in Central America. This helped OAS credibility and made future successes for the OAS less likely throughout the region, and it also meant that Ecuador and other countries would be less likely to draw on OAS resources.

Finally, Ecuadoran foreign-policy makers account in part for the nation's limited participation in the OAS. Foreign-policy making in Ecuador remains a personalistic enterprise. The Foreign Ministry has only recently begun to professionalize its corps. The Diplomatic Academy is now striving to train Ecuadorans from all parts of the country and to insist that they have diplomatic credentials and not simply personal ties to prominent politicos.[17] A change in foreign policy culture is nonetheless a slow process. Furthermore, the president holds constitutional control over foreign policy, and various presidents have employed foreign policy as a means to express their ideological differences with competitors. It is also important that presidents cannot be reelected. Hence, the peculiarities of presidential priorities, political needs, and sometimes whimsical preferences generate an Ecuadoran foreign policy that, as a body, is personalistic rather than reflective of a generally defined national interest. What is the effect of this highly variable foreign policy on Ecuador's use of the OAS? It creates little incentive for presidents to employ the OAS as a foreign policy instrument. Appealing to the OAS will necessarily be a relatively long process, in which careful negotiations, deal making and compromise will occur. This requires a long-term view of policy success and the patience to wait for policy outcomes. An Ecuadoran leader who has but four years to make a mark in international affairs, and especially one who may hope to undermine the potential success of his or her followers in office, will be unlikely to go to the OAS to attain foreign policy objectives. Instead, he or she will use unilateral and bilateral endeavors in an attempt to maximize short-term foreign policy in regional and domestic audiences.

President Hurtado's decision to hold CEL in Quito as opposed to promoting it within the OAS illustrates this point. Although Hurtado was certainly concerned about the burgeoning debt problem in Latin America, his approach was also designed to promote himself as the individual leader of the debt resolution movement. This is reflected in what some might call the hubris with which he describes the conference in his memoirs. CEL, he explains, was "perhaps the sole foreign policy initiative in Ecuador's diplomatic history that has been successful."[18] Similarly, rather than expressing satisfaction that CEL had launched a series of regional debt conferences, Hurtado reflected with marked irritation that subsequent debt conferences did not sufficiently acknowledge his role in starting the process.[19] Not surprisingly, Ecuador did not participate in most subsequent meetings. Had Hurtado instead used OAS offices to begin the regional discussion on debt, his own position and prestige in the affair would have been minimized, but the policy outcome for Ecuador may well have been stronger. Hurtado should not be singled out among Ecuadoran presidents for failing to use the OAS when he might have done so. Indeed, Hurtado's sympathies toward multilateral efforts are stronger than many of his peers in the presidential palace. CEL is only one example of an Ecuadoran president's unilateral policy choice that enhanced his political visibility.

Ultimately, there is evidence at every level of analysis that helps to account for Ecuador's limited participation in the OAS. At the individual level, there are Ecuadoran presidents who prioritize political and personal goals over long-term national interests. This contributes to them taking individualized routes rather than using the OAS in foreign policy. At the bureaucratic level, the presidency constitutionally controls foreign policy, a detail that is strengthened by a relatively weak Foreign Ministry. At the state level, Ecuador remains a country with few power-base resources, limiting its credibility and effectiveness within the OAS. At the system level operates a regional and global distribution of power and wealth that continues to work in favor of the United States and other powerful actors over weaker ones like Ecuador. Also at the system level is the OAS itself, an organization that on paper promises much but in fact offers very little on which a country like Ecuador can count. Taken together, these factors form a strong explanation for why Ecuador does not play a more prominent role within the OAS, even though a first glance would suggest that it should.

NOTES

1. Francisco Carrión Mena, *Política exterior del Ecuador: Evolución, teoría, práctica*, 2nd ed. (Quito, 1989).

2. See Carrión Mena; Arturo Lecaro Bustamante, *Política internacional del Ecuador, 1809–1984*, 2nd ed. (Quito, 1988); Osvaldo Hurtado, *El poder político en el Ecuador* (Quito, 1990); Jeanne A. K. Hey, *Theories of Dependent Foreign Policy and the Case of Ecuador in the 1980s* (Athens, OH, 1995).

3. Ministerio de Relaciones Exteriores (MRE), *Informe a la Nación* (Quito, 1990), 156–57.

4. Jeanne A. K. Hey, "Political Manipulation of Foreign Policy in the Durán Ballén Presidency," *The Canadian Journal of Latin American and Caribbean Studies* 21, no. 42 (1996): 306–7.

5. Jeanne A. K. Hey, *Theories*, 89.

6. Conceptual issues related to defining Ecuador's general foreign policy interests relative to those of the United States are explored in Jeanne A. K. Hey, "Compliance, Consensus and Counterdependence: Foreign Policy in Ecuador," *International Interactions* 19, no. 3 (1994): 241–61.

7. Osvaldo Hurtado, *Political Power in Ecuador* (Albuquerque, 1980), 89–90.

8. Hurtado, *Political Power*, 278, 280.

9. Osvaldo Hurtado, *El poder político*, 226, 273, 309.

10. Lecaro Bustamante, 382.

11. Interview with Rodrigo Borja, 26 June 1994; Hey, "Political Manipulation." 298–300.

12. Interview with U.S. Ambassador to Quito Peter Romero, 15 June 1994.

13. Interview with Diego Cordovez, 26 June 1994; interview with Mario Alemán, 26 June 1994.

14. John Martz, "The Face of a Small State: Ecuador in Foreign Affairs," in *American Nations in World Politics*, edited by Heraldo Muñoz and Joseph S. Tulchin, 2nd ed., (Boulder, 1996), 130.

15. Rachelle L. Cherol and José Nuñez del Arco, "Andean Multinational Enterprises: A New Approach to Multinational Investment in the Andean Group," *Journal of Common Market Studies* 21 (1983): 409–28.

16. William P. Avery, "The Politics of Crisis and Cooperation in the Andean Group," *Journal of Developing Arenas* 17, no. 2 (1983): 159–61.

17. Interview with Horacio Sevilla, 29 July 1994.

18. Osvaldo Hurtado, *Política democrática: Los últimos veinte y cinco años* (Quito, 1990), 149.

19. Interview with Osvaldo Hurtado, 27 May 1991.

15

The Inter-American Human Rights System: A Force for Positive Change in the Americas

Jo M. Pasqualucci

INTRODUCTION

In the last half of the twentieth century the nations of the Americas have joined together to combat human rights abuses in the Western Hemisphere. Under the auspices of the Organization of American States (OAS), they have adopted a series of treaties to protect human rights and have structured a system to enforce those rights. The OAS member states that have ratified these treaties have voluntarily relinquished sovereignty in the area of human rights and have made human rights violations in their territory subject to international law and the oversight of regional enforcement organs.[1] The principle OAS human rights instruments include the Charter of the OAS,[2] which has over time been amended to incorporate human rights provisions; the American Declaration of the Rights and Duties of Man,[3] which established approximately twenty-seven human rights and ten duties; and the American Convention on Human Rights,[4] including two protocols—the Additional Protocol to the American Convention on Human Rights in the Area of Economic, Social, and Cultural Rights, "Protocol of San Salvador,"[5] and the Protocol to Abolish the Death Penalty.[6] Recent specialized OAS human rights treaties are the Inter-American Convention to Prevent and Punish Torture,[7] the Inter-American Convention on the Forced Disappearance of Persons,[8] and the Inter-American Convention on the Prevention, Punishment, and Eradication of Violence Against Women.[9] A Declaration of the Rights of Indigenous Peoples is also in progress. Together these instruments and the enforcement organs they empower make up an effective regional system to promote and protect human rights in the Americas.

THE AMERICAN CONVENTION

The most influential of these instruments is the American Convention on Human Rights. The American Convention protects twenty-six substantive rights, including the rights to life, humane treatment, personal liberty, a fair trial, privacy, and freedom of thought, expression, and religion.[10] This treaty has been ratified by twenty-five American states.[11] The Convention does more than enumerate rights, however, it also empowers two bodies, the Inter-American Commission on Human Rights[12] and the Inter-American Court of Human Rights,[13] to enforce those rights. The drafters of the American Convention modeled it on the United Nations International Covenant on Civil and Political Rights[14] and the European Convention for the Protection of Human Rights and Fundamental Freedoms.[15] They were not content to merely replicate those treaties, however. Instead they structured the American Convention to respond more effectively to the types of human rights abuses and the socioeconomic realities of the Western Hemisphere.[16] Delegates to the drafting conference argued that if the American states were to conclude their own convention after the completion of the UN covenants, "then it was appropriate to introduce any modifications that were desirable in the light of circumstances prevailing in the American Republics."[17] In doing so, they modified traditional international law to enhance the protection of human rights within the unique circumstances of the Western Hemisphere.

One of the most important of these modifications is expanded individual access to the enforcement process. Individual victims must have both de jure and de facto access to an international human rights system if the system is to be optimally effective. Traditionally, even in international human rights law, which was created to protect individuals, only another state had automatic standing to file a complaint against a state. Under the American Convention, state parties automatically agree to the right of an individual to petition against a state.[18]

Even the direct authority to file complaints of a human rights abuse, however, will not allow all individuals to avail themselves of international human rights protection. Poverty, lack of education, and a lack of access to legal counsel may all restrict access. Many victims of human rights violations have limited education or are too poor to hire a lawyer. In addition, victims and their families may be intimidated and fear retaliation if they complain of human rights violations. Even a victim who is willing to suffer the consequences can seldom find a lawyer willing to take the case, because the lawyer is often threatened and sometimes becomes the next victim.[19] The American Convention is the only human rights treaty that attempts to counteract such problems of access or intimidation by allowing unrelated parties to complain of human rights violations on behalf of the victim.[20] Thus, the petitioner may be an international nongovernmental organization (NGO), such as Amnesty International or America's Watch. These NGOs can be effective because they often have more extensive resources than individuals and fewer security problems in investigating and filing complaints.[21] It was the World Council of Journalists that interceded and filed a complaint with the Inter-American Commission when a Peruvian journalist was murdered allegedly by the military and the witnesses were killed or threatened.[22] The publicity that an international NGO can generate focuses attention on the state and thereby provides some protection for the domestic witnesses while the enforcement organs, the Inter-American Commission and the Inter-American Court, consider the case.

THE INTER-AMERICAN COMMISSION

The Inter-American Commission is composed of seven commissioners who are elected in their individual capacity by the OAS General Assembly.[23] The seat of the Commission is in Washington, D.C. The Commission was originally established as a consultative organ of the OAS by its charter.[24] Under the charter, the Commission has the authority to oversee the human rights obligations of all member states of the OAS. Its principle charter-based functions include the preparation of country studies and an annual report, and the performance of on-site fact-finding investigations.

The Commission made such a fact-finding investigation in Argentina in 1979 in response to numerous complaints that the ruling junta was perpetrating acts of torture, extrajudicial killings, and disappearances.[25] While in the country, the Commission announced that it would take live testimony from people alleging human rights violations. Until that time, many victims or relatives of missing persons had not spoken publicly or even searched for their loved ones for fear of government retaliation. The Commission's request for information, however, brought out thousands of people who waited in the street in front of the Commission's Buenos Aires office to be heard. That public display reportedly inspired confidence in many persons to come forward and demand information on the whereabouts of their friends and relatives.[26] The Commission's report on the human rights abuses was then widely disseminated outside Argentina. Although it cannot be proved that the Commission's visit was instrumental in ending the repression, the number of disappearances declined drastically after that visit.

The American Convention grants the Commission additional authority to respond directly to individual petitions alleging human rights violations against those states that have ratified the human rights treaty.[27] The Commission has the initial role in considering human rights petitions from individuals who allege that a state party to the Convention has violated their human rights. Generally, the Commission receives more than 500 individual petitions each year.[28] The petition must state facts that tend to establish that there has been a violation of a right guaranteed by the treaty.[29] The Commission then determines whether the complaint meets the Convention's requisites of admissibility.[30] If the petition lacks the required information, the Commission may ask the petitioner to complete it. When the complaint is prima facie admissible, in that it complies with these requirements of admissibility, the Commission informs the government involved of the relevant portions of the complaint and requests pertinent information. The Commission withholds the identity of the petitioner from the government, however, unless the petitioner has expressly authorized disclosure. When the government provides the requested information, the Commission then forwards portions of it to the petitioner, along with a request for additional observations and evidence. If the government does not respond, as has frequently been the case, the Commission may treat the petition's allegations as presumptively true. During its processing of the case, the Commission may hold hearings for the purpose of receiving evidence and attempt to bring about a friendly settlement of the case between the state and the petitioner.[31] If, however, no friendly settlement is reached, the Commission draws up a report and transmits it to the state concerned. The Commission may then refer the case to the Inter-American Court if it has found that the state violated a protected right. In that case the Commission appears before the Court as the representative of the victim.[32]

THE INTER-AMERICAN COURT

Only after procedures before the Commission have been exhausted can the Commission or the state party submit the case to the Inter-American Court.[33] The individual petitioner has no standing to bring the case before the Court. Moreover, the Commission may only submit the case to the Court if the state involved recognizes the Court's jurisdiction.[34] To date, nineteen state parties to the American Convention have expressly accepted the jurisdiction of the Court.[35] The Court is composed of seven judges who must be nationals of a member state of the OAS. The nationality of judges is not limited, however, to jurists from states that have ratified the American Convention or accepted the jurisdiction of the Court. It was this provision that allowed Costa Rica to nominate the respected American international law scholar Thomas Buergenthal to the Court. The judges who have served on the Court have been some of the most impressive names in human rights law in the Western Hemisphere. Moreover, some of the judges have personally been subjected to human rights violations. Four of the judges initially elected to the Court had been imprisoned for political reasons at some time in their lives.[36]

The seat of the Court is in San Jose, Costa Rica, although the Court may convene in any OAS member state. The Court meets on a part-time basis. In the early years of the Court, when its caseload was light, the infrequent meetings were adequate. In recent years, however, the Court's workload has increased significantly, and it is now generally acknowledged that the Court should convene more frequently to deal in a timely fashion with the submissions of contentious cases and the many requests for advisory opinions and provisional measures.

Contentious Cases

The Court's contentious jurisdiction empowers it to adjudicate cases arising from alleged governmental violations of an individual's human rights. In this capacity, the Inter-American Court has heard cases involving some of the most egregious human rights violations ever to come before an international court. For instance, the Inter-American Court was the first international tribunal to confront the governmental policy of "forced disappearances."[37] A forced disappearance occurs when government agents kidnap and hold a person incommunicado in a clandestine prison. The kidnappers may torture and execute the prisoner and then destroy or conceal the body.[38] In such cases, the government often refuses to acknowledge that the person has been in custody, and the victims' loved ones live with long-term uncertainty, not knowing if the victim is living or dead. Perpetrators of disappearances attempt to avoid accountability by eliminating all evidence of the kidnapping or of the victim's fate.[39] Consequently, the complainant can seldom produce direct evidence of the kidnappers' identity or of the involvement of the government.

In the initial disappearance cases against Honduras, the Court fashioned an innovative two-pronged test to satisfy this burden. Under the first prong, the Commission must show that the state engaged in an official practice of disappearances or at least tolerated such a practice. Under the second prong, the Commission must establish a link between the disappearance of the individual and the state practice. In the Honduran cases, the Commission established that a state practice of disappearances existed in Honduras from 1981–1984.[40] It proved to the Court that between 100 and 150 persons disappeared during that time and that "[i]t was public and notorious knowledge in Honduras that the kidnappings were carried out by military personnel or the police, or persons acting under their orders."[41] The modus operandi was well known. The victims were often labor leaders, student leaders, or persons that the government deemed a threat to state security.[42] Many of them had been under surveillance before their disappearances. The kidnappers drove vehicles with tinted glass, which required official authorization, and carried arms reserved for use by the police and military. At times, state security agents even cleared an area of bystanders just prior to a kidnapping.

The Commission then established a link between the government policy and the disappearance of the particular victims. In the *Velásquez Rodríguez Case*, the Commission demonstrated the requisite link by showing that the victim was a student leader who had been under governmental surveillance and who was kidnapped in broad daylight under circumstances similar to those shown to be common in Honduras at that time.[43] When the Commission has met its burden of proof, a rebuttable presumption is established that the government is responsible for the disappearance. The burden then shifts to the government to refute the presumption.[44] The government may do so by showing that the alleged victim was not the type of person who traditionally disappeared, or that there were other likely reasons for the disappearance. In the first disappearance cases, however, Honduras did not present evidence to rebut the presumption. The state, therefore, was found liable for the disappearance of two of the victims and was ordered to make reparation to their families.[45]

Advisory Opinions

Under the Court's advisory jurisdiction, any member state or organ of the OAS may request an interpretation of the American Convention or other human rights treaty.[46] A state may also request the Court's opinion on the compatibility of its domestic laws with international human rights instruments.[47] In this way, the Court's advisory jurisdiction assists "the American States in fulfilling their international human rights obligations."[48] The Court's advisory opinions are now being relied on by domestic courts in interpreting their own laws. For example, the Costa Rican Supreme Court's Constitutional Chamber has nullified or re-interpreted domestic laws that the Inter-American Court found incompatible with the American Convention.[49] One law nullified by the Constitutional Chamber required the compulsory membership of journalists and reporters in an association that was open only to university graduates who had specialized in certain fields of study, such as journalism.[50] In an advisory opinion the Inter-American Court advised Costa Rica that the law was incompatible with freedom of expression under Article 13 of the Convention because it denied "any person access to the full use of the news media as a means of expressing opinions or imparting information."[51] The Costa Rican Constitutional Chamber later cited the reasoning of the Inter-American Court in voiding the law.[52] In another opinion, the Costa Rican Constitutional Chamber declared, in accordance with an Inter-American Court advisory opinion,[53] that a state law on nationalization of spouses could not discriminate on the basis of gender.[54] Similarly, the Argentine Supreme Court held that the American Convention on Human Rights created a directly enforceable right of reply in Argentina.[55] In doing so, it relied on an advisory opinion of the Inter-American Court holding that an injured individual's right to reply to an inaccurate or offensive statement made in the media is the law in Argentina without separate domestic legislation to that effect.[56] Thus, the Court's advisory opinions are contributing to the development of human rights law both nationally and internationally.[57]

Provisional Measures

Many human rights violations in the Inter-American system require urgent action; a person's life or physical well-being may be threatened. The Inter-American Court has the unprecedented authority to order that a state protect a person who is in danger of grave and irreparable harm, even when the case is not yet before the Court.[58] In these urgent cases, the Inter-American Commission can circumvent its time-consuming procedures and immediately ask the Court to adopt provisional measures.[59] In adopting such measures, the Court may order the government to take or refrain from taking certain actions. For instance, the Court may order a state to stay the execution of a prisoner or to provide protection to certain individuals.

One such example of the successful use of provisional measures occurred in a matter involving Guatemala. In that case, four Guatemalan human rights activists near the village of Chunima were murdered, and one was seriously wounded, in separate attacks during a five-month period.[60] The victims were members of an Indian group that monitored human rights abuses in the highlands.[61] The army refused to protect those threatened, and the police were unable to act even though civil defense patrol leaders[62] had publicly threatened the victims and then bragged about committing the murders. Even the two local judges who investigated the murders and issued arrest warrants for the civil patrol leaders received death threats and were forced to go into hiding. The remaining group members and their families also went into hiding. Their precautions were ineffective, however, and another member was murdered. The Commission then requested that the Court order Guatemala to take provisional measures. The Court ordered the Guatemalan government to provide protection for the threatened persons.[63] The government complied, and the measures were successful in that no additional members of the group were killed. Provisional measures may also be requested to protect witnesses who have testified or will testify before the Inter-American Court.[64] In recent years the Commission has increased its requests for provisional measures in both situations.

SPECIALIZED HUMAN RIGHTS INSTRUMENTS

Two protocols to the American Convention have been adopted by the General Assembly, with one provision requiring the progressive development of economic, social, and cultural rights. In 1988, the Protocol of San Salvador was signed. The Preamble to the Protocol recognizes that "the ideal of free human beings enjoying freedom from fear and want can only be achieved if conditions are created whereby everyone may enjoy his economic, social and cultural rights as well as his civil and political rights." The rights enumerated in the Protocol include the rights to work; to just, equitable, and satisfactory conditions of work; to organize trade unions; to social security; to health services; to a healthy environment; to food; to education; and to protection of the elderly. The principal monitoring mechanism provided for in the Protocol is state submission of periodic reports on the measures they have taken to ensure respect for the enumerated rights.[65] The violation of certain specific rights, however, can result in recourse to the Inter-American Commission and the Inter-American Court. These include the rights to organize or join a trade union, to strike, to have a free primary education, and to select the type of education for one's children.[66] A second protocol to the American Convention on Human Rights abolishes the death penalty and specifies that "[t]he States Parties to this Protocol shall not apply the death penalty in their territory to any person subject to their jurisdiction."[67]

The OAS has also promulgated treaties that deal with specific human rights violations. The Inter-American Convention to Prevent and Punish Torture provides that the existence of war, a state of emergency, political instability, or disaster never may be used to justify torture. Moreover, the Convention specifically negates the validity of the common justification that the torturer was merely acting "under orders of a superior." State parties to the Convention have made a commitment to exclude evidence obtained through torture and to emphasize the prohibition of torture in the training of police officers.[68] In addition the Inter-American Convention on the Forced Disappearance of Persons and the Inter-American Convention on the Prevention, Punishment, and Eradication of Violence Against Women[69] were adopted by the OAS General Assembly in 1994. The latter Convention defines violence against women to include physical, psychological, and sexual violence within or outside the home.[70]

EFFECTIVENESS OF THE SYSTEM

Some OAS member states may have ratified human rights instruments mainly for the sake of appearance, without the intention of modifying their actions to comply with treaty requirements. However, what a state may have intended merely as a gesture is being taken seriously by citizens of the state and the international community. Governments are finding that they are being held to their commitments and that individuals are demanding fulfillment of the government's international responsibilities. The inter-American system is thus proving to be effective in raising the expectations of the people of the Western Hemisphere and in improving the observance of human rights.

Formal Effectiveness

To date, all but two states have complied with the judgments of the Inter-American Court. Most states are actively participating in cases despite some grumbling and delay tactics. Governments summoned to appear before the Court present written arguments and then make oral arguments at public hearings. Moreover, when the evidence of state responsibility for a human rights violation is overwhelming, states are now preempting a Court decision on the merits by accepting international responsibility for violations of the Convention. For example, in the *El Amparo Case* against Venezuela, in which members of the military murdered fourteen fishermen, Venezuela accepted international responsibility for its acts.[71] Also, in the *Garrido and Baigorria Case* against Argentina, involving the disappearance of two Argentine citizens who were taken into custody by the state police in front of eyewitnesses, Argentina accepted international responsibility.[72] Suriname accepted liability in the *Aloeboetoe Case*, which involved the kidnapping and murder by the Surinamese military of seven young men of the Saramaca tribe.[73] In each of these cases, the governments involved had refused to accept responsibility before the Inter-American Commission. When they admitted responsibility before the Court, the only issue left to be decided by the Court was the type and amount of reparations that the state was to make to the families of the victims. States are also complying with these Court-ordered reparations, although compliance is not yet universal. In *Aloeboetoe*, the government of Suriname complied with the Court's order, and in the Honduran disappearance cases, in which the Court determined that Honduras was responsible for the disappearance of two of the victims, the government has paid the full amount of compensation ordered by the Court. Peru released a college professor from prison in response to the Court's holding in the *Lonyza Tamayo Case*.[74]

Governments have also consistently made an effort to comply with Court orders for provisional measures, as seen above in the *Chunima Case*. In some instances, state compliance with interim urgent orders made by the president of the Court when the full Court is not in session[75] has obviated the need for the plenary court to order provisional measures. This occurred in the *Suarez Rosero Case*, in which Ecuador, at the request of the president of the Court, released a prisoner who had been held for more than three years without trial.[76] Likewise, in the *Reggiardo-Tolosa Case*, Argentina complied with the president of the Court's initial order of urgent measures and thus obviated the need for further relief by the full Court. In that case, the Argentine organization, Grandmothers of the Plaza de Mayo, had filed a complaint with the Inter-American Commission requesting the return of male twins to their biological family.[77] The twins had been born while their mother was illegally and clandestinely imprisoned during Argentina's "dirty war."[78] Immediately after their birth, the boys were taken and registered as the children of a police officer who has since been formally accused of torture, rape, and murder by former victims.[79] Although the natural parents of the boys remained disappeared, biological relatives fought without success for many years in the Argentine courts for the boys' return. In response to the Commission's request for provisional measures, the acting president of the Court ordered the government of Argentina to take all measures necessary to protect the well-being of the boys and to provide a full report to the Court.[80] In its subsequent report, the Argentine government informed the Court that the boys had been removed from the home of the abductor and had been put into the substitute custody of their biological uncle. Thus, there was no further need for the Court to order provisional measures. States are also beginning to comply with requests from the president of the Commission for provisional measures. Reportedly, Commission President Claudio Grossman issued thirty requests for provisional measures in 1996, and twenty-nine of the persons who had been threatened were not injured.[81]

Informal Effectiveness

The mere referral of a case to the Court and the accompanying negative publicity often improve the human rights situation in the state involved. Most states are surprisingly concerned about their world image and international reputation. During the "dirty war" in Argentina the government went to the extent of hiring a high-powered public relations firm in New York to improve its image internationally. As explained by a former member of the UN Commission of Human Rights:

[d]espite the harsh realities of power politics, world opinion is a force to be reckoned with. Governments do devote much time and energy, both in and out of the UN, to defending and embellishing their own human rights image and demeaning that of others.[82]

The threat of negative publicity as a persuasive force that compels governments to comply with international human rights norms has been demonstrated many times in the Inter-American system. The adverse international publicity caused by the submission of a case to the Court has served to curtail governmental policies of human rights violations. After the referral of the Honduran disappearance cases to the Inter-American Court, the Honduran death squad was dismantled and politically inspired disappearances virtually ended in that state. Another example of government compliance was evidenced at a public hearing on an advisory opinion request concerning the death penalty.[83] Following the coup by General Rios Montt in 1982, Guatemala had extended the death penalty to crimes that had not been punishable by death at the time Guatemala ratified the American Convention. This state action contravened the Convention, which provides that the death penalty "shall not be extended to crimes to which it does not presently apply."[84] Guatemala had not yet accepted the Court's jurisdiction and thus could not be brought before the Court in a contentious case. Nevertheless, the Commission sought an advisory opinion from the Court. Although objecting to the admissibility of the advisory opinion petition, Guatemala attended the public hearing on the matter. At the hearing Guatemala announced that it had suspended the executions. Presumably the public exposure caused by the Court's consideration of the issue resulted in this change of policy. Earlier pleas to stop the executions from the Inter-American Commission and Pope John Paul II had been ineffective. Guatemala also responded to the Inter-American Court at the public hearing on provisional measures in the matter of Chunima. There, Guatemala made the surprise announcement that it had already arrested and imprisoned the civil patrol leaders charged with murdering the human rights monitors.[85]

THE FUTURE OF THE SYSTEM

The inter-American system has made progress in the protection of human rights in the Americas. The system is not without its problems, however. Trinidad and Tobago have denounced the American Convention, and Peru has rejected the jurisdiction of the Inter-American Court. It is not certain what effects these withdrawals may have on the future of the system.

A positive addition to the system would be the full participation of the most economically powerful states, which would serve as a positive example to smaller nations. It is unfortunate that some of the most powerful states in the Western Hemisphere have yet to ratify the Inter-American human rights treaties or to accept the jurisdiction of the Inter-American Court. Neither the United States nor Canada has done so. Mexico and Brazil have ratified the Convention but have not accepted the jurisdiction of the Court. Although the United States and Canada have relatively good human rights records and may not recognize the advantages of international intervention in what they perceive to be their domestic affairs, they do have a vested interest in improving the human rights situation worldwide. It would lend force and credibility to the human rights system if these states were to voluntarily submit to the international monitoring of their human rights practices.

The secretary general of the OAS, Cesar Gaviria, has proposed a number of modifications to the system. Several of his suggestions deal with the role of the Inter-American Commission and would result in a more efficient and transparent processing of cases. Furthermore, the secretary general focused on the Commission's multiple and often conflicting roles in dealing with individual petitions. At present, the Commission serves as the investigator of individual complaints, the mediator in efforts to reach a friendly settlement, and the functional equivalent of the prosecutor before the Court. Its prosecutorial role in one case involving a particular state, however, may jeopardize its role as mediator in another case involving the same state.[86] Although the Convention requires that the Commission appear in all cases before the Court, it does not require that the Commission serve as the representative of the complainant or the prosecutor. The secretary general proposed that the Commission could instead fill the role of the *ministerio publico*, serving as an advocate for the integrity of the system rather than an advocate of a party to the dispute. The secretary general also proposed increasing and lengthening the sessions of the Commission and the Court and studying the possibility of the creation of a full-time Commission and Court. This would allow these organs to process their caseloads more efficiently and minimize current delays. At the least, he proposed that the positions of president and vice president of the Court and Commission be made permanent. Alternatively, he raises the possibility of a radical structural change that would merge the Commission and the Court, a change that has been adopted in the European human rights system.

Continual pressure must be placed on the OAS to increase financing to the human rights enforcement organs. The limitation of financial resources is an insidious but effective way to impair the functioning of the Commission and the Court. Likewise, advocates of the system must be continually vigilant to ensure that commissioners and judges have the required experience and dedication to serve the system.[87]

CONCLUSION

Human rights violations continue in the Western Hemisphere. Since the mid-1970s, however, there has been significant improvement in state observance of human rights. In the last two decades the governance of many states in Latin America has changed from dictatorship to democracy. Whereas at one time human rights advocates were labeled "subversives" and were in danger, today government representatives frequently advocate human rights. These developments have also resulted in a change in the type of human rights violations. Formerly, the inter-American system was repeatedly confronted with gross and systematic violations of human rights in which governments intentionally engaged in extrajudicial killings or forced disappearances. Today's violations are more individual in nature.

Against many odds, the inter-American human rights system is contributing to the recognition and enforcement of human rights in the American states. Progress is slow, of course. Governments are always resistant to change, especially when that change means the relinquishment of power. Still, a functioning human rights system has taken shape. It must be nurtured and encouraged. Although activists sometimes complain that the formal system does too little too late, it is making progress in supplanting the rule of man with the rule of law. As explained by Judge Buergenthal, "[e]ven some success in the international human rights field, however small, will make this world a little better place to live in. And that, after all, is what law is all about."[88]

NOTES

1. Sovereignty allows states almost complete freedom to act within their domestic jurisdiction and forbids external interference in a state's domestic affairs. The state, however, can voluntarily relinquish sovereignty by ratifying a treaty. The subject matter of the treaty then becomes subject to international law, and the state can no longer claim absolute authority over it. See Ian Brownlie, *Principles of Public International Law* (Oxford, 1990), 287–97.

2. Charter of the Organization of American States, entered into force on 13 December 1951.

3. Adopted at the Ninth Conference of American States, Bogotá, Colombia, 1948, reprinted in *Basic Documents Pertaining to Human Rights in the Inter-American System*, updated to April 1997. [hereafter *Basic Documents*]

The Inter-American Court of Human Rights has held the American Declaration of the Rights and Duties of Man to be an authoritative interpretation of the Charter of the OAS. Interpretation of the American Declaration of the Rights and Duties of Man within the Framework of Article 64 of the American Convention on Human Rights, I-A.CT.H.R., Advisory Opinion OC-10, 14 July 1989.

4. American Convention on Human Rights, 22 November 1969, 9 I.L.M. 673, OEA/ ser.K/XVI/L 1, doc. 65 rev. 1 corr. I (1970) [hereafter Convention or American Convention], reprinted in *Basic Documents*.

5. Signed in San Salvador on 17 November 1988, reprinted in *Basic Documents*.

6. Signed at Asuncion, Paraguay, on 8 June 1990, at the Twentieth Regular Session of the General Assembly, entered into force on 28 August 1991, reprinted in *Basic Documents*.

7. *Basic Documents*.

8. Resolution adopted at Belem Do Para, Brazil, 9 June 1994 at the Twenty-fourth Regular Session of the General Assembly of the Organization of American States, entered into force on 29 March 1996 on the thirtieth day from the date of the deposit of the second instrument of ratification. The Convention has been ratified by Argentina, Costa Rica, Panama, and Uruguay.

9. Adopted in Belem de Para, Brazil on 9 June 1994 during the Twenty-fourth Regular Session of the General Assembly of the OAS, entered into force on 5 March 1995.

10. American Convention, arts. 4, 5, 7, 8, 11, 12, and 13.

11. The twenty-five states include: Argentina, Barbados, Bolivia, Brazil, Chile, Colombia, Costa Rica, Dominica, Ecuador, El Salvador, Grenada, Guatemala, Haiti, Honduras, Jamaica, Mexico, Nicaragua, Panama, Paraguay, Peru, the Dominican Republic, Suriname, Trinidad and Tobago, Uruguay, and Venezuela. However, Trinidad and Tobago denounced the American Convention on 26 May 1998, effective 26 May 1999. The United States has signed but has not ratified the American Convention. See *Basic Documents*.

12. American Convention, *American University Journal of International Law and Policy* 9, art. 37. [hereafter "Commission" or "Inter-American Commission"]

13. Ibid., art. 33. [hereafter "the Court" or the "Inter-American Court"]

14. International Covenant on Civil and Political Rights, opened for signature 16 December 1966, G.A. Res. 2200, U.N. *GAOR*, 21st Sess., Supp No. 16, at 52, U.N. Doc. A/6316 (1967); 999 *U.N.T.S.* 171, 61 *I.L.M.* 368 (1967) (entered into Force 3 January 1976).

15. Convention for the Protection of Human Rights and Fundamental Freedoms, 4 November 1950, 213 U.N.T.S. 222, Europ. T. S. No. 5, [hereafter the European Convention] reprinted in Ian Brownlie, *Basic Documents on Human Rights* (New York, 1992), 326.

16. Habeas corpus in Emergency Situations, arts. 27(2), 25(1), and 7(6), American Convention on Human Rights, Advisory Opinion, 8 I.-A, Ct H.R., Ser. A, para. 36 (1987).

17. Thomas Buergenthal and Robert Norris, *2 HUM, RTS., The Inter-American System*, part 2, chap. 3. Council of Europe, *Report on The Inter-American Specialized Conference on Human Rights*, 71. While the American Convention was still in the stage of proposals and drafts, the U.N. General Assembly in December 1966 approved the text of the U.N. Covenants on Civil and Political Rights and Economic, Social, and Cultural Rights. At that time, the member states of the OAS, on being polled by the Council of the OAS, chose to go ahead with a separate Inter-American human rights treaty. Council of Europe, 68.

18. American Convention, art. 44.

19. See Exceptions to the Exhaustion of Domestic Remedies in Cases of Indigence or Inability to Obtain Legal Representation Because of a Generalized Fear within the

Legal Community, Advisory Opinion of 10 August 1990, Ser. A, OC-I 1/90, reprinted in *Human Rights Law Journal* 12 (1991): 20.

20. American Convention, art. 44. Any state party to the Convention automatically agrees to the right of individual petition, not only by the victim or relative of the victim, but also by "any nongovernmental entity legally recognized in one or more member States" of the OAS.

21. See David Padilla, "The Inter-American Commission on Human Rights of the Organization of American States: A Case Study," 95, (1993): 97–115.

22. Bustios-Rojas Case, Provisional Measures, Resolution of the I.-A.Ct.H.R. of 8 August 1990, 17, para.1.

23. American Convention, art. 36. The commissioners are chosen from the member states of the OAS and must be of recognized competence in the field of human rights. No two Commission members may be nationals of the same State (art. 37). The Commission is in session for approximately eight weeks a year.

24. Charter of the OAS, art. 112.

25. These complaints were confirmed by the truth commission established by the subsequent democratic government in Argentina, which reported that the military junta in power in Argentina from 1976 to 1983 tortured, murdered, and disappeared approximately 9000 people. Comisión Nacional Sobre la Desaparición de Personas, *Nunca Más* (Buenos Aìres, 1984). [hereafter *"Nunca Más"*]

26. David Weissbrodt and Maria Luisa Bartolomei, "The Effectiveness of International Human Rights Pressures: The Case of Argentina, 1976–1983," *Minnesota Law Review* (1991): 1009, 1021.

27. American Convention, art. 41. The Convention grants the Commission several functions, including the power to make human rights recommendations to governments, to prepare human rights studies and reports, to request information from states, and to take action on individual petitions alleging human rights abuses.

28. Cesar Gaviria, "Toward a New Vision of the Inter-American Human Rights System," *Journal of Latin American Affairs* 4 (1997): 4–6.

29. American Convention, art. 47.

30. Ibid., art. 48(1)(a).

31. American Convention, art. 48(1)(f). See Charles Moyer, "Friendly Settlement in the Inter-American System: The Verbitsky Case—When Push Needn't Come to Shove," in *La Corte y El Sistema Interamericana de Derechos Humanos*, (San José, Costa Rica, 1994), 347 (analyzing a case in which the Commission successfully used its good offices to bring about a friendly settlement).

32. American Convention, art. 50(1), 57.

33. "In the Matter of Viviana Gallardo *et al.*," I.-A. Ct. H.R., No. G101/81, para. 11 (1981).

34. American Convention, art. 62(1). The declaration of recognition of the jurisdiction of the Court "may be made unconditionally, on the condition of reciprocity, for a specific time, or for specific cases"—art. 62(2).

35. The following states have accepted the jurisdiction of the Inter-American Court: Argentina, Bolivia, Brazil, Chile, Colombia, Costa Rica, Ecuador, El Salvador, Guatemala, Haiti, Honduras, Mexico, Nicaragua, Panama, Paraguay, Suriname, Trinidad and Tobago, Uruguay, and Venezuela. See 1998 *Annual Report of the Inter-American Court*, 543–44, OAS/Ser.L/V/III.35, Doc.4, 3 February 1997.

36. Those judges were Carlos Roberto Reina, Rodolfo Piza Escalante, Maximo Cisneros, and Thomas Buergenthal.

37. In its first contentious cases the Court considered claims brought by the families of victims who had allegedly disappeared at the hands of persons acting on behalf of the Honduran government. Velásquez Rodríguez Case, (Merits), I.-A. Court H.R., Ser. C, No. 4 (1988); Godinez-Cruz Case, (Merits), 1989, Ser., C, No. 5 (1989); Fairen Garbi and Solis Corrales Case, (Merits), Ser. C, No. 6 (1989). [hereafter "The Honduran Cases"]

See also Jo Pasqualucci, "The Whole Truth and Nothing but the Truth: Truth Commissions, Impunity and the Inter-American Human Rights System," *Boston University International Law Journal* 12 (1994): 321, 352.

38. Velásquez Rodríguez Case, (Merits), I.-A. Ct. H.R., Ser. C, No. 4, paras. 147–48 (1988). In Argentina during the "dirty war," the armed forces eliminated bodies by drugging victims and then dropping them live from airplanes into the ocean. *Nunca Mas*, 235–36; Calvin Sims, "Argentine Tells of Dumping 'Dirty War' Captives Into Sea," *New York Times*, 13 March 1995, p. 22.

39. Velásquez Rodríguez Case, (Merits), I.-A. Ct. H.R., Ser. C, No. 4, para. 130 (1988).

40. Ibid., paras. 124, 125, 147(a).

41. Ibid., para. 147(b)&(c).

42. Velásquez Rodríguez Case (Merits), I.-A. Ct. H.R., Ser. C, No. 4, para. 147(i) (1988). The usual targets of the state-sponsored violence included opposition political groups, union leaders, student leaders, religious persons who assisted the poor, and virtually anyone who threatened the status quo. *Comisionado nacional de protección de los derechos humanos, los hechos hablan por is mismos, informe preliminar sobre los desaparecidos en Honduras, 1980–1993* (January 1994): 385.

43. Ibid., para. 147.

44. Thomas Buergenthal, "Judicial Fact-Finding: Inter-American Human Rights Court," in *Fact-Finding before International Tribunals*, edited by Richard Lillich (Ardsley-on-Hudson, NY, 1991), 261, 269.

45. Velásquez Rodríguez Case (Compensatory Damages), I-A. Ct. H.R., Ser. C, No. 7, judgment of 21 July 1989.

46. American Convention, art. 64(1). The Convention also grants this authority to any of the organs of the OAS listed in Chapter X of the Charter of the Organization, provided that the issue of the advisory request is "within its sphere of competence."

47. Ibid., art. 64(2).

48. "Other Treaties" Subject to the Advisory Jurisdiction of the Court (Art. 64 American Convention on Human Rights), (Advisory Opinion) OC-I/82 of 24 September 1982, I-A. Ct. H.R., Ser. A, No. I, para. 25 (1982).

49. Acción de Incost, No. 421-S-80, Roger Ajun Blanco, Art. 22 Ley Org. Col. de Periodistas, Sala Constitucional de la Corte Suprema de Justicia (9 May 1995) (Costa Rica). Other states have not necessarily revised their internal laws to correspond with the Court's advisory opinions. Some states, for instance, continue to have laws that authorize the derogation of the right of habeas corpus during a state of emergency. This practice ignores two advisory opinions interpreting the American Convention as prohibiting the suspension of habeas corpus. See Judicial Guarantees in States of Emergency, arts. 27(2), no. 25, and 8, American Convention on Human Rights (Advisory Opinion) I-A. Ct. H.R., Ser. A, No. 9 (1987); Habeas Corpus in Emergency Situations, arts. 27(2), 25(1), and 7(6), American Convention on Human Rights (Advisory Opinion), I-A. Ct. H.R., Ser. A, No. 8, para. 36 (1987).

210   Beyond the Ideal

50. Compulsory Membership in an Association Prescribed by Law for the Practice of Journalism (arts. 13, 29 of American Convention on Human Rights), Advisory Opinion OC-5/85, 13 November 1985, Ser. A., No 5, para. 81 (citing Costa Rican Law No. 4420).

51. Ibid., para 85.

52. Acción de Incost, No. 421-S-80, Roger Ajun Blanco, Art. 22 Ley Org. Col. de Periodistas, Sala Constitucional de la Corte Suprema de Justicia (9 May 1995) (Costa Rica).

53. Proposed Amendments to the Naturalization Provisions of the Constitution of Costa Rica, Advisory Opinion OC-4/84, I-A.Ct.H.R. Ser. A, No. 4 (1984).

54. Expediente 2965-S-91, Voto: 3435–92, *Ricardo Fliman Wargraft v. Director y Jefe de la Seccion de Opciones y Naturalizaciones*, Sala Constitucional de la Corte Suprema de Justicia (11 November 1992) (Costa Rica).

55. *Ekmekdjian v. Sofovich*, Case No. E. 64, 23, (Arg., CSJN, 1992). See Thomas Buergenthal, "International Tribunals and National Courts: The Internationalization of Domestic Adjudication," *Recht Zwischen Umbruck und Bewahrung Festschrift fur Rudolf Berhnardt* (1995), 687, 695. Article 14 (1) of the American Convention provides: "Anyone injured by inaccurate or offensive statements or ideas disseminated to the public in general by a legally regulated medium of communication has the right to reply or to make correction using the same communications outlet, under such conditions as the law may establish."

56. Enforceability of the Right to Reply or Correction, Advisory Opinion OC-7/86, I-A. Ct. H.R., Ser. A, No. 7 (1986).

57. See Thomas Buergenthal, "The Advisory Practice of the Inter-American Human Rights Court," *American Journal of International Law* 79 (1985): 1, 25.

58. American Convention, art. 63(2). See Jo Pasqualucci, "Provisional Measures in the Inter-American Human Rights System," 26 *Vanderbilt Journal of Transnational Law* (1993): 803, 820–21. Jo Pasqualucci, "Medidas Provisionales en la Corte Interamericana de Derechos Humanos: Una Comparacion con La Corte Internacional de Justiciay la Corte Europea de Derechos Humanos," 19 *Revista del Instituto Interamericano de Derechos Humanos [Journal of the Inter-American Institute of Human Rights]* (1994): 47.

59. American Convention, art. 63(2) provides: "In cases of extreme gravity and urgency, and when necessary to avoid irreparable damage to persons, the Court shall adopt such provisional measures as it deems pertinent in matters it has under consideration. With respect to a case not yet submitted to the Court, it may act at the request of the Commission."

60. Chunima Case, (Provisional Measures) Resolution of the President of the I.-A. Ct. H.R., Ser. E, 27, 15 July 1991.

61. In 1988, several hundred villagers from Quiche province founded the Council of Ethnic Communities Runujel Juman (CERJ), the first organization established to defend the rights of Guatemala's Maya population. See *1990–91 Annual Report of the Inter-American Commission on Human Rights*, Status of Human Rights in Several Countries, Guatemala, (1990–91): 447–48.

62. The civil patrols were established by the Guatemalan government in 1982, ostensibly to protect villages from guerrillas, and "are military structures established by the military." *Inter-American Yearbook on Human Rights* (1990): 242.

63. Chunima Case, (Provisional Measures) Resolution of the I.-A. Ct. H.R., Ser. E, 37, 29 July 1991.

64. José Miguel Vivanco and Juan E. Mendez, "Medidas de Protección para Testigos

en Casos ante La Corte Interamericana de Derechos Humanos," *Revista del Instituto Interamericano de Derechos Humanos* 19 (1994): 157.

65. Protocol of San Salvador, arts. 19, 26.

66. Ibid., art 19(6), 8, and 13.

67. Ibid., art. 1. As stated above, the Convention as originally ratified provided only that the death penalty "shall not be extended to crimes to which it does not presently apply." American Convention, art 4(2).

68. Signed at Asunción (note 6), arts. 5, 4, 10, and 7.

69. Resolution adopted at Belem do Para (note 8).

70. Ibid., art 2.

71. Judgment of 18 January 1995, I.-A. Ct.H.R., Ser. C, para. 19 (1995).

72. Judgment of 2 February 1996, I.-A. Ct. H.R., Ser. C, para. 25.

73. Judgment of 4 December 1991, I.-A. Ct. H.R., Ser. C, para. 22.

74. Letter from the State of Peru of 20 October 1997, reprinted in the *Annual Report of the Inter-American Court of Human Rights*, (1997): 245.

75. Art. 25(4) of the Rules of Procedure of the Inter-American Court of Human Rights, approved 16 September 1996 provides: "If the Court is not sitting, the President, in consultation with the Permanent Commission and, if possible the judges, shall call upon the government concerned to adopt such urgent measures as may be necessary to ensure the effectiveness of any provisional measures subsequently ordered by the Court at its next session."

76. *Annual Report of the Inter-American Court of Human Rights* (1996): 16.

77. Request for Provisional Measures involving Argentina, (Reggiardo-Tolosa Case), Case 10.959, I.-A. Comm. H.R. (1993), 1993 *Annual Report of the Inter-American Court of Human Rights*, 92.

78. Theo Van Boven, *Report to the U.N. on the Prevention of the Disappearances of Children in Argentina*, U.N. Hum. Rts. Comm., 40th Sess., 8, E/CN.4/Sub2/1988/19 (1988).

79. Carlos Ernesto Rodriguez, "Los Crimenes Impunes del Comisario Miara," *Madres de la Plaza de Mayo*, May 1989, at 20.

80. Resolution of the President of the Inter-American Court of Human Rights, Reggiardo-Tolosa Case, Provisional Measures Requested by the Inter-American Commission on Human Rights in the matter of The Republic of Argentina, 19 November 1993, reprinted in the *Annual Report of the Inter-American Court of Human Rights* (1993).

81. Douglass Cassel, "Will the Inter-American Human Rights System Come of Age," *Journal of Latin American Affairs*, 4 (1997): 45, 46.

82. Morris Abraham, "The U.N. and Human Rights," *Foreign Affairs* 47 (1969): 363–71.

83. Restrictions to the Death Penalty, arts. 4(2) and 4(4) American Convention on Human Rights, Advisory Opinion, I-A. Ct. H.R. OC-3/83 of 8 September 1983, Series A, No. 3.

84. American Convention, art. 4(2).

85. Chunima Case, (Provisional Measures) Resolution of the I.-A. Ct. H.R. of 1 August 1991, Ser. E, No 1. para. 4.

86. Jo Pasqualucci, "The Inter-American Human Rights System: Establishing Precedents and Procedure in Human Rights Law," *Inter-American Law Review* 26 (1994–95), 297, 317.

87. See Douglas Cassel Jr., "Somoza's Revenge: A New Judge for the Inter-American Court of Human Rights," *Human Rights Law Journal* 13 (1992), 137.

88. Remarks by Thomas Buergenthal, American Society of International Law, Annual Meeting, 24 April 1981.

16

Eclectic Ideal: Bringing a Positivist Order to the Literature of Pan Americanism

David Sheinin

The broad range of themes and approaches reflected in this collection identify two important keys to the literature of Pan Americanism. First, because there are multiple definitions and understandings of Pan Americanism, the scholarly and popular literature on this theme crosses a variety of disciplines and methodologies. Second, the concept of Pan Americanism is so ample that, in creating a comprehensive bibliography of Pan Americanism, it would be difficult to leave out works that touch on most aspects of inter-American ties, broadly conceived. Or, in a related twist, someone setting out to study an element of Pan Americanism could not begin and end his or her research bounded by the literature explicitly addressing that topic. A researcher interested, for example, in Pan Americanism and human rights in Argentina after 1975 could not be limited to the growing literature on the Inter-American Court of Human Rights and the Inter-American Commission on Human Rights, in reference to the last Argentine dictatorship (1976–1983) and the transition to democracy of the mid-1980s. He or she would have to study works on President Jimmy Carter's human rights policies in Latin America and beyond; military authoritarianism in Argentina and in Latin America in general; Argentina's relations with the Organization of American States (OAS) and foreign governments; and the politics and cultures of the Argentine dictatorship's defense of its human rights record.

The catch-22 of Pan Americanism, then, as an ideal, a methodology, or a set of problems that inspires such ranging—and at times contradictory—visions of inter-American affairs, is that its literature varies according to approach and subtheme. My goal in this brief bibliographical essay is not to provide a comprehensive list of useful studies but to orient readers in a number of the important works in several disciplines that specifically identify themeselves as addressing Pan Americanism or Pan American affairs. Because Pan Americanism has been criticized for more than a century by both North and South Americans as classist, racist, and a hostile imperialist invention of the United States, the critics of Pan Americanism and many others have simply set it aside as an appropriate organizing theme. As a result, the literature of Pan Americanism tends to be dominated by those interested in what supporters of Pan Americanism have held up as its accomplishments: the bureaucratic, legal, political, diplomatic, and social accomplishments of Pan Americanism as measured by its exponents within the Pan American Union, the OAS, and governments in the hemisphere.

Several bibliographies and other resource works chart the literature of Pan Americanism, mainly as related to the activities of the OAS, the Pan American Union, and their associated organs. The Columbus Memorial Library's *Guide to the Columbus Memorial Library* (Washington, 1988) offers a thorough listing of catalogued works in the OAS library, while the OAS's *A Classification Manual for the OAS Official Records Series: A Manual for the Maintenance of the Series* (Washington, 1977) provides insights into how the OAS has organized and catalogued its published series from the General Assembly, the Pan American Conferences of Foreign Ministers, the Permanent Council, the Inter-American Human Rights Commission, and a handful of others. Two recent bibliographies on the OAS that contain much that is specifically relevant to Pan Americanism in its various forms are Thomas L. Welch and René L. Gutiérrez, *The Organization of American States: A Bibliography* (Washington, 1990) and David Sheinin, *The Organization of American States* (Oxford, 1995).

General works include Alonso Aguilar's *Pan-Americanism from Monroe to the Present: A View from the Other Side* (New York, 1965) and Ezequiel Ramos Novoa's *La farsa del panamericanismo y la unidad indoamericana* (Buenos Aires, 1955), two Marxist attacks on Pan Americanism as an arm of U.S. imperialism in Latin America in the twentieth century. On the other end of the political spectrum are Henry H. Han's *Problems and Prospects of the Organization of American States: Perceptions of the Member States' Leaders* (New York, 1987) and Germán Arciniegas (ed.), *O.E.A.: La seurte de una institución regional* (Bogotá, 1985). The latter is a collection that trumpets Pan American accomplishments in diplomacy, economic development, and inter-American security, in the words of Colombian President Belisario Betancur, OAS Secretary General Joao Clemente Baena Soares, U.S. Ambassador to the OAS J. William Middendorf, and other Pan American "insiders." John Edwin Fagg's *Pan Americanism* (Malabar, 1982) remains a good introduction to the ideas and institutions in twentieth century Pan Americanism while Richard L. Millett's "Beyond Sovereignty: International Efforts to Support Latin American Democracy," *Journal of Inter-American Studies and World Affairs* 36, no. 3 (Fall 1994): 1–23, and Mark Peceny's "The Inter-American System as a Liberal 'Pacific Union'?," *Latin American Research Review* 29, no. 3 (1994): 188–201, are two of many recent studies to address the place of Pan Americanism in the building of democratic institutions in the Americas.

Many good studies highlight the importance of Pan Americanism during specific historical periods, although these often stress Pan American meetings only. A U.S. delegate to many Pan American gatherings, Samuel Guy Inman wrote *Inter-American Conferences, 1826–1954* (Washington, 1965) as a core reference tool to the Pan American conferences. An account from a Colombian delegate to the First Pan American Financial Conference, *The Pan-American Financial Conference of 1915* (London, 1915) by Santiago Pérez Triana, remains the most detailed report of that meeting. *La trascendencia de las reuniones interamericanas* by Teodoro Alvarado Garaicoa (Guayaquil, 1949) is an outstanding review of Pan Americanism during World War II. Because the United States played so prominent a role in shaping Pan Americanism after 1890, many studies highlight U.S.–Latin American relations. Mark T. Gilderhus's *Pan American Visions: Woodrow Wilson in the Western Hemisphere, 1913–1921* (Tucson, 1986) is an insightful analysis of U.S. foreign policy and Pan Americanism during the Wilson administration. Robert Neal Seidel's doctoral dissertation, *Progressive Pan Americanism: Development and United States Policy Toward South America, 1906–1931* (Ithaca, 1973) remains the most compelling analysis of finance- and commerce-based Pan Americanism as a core of U.S. foreign policy during the early twentieth century. Christián Guerrero Yoacham's *Las conferencias del Niagara Falls: La mediación de Argentina, Brasil, y Chile en el conflicto entre los Estados Unidos y México en 1914* (Santiago, 1986) is one of few studies on the 1914 ABC Conference, whereas Gregg Andrews's *Shoulder to Shoulder? The American Federation of Labor, the United States, and the Mexican Revolution, 1910–1924* (Berkeley, 1991) is one of several studies on Pan Americanism and international ties among labor organizations.

Much of the literature on Pan Americanism concerns historical episodes in which Pan Americanism, the Pan American Union, or the OAS figured prominently. Writings in this context on the Alliance for Progress include Paul J. Dosal, "Accelerating Dependent Development and Revolution: Nicaragua and the Alliance for Progress," *Inter-American Economic Affairs*, vol. 38, no. 4 (Spring 1985): 75–96; Marcos Gabay and Carlos María Gutiérrez, *Integración latinoamericana? De la Alianza para el Progreso a la OLAS* (Montevideo, 1967); and Edwin McCammon Martin, *Kennedy and Latin America* (Lanham, MD, 1994).

Among those who have placed the 1965 Dominican Crisis in a Pan American setting are Daniel I. Papermaster, "A Case Study of the Effect of International Law on Foreign Policy Decisionmaking: The United States Intervention in the Dominican Republic in 1965," *Texas International Law Journal* 24, no. 3 (1989): 463–497, and Bruce Palmer, Jr., *Intervention in the Caribbean: The Dominican Crisis of 1968* (Lexington, KY, 1989).

Many studies have addressed the 1989 U.S. invasion of Panama: Alan Berman, "In Mitigation of Illegality: The U.S. Invasion of Panama," *Kentucky Law*

Journal 79, no. 4 (1990–1991): 735–800; Lawrence S. Eagleburger, "The OAS and the Panama Crisis," *Department of State Bulletin* 89, no. 2152 (November 1989): 67–68; and Ved P. Nanda, "Validity of United States Intervention in Panama under International Law," *American Journal of International Law* 84, no. 2 (April 1990): 494–503.

Like the majority of works in this collection, a broad sector of the literature addresses Pan Americanism as related to a specific region or country. Works concerning Argentina highlight U.S.-Argentine relations: David Sheinin, *Searching for Authority: Pan Americanism, Diplomacy, and Politics in United States-Argentine relations, 1910–1930* (New Orleans, 1998); Pan American diplomacy: Pablo Yankelevich, *La diplomacia imaginaria: Argentina y la revolución mexicana, 1910–1916* (México, 1994); Pan American conferences: David Sheinin, *Argentina and the United States at the Sixth Pan American Conference (Havana 1928)* (London, 1991); the Falklands/Malvinas War: Heraldo Muñoz, "Beyond the Malvinas Crisis: Perspectives on Inter-American Relations," *Latin American Research Review* 19, no. 1 (1984): 158–172; and the course of Argentine foreign policy during the Cold War: Juan Archibaldo Lanús, *De Chapultepec al Beagle: Política Exterior Argentina, 1945–1980* (Buenos Aires, 1984).

Publications on the Caribbean have emphasized the work of the Pan American Health Organization: Mervyn U. Henry, "Primary Health Care—Caribbean Update," in Pan American Health Organization, *Primary Health Care and Local Health Systems in the Caribbean* (Washington, 1989), 3–15; and problems in international law: Val T. McComie, "Legal Contribution of the Caribbean to the Inter-American System," in B. G. Ramcharan, L. B. Francis, eds., *Caribbean Perspectives on International Law and Organizations* (Dordrecht, 1989).

On Central America, authors have stressed human rights: Claudio Grossman, "Disappearances in Honduras: The Need for Direct Victim Representation in Human Rights Litigation," *Hastings International and Comparative Law Review* 15, no. 3 (Spring 1992): 363–389; the low intensity warfare in the region during the 1980s: Joseph G. Sullivan, "How Peace Came to El Salvador," *Orbis* 38, no. 1 (Winter 1994): 83–98; and the Nicaraguan revolution: Philip J. Williams, "Elections and Democratization in Nicaragua: The 1990 Elections in Perspective," *Journal of Inter-American Studies and World Affairs* 23, no. 4 (Winter 1990): 13–34.

There are still very few works on Pan Americanism and women. They include Carol S. Bruch, "The 1989 Inter-American Convention on Support Obligations," *American Journal of Comparative Law* 40, no. 4 (Fall 1992): 817–863; Rebecca J. Cook, "International Human Rights Law Concerning Women: Case Notes and Comments," *Vanderbilt Journal of Transnational Law* 23, no. 4 (1990): 779–818; June E. Hahner, *Emancipating the Female Sex: The Struggle for Women's Rights in Brazil, 1850–1940* (Durham, 1990); Francesca Miller, "The International Relations of Women in the Americas, 1890–1928," *The Americas* 43, no. 2 (October 1986): 171–182; and K. Lynn Stoner, *From the House to the Streets: The Cuban Women's Movement for Legal Reform, 1898–1940* (Durham, 1991).

Problems in health and technology are addressed in Miguel E. Bustamante, *The Pan American Sanitary Bureau: Half a Century of Health Activities, 1902–1954* (Washington, 1955); Humberto de Moraes Novaes, *Acciones integradas en los sistemas locales de salud* (Washington, 1990); and Ernest B. Haas, "Technological Self-Reliance for Latin America: The OAS Contribution," *International Organization* 34, no. 4 (Autumn 1980): 541–570.

Recent progress in human rights protection as a Pan American concern is documented in Antonio Augusto Cançado Trindade, "The 1992 Brasilia Seminar on Human Rights Protection and Environmental Protection," *Human Rights Law Journal* 13, no. 7–8 (31 August 1992): 317–318; Michael José Corbera, "In the Wrong Place at the Wrong Time; Problems with the Inter-American Court of Human Rights Use of Contentious Jurisdiction," *Vanderbilt Journal of Transnational Law* 25, no. 5 (February 1993): 919–950; and Elizabeth Faulkner, "The Right to habeas corpus: Only in the Other Americas," *American University Journal of International Law and Policy* 9, no. 3 (Spring 1994): 653–687.

Because the elimination of military intervention in the Americas was central to Pan American debates throughout the twentieth century, intervention and nonintervention are taken up by a number of authors, including Gerardo Bra, *La doctrina Drago* (Buenos Aires, 1990); Yale H. Ferguson, "Reflections on the Inter-American Principle of Nonintervention: A Search for Meaning in Ambiguity," *Journal of Politics* 32, no. 3 (August 1970): 628–654; and Caroline Thomas, *New States, Sovereignty and Intervention* (Aldershot, 1985).

Other problems of Pan Americanism in international law are dealt with in César Augusto Bunge and Diego César Bunge, "The San José de Costa Rica Pact and the Calvo Doctrine," *University of Miami Inter-American Law Review* 16, no. 1 (Spring 1984): 13–52; Rafael Eyzaguirre, "Arbitration in Latin America: The Experience of the Inter-American Commercial Arbitration Commission," *International Tax and Business Lawyer* 4, no. 2 (Fall 1986): 288–296; W. C. Gilmore, *International Efforts to Combat Money Laundering* (Cambridge, England, 1992); César Sepúlveda, *Las fuentes del derecho internacional americano* (Mexico City, 1975); and Keith W. Yundt, "International Law and the Latin American Political Refugee Crisis," *University of Miami Inter-American Law Review* 19, no. 1 (Fall 1987): 137–154.

Several recent studies have taken important new methodological steps to recast Pan Americanism. In *The Enormous Vogue of Things Mexican: Cultural Relations between the United States and Mexico, 1920–1935* (Tuscaloosa, 1992), Helen Delpar discusses the growing American affinity for Mexican art, literature, and archaeology. Strong Pan American sentiment in the United States during the 1930s can be explained in part by an American empathy for Mexican culture. Alexandra Stern's *Mestizophilia, Biotypology, and Eugenics in Post-Revolutionary Mexico: Towards a History of Science and the State, 1920–1960* (University of Chicago, Mexican Studies Program, Working Paper No. 4, 1999) offers a new basis for conceiving health and problems of race and ethnicity in inter-American cultural relations. "The Enterprise of Knowledge" by Ricardo

Salvatore, in Gilbert M. Joseph, Catherine C. LeGrand, and Ricardo D. Salvatore, eds., *Close Encounters of Empire: Writing the Cultural History of U.S.–Latin American Relations* (Durham, 1999), reformulates Pan Americanism as an imagined set of cultural practices associated with an informal American empire. Fredrick B. Pike's *The United States and Latin America: Myths and Stereotypes of Civilization and Nature* (Austin, 1992) characterizes Pan Americanism as a function of American cultural constructions of race and ethnicity in the Americas.

Index

Aboriginal people: Brazil, 127; Chile, 127
Alegría, Fernando, 154
Alliance for Progress, 49, 50, 52
American Convention on Human Rights, 195, 196–97, 201
American Declaration of the Rights and Duties of Man, 195
Andean Pact, 191
Anti-imperialism, 57–65
Aranha, Oswaldo, 6–7, 133–49
Argentina: environment, 118; human rights violations, 203

Bagehot, Walter, 36–37
Baron of Rio Branco (José Maria da Silva Paranhos), 135
Blaine, James G., 2, 20–22, 25–30
Bolívar, Simon, 9–16
Bolton, Herbert, 38, 47, 154, 156, 163
Brazil, 6–7, 23; aboriginal people, 127; coffee prices, 145; environment, 120, 121; finance and credit policy, 144; foreign policy, 133–49
Buergenthal, Thomas, 198
Bureau of American Republics, 29

Bush, George, 51, 52
Bustamante, Cecilio, 72–73

Caribbean Defense Command (CDC), 103
Catt, Carrie Chapman, 90
Central America, 6, 25–26, 50–51, 89, 95–109, 167–77
Central American Treaty (1923), 98
Chevigny, Bell Gale, 158–59
Chile, 23, 72–73; aboriginal people, 127
Club Femenino de Cuba, 84
Cold War, 3–4, 6, 7, 49, 50–52, 95, 104, 142–49, 167–77
Colombia, 14–15, 23, 26
Commercial Bureau of the American Republics, 27–30
Congress of Panama (1826), 1, 14–15
Continental Congress of Santiago (1856), 2
Cooke Mission (1942–1943), 141
Coolidge, Calvin, 82–83, 85
Cuba, 83, 175–76, 187
Cuban Missile Crisis, 175–76
Curtis, William E., 23–25, 28–29

Darío, Rubén, 5, 57–65
Diplomatic recognition, 98–99, 103, 105
Disappearances, 199–200
Draft Convention on Nature Protection
and Wild Life Preservation in the
Western Hemisphere (1940), 117–21
Durán Ballén, Sixto, 185

Ecuador, 7–8, 183–93; human rights viola-
tions, 203
Eighth Conference of American States
(1938), 3, 117, 139
Eisenhower, Dwight D., 170–74, 177
El Salvador, 98, 105
Enterprise for the Americas Initiative, 52
Environment, 115–28; Argentina, 118;
Brazil, 120; Uruguay, 120

Feminism, 79–93
Fernández Retamar, Roberto, 158
Fifth Conference of American States
(Santiago, 1923), 1, 2–3, 6, 72, 75
First Conference of American States
(1889–1890), 2, 4, 19–30, 81
First Pan American Financial Conference
(1915), 2

Galapagos Islands, 123
Gaviria, César, 188–89, 205
Good Neighbor policy, 3, 41, 48, 96, 97,
138
Guatemala, human rights violations, 201,
204

Harrison, Lawrence E., 53
Haya de la Torre, Victor Raúl, 1
Hernández Martínez, Maximiliano, 98,
101, 103
Hispanismo, 5–6, 67–75
Honduras, human rights violations, 199–
200, 204
Hoover, Herbert, 40
Hull, Cordell, 99–100, 137–39
Human rights, 8, 195–206; American
Convention on, 195, 196–97, 201; Ar-
gentina, 203; Ecuador, 203; Guatemala,
201, 204; Honduras, 199–200, 204;
Inter-American Commission on, 8, 196–

98; Inter-American Court of, 196, 198–
205
Humphrey, George W., 154
Hurtado, Osvaldo, 185, 187, 192

Inman, Samuel Guy, 48
Inter-American Commission of Women,
6, 79–93
Inter-American Commission on Human
Rights, 8, 196–98
Inter-American Conference for the Main-
tenance of Peace (1936), 97
Inter-American Convention on the Forced
Disappearance of Persons, 195
Inter-American Convention on the Pre-
vention, Punishment, and Eradication
of Violence Against Women, 195
Inter-American Convention to Prevent
and Punish Torture,195
Inter-American Court of Human Rights,
196, 198–205
Inter-American High Commission, 40
Inter-American literature, 153–64
International American Union, 27

Juridical Congress of Lima (1877–1879),
2

Kennedy, John F., 170–74, 177
Kroeber, Karl, 155–56
Kubitschek, Juscelino, 147–48

Laguardia, Gary, 158–59
Langley, Lester D., 51–52, 156
Latin American Free Trade Agreement
(LAFTA), 191
Latin American studies, 45–54
Latin American Studies Association
(LASA), 50
Liberal developmentalism, 170–71
Lowenthal, Abraham F., 50–52

Machado, Gerardo, 82–83, 85
Martí, José, 2, 19, 26, 85
Martin, Robert, 155, 157–58
McCreary-Frye Act, 22, 28
McKinley, William, 25
McKinley Tariff, 25

Mecham, J. Lloyd, 49, 50
Mexico, 23, 25–26, 37–38
Modernismo, 58–65
Monroe Doctrine, 1, 40, 81, 169
Muñoz Marín, Mona Lee, 87–88

National Women's Party, 84
Nicaragua, 98–99, 105
Niehaus, Bernd, 188–89
Ninth Conference of American States
  (1948), 104
Nixon, Richard M., 173
Nonintervention, 36, 96, 98, 106, 108
North American Free Trade Agreement
  (NAFTA), 53

Office of the Coordinator of Inter-
  American Affairs (CIAA), 48–50, 100
Organization of American States (OAS),
  3, 183–93, 195–206

Pan American Union (PAU), 1, 20, 27–
  30, 79, 80, 81, 84, 92, 115–17; Nature
  Protection Section, 124
Pan Hispanism, 58–59, 63
Paraguay, 23
Parkinson Zamora, Lois, 161
Peru, 14–15
Prieto, René, 160
Protocol of San Salvador (1988), 201

Québec, 160, 163

Reagan, Ronald, 50–51
Rodó, José Enrique, 68
Rodríguez Monegal, Emir, 160
Roldós, Jaime, 187
Roosevelt, Franklin D., 124
Roosevelt, Theodore, 2
Rowe, Leo Stanton, 4–5, 33–42, 46–47
Rubottom, Roy R., Jr., 169–70

Sabas Alomá, Mariblanca, 90
Saldívar, José David, 158
Schmitt, Waldo LaSalle, 116, 122–23
Schurz, Carl, 21
Science, 115–28

Second Conference of American States
  (1901–1902), 2, 30
Security, 3–4
Seventh Conference of American States
  (1933), 3, 91, 95
Shouldice, Larry, 157
Sixth Conference of American States
  (1928), 2–3, 6, 74, 82, 83–84, 97
Slavery, 9–16
Smithsonian Institution, 122
Somoza, Anastasio, 98–99, 101–2, 103
Spain, 67–75
Spanish-Cuban-American War, 61–62,
  67, 121
Stevens, Doris, 84, 86, 87, 88, 90
Suriname, 203

Taylor Grazing Act, 124
Tenth Conference of American States
  (1954), 108, 173–74
Third Conference of American States
  (1906), 2
Third Meeting of Consultation of Foreign
  Ministers (1942), 101
Trade, 21–22, 37, 53, 69, 99, 100
Treaty of Rio de Janeiro (1947), 104,
  134, 142–43, 169

Ugarte, Manuel, 1, 2
United States, lumber contractors in Latin
  America, 121; parks, 118, 124–26; rela-
  tions with Brazil, 133–49; relations
  with Central America, 95–109; rela-
  tions with Cuba, 175–76; relations with
  Ecuador, 186–93, 190; relations with
  Latin America, 5, 19–30, 35–42, 45–
  54, 60–61, 71, 74–75, 81, 82–83, 89,
  115–28, 167–77; wildlife initiatives in
  Latin America, 123–24
Uruguay, environment, 120

Vargas, Getulio, 133–49
Velásquez Rodríguez Case, 199–200
Venezuela, 11, 13

Wasserman, Renata R. Mautner, 161–62
Wetmore, Alexander, 117

Wildlife, 6, 115–28
Wilson, Edmund, 154–55
Wilson, Woodrow, 2
Women, 6, 79–93

World War II, 95, 100, 101–5, 118, 138–41

Zaldívar, Angela M., 86

About the Editor and Contributors

MARK T. BERGER is Senior Lecturer in the Department of Spanish and Latin American Studies at the University of New South Wales. He is the author of *Under Northern Eyes: Latin American Studies and U.S. Hegemony in the Americas, 1898–1990* (1995).

PETER BLANCHARD is Professor of History at the University of Toronto. His published works include *The Origins of the Peruvian Labor Movement, 1883–1919* (1982), *Markham in Peru: The Travels of Clements R. Markham, 1852–1853* (1991), and *Slavery and Abolition in Early Republican Peru* (1992). He is presently working on a book on slaves and slavery during the Latin American wars of independence.

DAVID BARTON CASTLE, Assistant Professor of History at Ohio University—Eastern, holds a Ph.D. from the University of Oregon. He is working on a study of the intellectual framework for U.S. policy in Latin America in the early twentieth century.

EARL E. FITZ is Professor of Portuguese, Spanish, and Comparative Literature at Vanderbilt University. His publications include *Machado de Assis* (1989), *Rediscovering the New World: Inter-American Literature in Comparative Context* (1991), and *Ambiguity and Gender in the New Novel of Brazil and Spanish America*, co-edited with Judith Payne (1993).

JEANNE A. K. HEY is Associate Professor of Political Science and International Studies at Miami University. She has written *Theories of Dependent For-*

eign Policy and the Case of Ecuador in the 1980s (1995) and is the co-editor of *Foreign Policy Analysis: Continuity and Change in Its Second Generation* (1995).

THOMAS M. LEONARD is Distinguished Professor of History and Director of the International Studies Program at the University of North Florida. He is the author of nine books, his most recent publications being *Castro and the Cuban Revolution* (Greenwood, 1999) and *The United States and Latin America, 1850–1903* (1999).

JO M. PASQUALUCCI is Associate Professor of international law at the University of South Dakota School of Law. Now a Doctor of Judicial Science candidate at the George Washington University Law School, she was formerly affiliated with the Inter-American Court of Human Rights in Costa Rica.

ALBERTO PRIETO-CALIXTO is Assistant Professor of Spanish at Rollins College. He has written several articles on Spanish and Latin American literatures and is completing a book, *Ambiguous Encounters: Indian and Moorish Captivity in Hispanic Literatures, 1550–1650.*

RICHARD V. SALISBURY, a former Peace Corps volunteer in Venezuela and Senior Fulbright lecturer in Costa Rica, is Professor of History at Western Kentucky University. He is the author of *Costa Rica y el istmo, 1900–1934* (1984) and *Anti-Imperialism and International Competition in Central America, 1920–1929* (1989).

DAVID SHEININ is Associate Professor of History at Trent University. He has published *Searching for Authority: Pan Americanism, Diplomacy and Politics in United States–Argentine Relations, 1910–1930* (1998), *The Organization of American States* (1995), *The Jewish Diaspora in Latin America* (1996) and *Es Igual Pero Distinto: Essays in the Histories of Canada and Argentina* (1997), coedited with Carlos A. Mayo. He is now working on a history of U.S.-Argentine relations from 1800.

JOSEPH SMITH is Reader in American Diplomatic History at the University of Exeter. His publications include *Illusions of Conflict: Anglo-American Diplomacy Toward Latin America, 1865–1896* (1979), *Unequal Giants: Diplomatic Relations Between the United States and Brazil, 1889–1930* (1991), and *The Spanish-American War: Conflict in the Caribbean and the Pacific, 1895–1902* (1994).

K. LYNN STONER is Professor of History and past Director of the Center for Latin American Studies at Arizona State University. Her many publications include *From the House to the Streets* (1991).

STEPHEN M. STREETER is Assistant Professor of History at Wilfrid Laurier University. He is the author of numerous articles on U.S.–Central American relations and a forthcoming book from Ohio University Press.

W. MICHAEL WEIS is Professor and Chair of History at Illinois Wesleyan University. He is the author of *Cold Warriors and Coups d'Etat* (1993) as well as several articles on U.S. foreign relations.